The Organic City

THE
Organic City
Urban Definition
& Community
Organization
1880-1920

PATRICIA MOONEY MELVIN

THE UNIVERSITY PRESS OF KENTUCKY

Library of Congress Cataloging-in-Publication Data

Melvin, Patricia Mooney.
    The organic city.

    Bibliography: p.
    Includes index.
    1. Community organization—United States—History
—20th century.   2. Community development, Urban—
United States—History—20th century.   I. Title.
HN90.C6M45   1987   307.7'6'0973   87-13322
ISBN 0-8131-1585-X

In memory of my father
PAUL ANDREW MOONEY
and my aunt
RUTH BARR MOONEY

Contents

List of Figures and Tables ix

Acknowledgments xi

Introduction 1

1 Neighborhood in the Organic City 11

2 Infant Health and Neighborhood Organization 27

3 The Social Unit Theory of Organization 57

4 The Social Unit Comes to Cincinnati 77

5 An Experiment in Neighborhood Health Care 98

6 Politics and the Social Unit, 1919-1920 124

7 Metropolitan Community to Fragmented
 Metropolis, 1920-1940 159

Notes 174

Bibliographic Essay 208

Index 223

Figures and Tables

Figure 1 Death Rate per Thousand under One Year of Age,
New York City, 1898-1911   33

Figure 2 Infant Deaths from Diarrhea, New York City,
1904-1912   34

Figure 3 City of Milwaukee and Ward Locations, 1911   48

Figure 4 Phillips's Social Unit Plan   61

Figure 5 Circle, Zone, and Hilltop Sections of Cincinnati,
1910   85

Figure 6 The Mohawk-Brighton Social Unit Organization
District   88

Table 1 Deaths of Children under One Year of Age, New
York City, 1902-1911   32

Table 2 Deaths of Babies in the New York Milk Committee
Experimental Program, June 17-August 31, 1908   40

Table 3 Babies Weighed at Consultations, Week Ending
August 31, 1908, New York Milk Committee
Experimental Program   41

Acknowledgments

During the preparation of this study I have accumulated many debts. I am especially grateful to Zane L. Miller who first suggested Wilbur C. Phillips's social unit plan as a possible thesis topic in 1971. Throughout the years he has been an excellent mentor, a sympathetic yet discerning critic, and a valued friend. His support and confidence in my work helped turn a dissertation into a book. Throughout the course of my work Robert Fisher and Henry D. Shapiro also have contributed to my understanding of the dynamics of community organization and of the problem of neighborhoods, cities, and the larger question of urban definition.

I want to thank the staffs at the Social Welfare History Archives Center at the University of Minnesota, the Manuscript Division of the Library of Congress, the National Archives, the State Historical Society of Wisconsin, the New York Public Library, the Folger Library at the University of Maine, the Houghton Library of Harvard University, the Boston Public Library, the George Arents Library at Syracuse University, the Butler Library at Columbia University, the Special Collections Department at the University of Cincinnati, the Public Library of Cincinnati and Hamilton County, and the Cincinnati Historical Society. All of these people helped me with the material under their care. Joan Phillips Reed, daughter of Wilbur and Elsie Phillips, kindly sent me copies of her father's papers still in her possession. Research funds from the University of Cincinnati's University Research Council in 1975 and a Charles P. Taft Fellowship (1975-1976) made it possible to collect the material necessary for this study.

Parts of *The Organic City* have appeared as articles. I wish to thank Greenwood Press, the *Journal of the West, Mid-America,* and the *Bulletin of the Cincinnati Historical Society,* now entitled *Queen City Heritage,* for permission to reprint portions of this material.

Over the years numerous people have shared their ideas, criticisms, and encouragement. In particular I would like to thank William D. Aeschbacher, Deborah Baldwin, Saul Benison, James Hodges, Carl Moneyhon, and Barbara N. Ramusack. Melissa Lee helped with the typing. In addition, I want to thank my family for its support and encouragement as I strove to make sense out of the world of the past my father unlocked for me during the all-too-few years we had together. My aunt, Ruth Mooney, made Cincinnati history come alive. Finally, my heartfelt appreciation to Eric for his help, moral support, and understanding.

Without the support of the individuals and institutions cited above, this project would have been difficult to pursue. They are responsible for its merits. I alone am responsible for its shortcomings.

Introduction

In 1926 Ernest W. Burgess, a pioneer in urban sociology at the University of Chicago, wrote that although urban reformers in the first two decades of the twentieth century had turned the city into " 'the happy hunting ground' of movements," they had lacked a basic conception or understanding of the city. Social scientists during the 1920s, on the other hand, especially those at the University of Chicago, had such a conception. They, said Burgess, thought of the city as an organism and, using the notion of the organic city as a base, attempted to study the city "to bring light to bear on the practical problems of city life."[1] Burgess, however, misinterpreted the position of many of those active in the movements of which he spoke with such disdain. A number of men and women active in city affairs during the late nineteenth and early twentieth century did articulate a basic conception of the city. Like the Chicago sociologists who followed them, they described the city as an organism—although they meant something very different than Burgess and his contemporaries. And these turn-of-the-century students of the city, using *their* conception of the city as a base, also attempted to understand the city and to devise programs designed to attack the problems found in the urban environment.

Of course, the prevalent conception of the city between 1880 and 1920 was no more right or wrong than the view held by the Chicago sociologists. It is not necessary, however, to determine the truth of either view. What is important is whether contemporaries believed that such views accurately described reality for a particular historical period. People organize reality differently at different points in time, and it is clear that despite Burgess's dismissal of the beliefs held by those active in the movements, no single model can describe the city over time. Although Burgess failed to realize it, his remarks are important not because he was celebrating the articulation of an ideal model to describe a timeless urban form and structure, but because in a sense he was certifying that a new mode of thought—a new conception of the city—had replaced one that had become less useful in describing America's urban landscape. By discussing notions of urban form contextually, we can begin to understand the particular configurations of reality popular during different historical periods and the attempts of contemporaries to address the various issues or problems confronting them on the basis of prevailing beliefs.[2]

Amid all the enthusiasm for neighborhood organization that characterized the 1970s, Milton Kotler, founder of the National Association of Neighborhoods, urged neighborhood proponents to analyze seriously why such localism should be supported. "We must remember," Kotler wrote, "where the neighborhood movement came from and what happened to create the present situation. The neighborhood movement did not fall from heaven yesterday. It began in the 1960s."[3] As Kotler's comments indicate, the history of the efforts to organize America's neighborhoods is little understood. Interest in the neighborhood as an arena for revitalizing urban areas is not an outgrowth of the urban crisis of the 1960s with its use of the neighborhood as a staging ground for solutions to contemporary problems. Instead, its roots reach back to the final decades of the nineteenth century as Americans sought to understand and shape the modern city.

As the modern city came into being during the late nineteenth century, Americans confronted the challenge of a seemingly new urban form. Out of their efforts to understand the turn-of-the-century city came the identification of the neighborhood as a discrete and manageable unit of the larger urban structure. Like those Americans attempting to impose order on a rapidly changing society caught in the throes of industrialization and urbanization, the men and women interested in urban affairs embraced the notion of interdependence popular in descriptions of society and started to view the city as an organism—as an interdependent system of complementary parts or neighborhoods.

Neighborhoods, turn-of-the-century urban analysts argued, functioned as the local units of citizen identification and participation and represented the cells of the new organic city. While each neighborhood exhibited differences, proponents of the organic view stressed the existence of a symbiotic relationship between the local units and the city as a whole. Insisting that the well-being of the whole depended on the health of the parts, numerous groups attempted to organize geographic areas according to their conception of the appropriate function of the neighborhood and to establish systems designed to facilitate communication and interaction between the city and its component parts. In the view of those who attempted to organize the city, such systems would create a sound city and, by implication, a healthy society.

With the emergence of the neighborhood as an identifiable unit, contemporaries interested in the city scrutinized the neighborhood and developed organizing strategies that facilitated interaction between the city as a whole and its constituent parts. The establishment of settlement houses, community centers, and neighborhood improvement associations are all examples of strategies used to further the development of a unified civic community. In terms of community organization practice, settlement houses and community centers fall within the social work tradition, while neighborhood improvement associations illustrate the neighborhood maintenance approach to neighborhood organizing.[4] These two approaches dominate the organizational activities undertaken during the formative years of community organization.

The social work tradition portrays the community as an organism, focuses on members of the working and lower classes, and identifies social disorganization and conflict as the major problems confronting local areas. The role of the organizer is to operate as an enabler, advocate, coordinator, and/or planner. Neighborhood residents act either as partners with the professional staff or as recipients of services. Tactics employed in this approach are consensual, gradualist, and designed to work with, rather than against, the existing power structure. Basic goals include group formation, social integration, and service delivery.

Neighborhood maintenance, on the other hand, defines the community explicitly as a residential area. Members of the middle and upper classes organize behind an elected spokesperson to combat threats to property values or neighborhood homogeneity, or to fight for better services. They use a variety of tactics, including consensus, peer pressure, political lobbying, and legislation.[5] Despite the differences between the social work and neighborhood maintenance traditions between 1880 and 1920, both approaches to neighborhood organizing encouraged interaction between the city and its component parts and had as a common goal the creation of a well-orchestrated metropolitan community.

Of all the attempts to perfect the organization of the organic city, Wilbur C. Phillips's social unit organization represents the quintessential example of the translation of the organic city into action. More than most of his contemporaries, Phillips tried to lay the basis for the development of strong neighborhood organizations that would provide residents with the potential to better both their own community and the city as a whole. In so doing, he wove together aspects of the social work and neighborhood maintenance approaches to community organization. While acknowledging social disorganization and conflict as problems, he focused not on particular classes but on residents of specific geographic areas. He saw the organizer as a facilitator, able to build a cooperative network of residents and experts who would learn how to work together to define neighborhood needs and devise plans to solve local problems. Phillips's social unit plan combined the protectionist urge inherent in the neighborhood maintenance approach with the integrative aspects of the social work tradition to foster a civic consciousness that identified with and yet transcended the neighborhood and incorporated it into the larger urban community.

Wilbur C. Phillips entered the drive to organize the nation's neighborhoods more by accident than by design. Born on March 10, 1880, in Hamilton, New York, Phillips grew to maturity under the guidance of his father, Baptist minister Wilbur Phillips, and the schoolmasters of Colgate Academy. After his graduation from Colgate, Phillips moved with his family to the neighboring town of Oswego. His father's death soon after led Phillips to work for the *Oswego Times* and the *Syracuse Post Standard* as an apprentice reporter covering local news events to support his family. At the same time, he prepared himself in Greek, Latin, French, English, and algebra for the Harvard entrance examinations. In the summer of

1900, after he passed the examinations, Phillips took his mother to Rochester, New York, to live with relatives and settled in Cambridge for his first year at Harvard.[6]

Phillips spent his Harvard years as part of a class that viewed demanding subjects, such as the classics and mathematics, as "greasy grinds." A survey by the Faculty Committee on Improving Instruction at Harvard in 1903 revealed that for the many undergraduates able to breeze through programs in only three years, reputed softness or convenient hours determined course selection. Many undergraduates felt that it was poor form to receive higher than a C, the "gentlemen's grade," in any course.[7] Not surprisingly, as a student not fond of reading and academic pressure, who was attending Harvard out of a feeling of duty toward a dead father, Phillips received little intellectual stimulation from his courses. In addition, having to support himself and, after 1903, his mother as well, Phillips directed his efforts toward earning a living rather than "preparing himself for life." Luther Wright Mott, an 1896 Harvard graduate whose father owned the *Oswego Times*, arranged for Phillips to work his way through Harvard by sending queries or stories about Harvard life to eighteen East Coast papers. Isolated from the Harvard community and overloaded with newspaper work, Phillips soon buckled under the strain and suffered a nervous breakdown. Nonetheless, Phillips finally received his A.B. degree in 1904 and left Cambridge to work for the *Philadelphia Press*.

The move to Philadelphia, however, failed to fulfill Phillips. Dissatisfied with his life and lacking either drive or direction, he soon quit this job and in 1906 joined former classmate Henry Masten in France. After a year of aimless drifting, Phillips resolved to try to forget about himself by helping others. He decided to return to the United States and wrote of his intent to his cousin, Dr. Margaret Doolittle, an acquaintance of many employees of New York City's social agencies. It so happened that one of Dr. Doolittle's friends, Robert Bruère, the general agent of the New York Association for Improving the Condition of the Poor (AICP), was looking for a young man with newspaper experience to serve as secretary of the newly formed New York Milk Committee. His cousin made the appropriate arrangements, and on his arrival in the United States, Phillips was greeted with the opportunity to join an organization committed to helping others. Two days after his return to America Phillips situated himself in New York City and found himself faced with the assignment of "waking people up to the need of doing something to improve the city's milk supply and to reduce the high rate of mortality among babies."[8]

As secretary of the New York Milk Committee from 1906 to 1911, Phillips helped mobilize community resources for the committee's campaign against infant mortality. Stressing social and personal as well as environmental aspects of community health, Phillips encouraged the New York Milk Committee to establish infant milk stations that not only dispensed milk but also offered maternal education in the principles of child hygiene. Later he assisted in the organization of a model dairy designed to demonstrate the practicality of pure milk production. From his work with the New York Milk Committee, Phillips found that he was more interested in the educational and social side of the milk depot work, which stressed the "whole child," than in the medical side. He grew restive in his work with the milk committee, and when offered a position as secretary of the newly formed Child Welfare Commission in Milwaukee, left New York City in the spring of 1911.

Building on the lessons learned in New York City, Phillips established under the auspices of the Child Welfare Commission the first urban health center in the United States. This health center represented the earliest large-scale attempt to organize a neighborhood so that residents could participate actively in the execution as well as the determination of the center's health programs. Focusing on the conservation of infant life in a district that registered the highest infant mortality rate in the city, Phillips and his corps of local doctors, nurses, midwives, and residents registered babies, provided pre- and postnatal maternal education, and offered creative clinical instruction in child welfare for the local medical profession. No other agency in the country provided such intensive care as the health center in St. Cyril's Parish, Milwaukee.

In 1912, however, a change in the municipal administration resulted in the creation of a division of child welfare under the Health Department and in the firing of Phillips as secretary. Phillips returned East and pondered the possibilities and techniques of health and community organization. The fruit of his labors, the Cincinnati

Social Unit Organization, commenced in January 1917 in the Mohawk-Brighton district of Cincinnati.

Using infant health care as his pilot organizational technique, Phillips focused more directly on building a neighborhood structure around the organization of citizens and producers. He hoped to create a sense of corporate identity or community within the confines of an arbitrarily defined territorial unit. Once functioning as an integrated whole, group members could exercise control over the social, economic, and political processes operating within neighborhood boundaries, efficiently matching needs with resources. Phillips then envisioned the replication of such units on a citywide and ultimately a national basis.

To achieve such control, Phillips sought to organize neighborhood groups into social units in which residents worked together, defined their needs, and arranged to have their needs met through a threefold process. First, Phillips subdivided the neighborhoods into block associations to promote face-to-face contact among the residents and encourage interchange. Second, to provide vehicles for the expression of block ideas, needs, and aspirations, Phillips set up neighborhood citizens' councils and producers' councils. Representatives from each block association sat in the neighborhood citizens' council to advance the needs of the locale, and representatives of the area's service sectors sat in the occupational council to suggest ways to meet the needs. Third, Phillips had both groups come together regularly to seek, through consensus, the appropriate balance between needs and solutions.

Once the process was functioning horizontally on the neighborhood level across the city, Phillips hoped to establish the process vertically to achieve intracity cooperation. He wanted each neighborhood group to send delegates to a citywide citizens' council and a citywide producers' council. These groups were to articulate city needs and strategies for action, the actual programs selected to be decided upon in joint meetings of the two bodies. Eventually, Phillips envisioned the reproduction of this organizational form on the county, state, and federal levels, where citizen participation combined with expert analysis in the neighborhood setting produced a working democracy with decision-making flowing from smaller centers outward toward the whole society. Phillips believed that such a structure permitted more group participation in the decision-making process, provided a sense of order throughout the city, and trained neighborhood residents to be responsible citizens. It was the organic model par excellence.

Although Phillips failed to plant his organization firmly enough to withstand an attack by Cincinnati's city fathers and charitable organizations during the post–World War I Red Scare, the social unit organization developed the most detailed organic organizational scheme and represented the major attempt to make the neighborhood in the organic city a reality. But just as the organic model reached its apogee in implementation, its adherents dwindled. By the mid-1920s, a variety of forces seemed to pull cities apart and produce an urban form characterized more by particularism than by the interaction described by Phillips and other proponents of the organic city. Social welfare practitioners and academics alike rejected the organic model of the early twentieth century city and replaced it with a new model that was pluralistic rather than syncretic. This study of the neighborhood in the organic city uses the social unit organization as a vehicle to illustrate the interplay of ideas and action primarily during the first two decades of the twentieth century. Specifically, it elucidates the context in which contemporaries developed a theory of the city and attempted to organize urban areas in an effort to harmonize their conception of the city with reality as they saw it.

Although the major focus of the study is on the social unit plan and urban organization, it does touch on important issues in both Progressive era historiography and the history of community organization. As far as the historiography of the Progressive era is concerned, the history of the social unit underscores the fact that reformers during this period were a heterogeneous group and were interested in a wide variety of issues. This study indicates that two important elements of progressivism—the desire to increase the influence of ordinary men and women and the fascination with experts—were not mutually exclusive. Instead, Progressives like Phillips and his supporters believed that democracy could be achieved through the interaction of the people and the experts. To some extent the discussion of Phillips's social unit organization points to the interest among Progressives in a transformation of politics and government. The multiplication of social units from the neighborhood to the national level as envisioned by Phillips certainly suggests a restructuring of American government. The implications of the spread of social units on the city level, for example, concerned Cincinnati's Mayor Galvin and other party regulars who feared that the proliferation of these units throughout Cincinnati would endanger the control of the Queen City's Republican party. Phillips's work with the New York Milk Committee emphasizes the importance of the environment in early twentieth century thought. And this study suggests that a democratic impulse, in addition to those of social justice and social control, did exist. Perhaps as a result of Phillips's affinity with Milwaukee-style socialism, the social unit plan stressed the importance of citizen participation in the decisions that shaped the lives of neighborhood residents.

This analysis of the social unit organization also represents an addition to the scant literature on the history of community organization. Kotler's comments about the history of the neighborhood movement point up the fact that little has been written on the history of neighborhood organizing. Most available literature in the field concentrates on the dynamics of a specific organization's successes and failures rather than on organizational activities viewed over time. A consciousness of time forces us to weigh the significance of events and ideas in relation to a particular historical setting. In so doing, we can better understand the origin of neighborhood efforts and the position of different organizations in the larger picture. An appreciation of the past is important if we are to understand fully the different motives, goals, failures, and successes of current activities. In addition, a look at the history of community organization can reveal the continuities that exist in the practice of neighborhood organization over time despite the unique historical contexts of the various efforts.

This examination of the social unit organization suggests that its experience is both peculiar and common. Because it occurred during a particular historical era, the shape of the organization, the goals of the organizers, and the tactics used are related to specific definitions of neighborhood and city. However, the social unit's experience also reveals certain constants. In many respects, for instance, the charges leveled at the organization are similar to charges currently faced by neighborhood organizers as they work with different community groups. The social unit's history indicates as well how the strategy that uses a particular service as an educational tool can backfire when residents see the tool as the end product rather than the means to a larger end.

In *The Organic City* the social unit organization is treated as symptomatic of the ways Americans during the years between 1880 and 1920 defined their world and attempted to structure their society to fit their definitions. The social unit organization is not a microcosm of all the forces that shaped American society during this period. But although the social unit organization does not epitomize the era, it serves as a medium through which to better understand it.[9] The actual configuration of the social unit organization was unique, but how that configuration came about was not. By focusing on the how, we can increase our understanding of the interplay of ideas and action, as well as the consequences of that interaction, during a particular period.

1
Neighborhood in the Organic City

During the second half of the nineteenth century rapid social and economic changes negated the antebellum definition of the city as an undifferentiated whole. When confronted with the disparity between the old urban definition and the new city of the late nineteenth century with its specialized land use pattern and system of socioeconomic segregation, concerned Americans searched for a new definition of the city that corresponded more closely to the segmented urban community around them. Borrowing the organic analogy popular in descriptions of society, these Americans portrayed the city as an organism composed of an interdependent system of complementary parts or neighborhoods. And once these Americans began to think in terms of interdependence, they sought to translate that belief into a workable system of urban organization that facilitated communication and interaction between the city and its component parts. In so doing, they isolated the neighborhood as the central unit of urban life and devised a series of programs to insure that the neighborhood contributed to the overall health of the American city. Thus, the notion of the organism provided both an appropriate definition of urban form and a prescription for action during the first two decades of the twentieth century.

Acceptance of the organic theory of society represented a major step in a process of reconceptualization that ultimately led to a series of attempts to create a feeling, however imprecise, of unity and order believed to be missing in late nineteenth century society. On a variety of levels, the Revolutionary Generation had commenced a national discussion on the "meaning and implementation of wholeness."[1] At the outset of the nineteenth century and despite increasing numbers of foreigners and the ever-widening impact of industrialization, technological sophistication, and urban growth, many Americans envisioned the nation as an ever-expanding composite whole[2] and believed America to be embarked on a process leading to the creation of what John Higham has called a "homogeneous future from a heterogeneous past."[3] Although the population mix during the first sixty years of the nineteenth century changed rapidly and the economic and physical landscapes of America began undergoing dramatic transformation, Americans held fast to the belief that America—at once homogeneous and diverse—forged unity out of diversity.[4]

This belief, however, was shaken after the Civil War. Rapid and disruptive economic and demographic changes negated the prevailing holistic vision of America. Between 1870 and 1890 immigration to the United States virtually doubled,[5] and industrialization and urbanization tore apart the seams of a localized, more rural, and seemingly less impersonal world. Instead of the amalgamated whole, society resembled a collection of entities that made America appear not unified but particularistic. Distance, rather than absorption, seemed to characterize society.[6] Under such conditions, old ideas and institutions seemed dysfunctional in the face of a society both distended and fragmented.[7]

When presented with a disparity between their belief that "America was becoming, . . . or ought to be a unified and homogeneous entity"[8] and the apparent reality of diversity and division, many concerned Americans sought to resolve the dilemma posed by the disjunction between their conception and their perception of American life. These Americans, including sociologists like Albion Small, social reformers like Robert A. Woods and Frederic Howe, philosophers like Josiah Royce, and students of government like Mary Follett, searched for a theoretical structure through which to understand, describe, and direct society.[9] By the 1880s the notion of interdependence appealed to many men and women who were anxious to impose order on the world around them,[10] and it soon dominated late nineteenth century thought. While not all championed the new beliefs and many described interdependence somewhat differently, a great number of Americans began to accept the notion that no part of life could be viewed in isolation and that all parts of society were interrelated in a larger whole. By adopting an organic theory of society that stressed the interdependence of parts, numerous Americans redefined wholeness to mean not homogeneity but rather group interaction in a large, ultimately smoothly functioning, composite whole. Armed with this redefinition or conceptual framework, they were able to come to grips with their environment.

When or how Americans acquired their new conceptual framework is not an easy or, for this book, an important issue to resolve. It is clear, however, that intellectuals in America in the latter part of the nineteenth century had become interested in European discussions about an organic society. Their reading of such theorists as Georg Wilhelm Friedrich Hegel, George Simmel, and Émile Durkheim had made American intellectuals familiar with theories that stressed interaction as the very essence of society.[11] But it is likely that the work of Herbert Spencer proved most useful in spreading notions of society as an organism outside of the intellectual community to an increasingly larger public.

Admittedly, it is not possible to quantify the impact of Spencer's ideas. But, as Sidney Fine points out in his study of post–Civil War American thought, Spencer enjoyed a wide following in the United States. Spencer's books sold well, and Edward Livingston Youman's *Popular Science Monthly*, begun in 1872, disseminated various versions of Spencer's ideas even more broadly. On the basis of his study, Fine found little reason to doubt William James's comment on Spencer's general popularity in America. According to James, unlike many theorists, Spencer was not the preserve of a small coterie of intellectuals. Instead, "Spencer was a philosopher who could be appreciated by those who had no other philosopher."[12]

Spencer, of course, influenced Americans in a variety of ways, for he was a political thinker as well as a proponent of evolution and societal interdependence. One of the aspects of Spencer's ideas, however, with particular appeal for those Americans concerned with social unity revolved around the notion of society as an organism. His organic theory, which essentially contended that greater specialization of function resulted in a greater interdependence of groups, provided many Americans with a coherent framework for explaining their conception of late nineteenth century society.[13] Americans whose interests ranged from philosophy, psychology, and sociology to child welfare, public health, and political reform promulgated a loosely Spencerian analysis of society and began to use an organic analogy to describe the nature of the new society.[14] They argued that society was not merely a "loose collection of self-sufficient individuals," but instead an organic whole composed of groups and territorial parts.[15] Henry Adams, professor of political economy and finance at the University of Michigan, captured the spirit of the new belief. "Modern life," he wrote in 1893, "has increased the dependence of men and classes to such a degree that interdependence is a thing which is felt, rather than an idea to be reasoned about. . . . Society is coming to be in fact organic, and the claim that all parts should find harmony of life in the recognition of a common aim, shows itself in the attitude of which large numbers of persons are assuming before the vexed problems of the day."[16]

Once Americans adopted the notion of an organic society, they sought to describe it. In so doing, they imparted a feeling of hope and purpose. Old bonds of union, such as the "political compact," declared prominent social reformer Robert A. Woods, no longer held Americans together. The "social organism, or the new bond of union" had replaced the older bonds that no longer worked.[17] And what was this social organism? According to Josiah Strong, a minister keenly interested in the state of society, it was a structure "whose life is one and whose interests are one. . . . [It] possesses different organs, having different functions, each of which exists, not for itself but to serve all the others. . . . If any organ refuses to perform its proper function, there is disease, perhaps death."[18] If nurtured properly, however, so that all parts remained healthy, a "genuine interweaving where each individual (or group composed of individuals) had a full part in the whole-a-making" occurred.[19] Those interested in reconstructing reality to conform to their new model began to study society to discover how best to hasten its perfection as a well-formed whole. Or as Edward Devine, editor of *Charities*, suggested, they began the process of putting "into orderly arrangement that which had been disarranged or badly arranged."[20]

Since the way a society defines itself influences how it defines its constituent parts, it is not surprising that proponents of an organic society interested in urban affairs, such as Robert A. Woods and Frederic Howe, adopted an organic analogy when confronted with an urban environment that failed to correspond with their conception of the city. They searched for a new image or definition of the urban landscape to replace "the inadequacies of what were once true and tried conceptions."[21] In response to this intellectual crisis provoked by the inapplicability of inherited images, these men and women came to view the city in a new way. They abandoned the pre–Civil War notion of the city as a residential community composed of congeries of densely settled individuals joined by a "quest for economic expansion and social improvement."[22] They began to see the city, instead, as an interdependent system of differentiated but complementary parts. Like the larger society of which it was a part, the city was an organism. As Robert A. Woods suggested in a review of his thirty years of work in Boston, the city of late nineteenth and early twentieth century America was a city of interdependence—an organic structure. It was, according to Woods, "a cluster of interlacing communities, each having its own vital ways of expression and action, but all together creating the municipality which shall render the fullest service through the most spirited participation of its citizens."[23]

This conception of the city represented an attempt to make sense of and to order an urban reality that was in fact changing rapidly. As the nineteenth century drew to a close, what we recognize as the modern metropolis gradually emerged. Although occurring at different times across the country, the transformation from the pedestrian city of the eighteenth and early nineteenth centuries to the expanded and differentiated urban structure of the twentieth century had taken place in most major urban centers by the dawn of the twentieth century.

Prior to the 1850s most major American cities were small, compact, and relatively integrated. Under conditions marked by a very rudimentary transportation technology, urban areas were walking cities in which the location of all activities—whether social, economic, religious, or political—depended on the time it took to walk from one place to another. These dense settlements rarely exceeded a two-mile radius from the center of the community. And, in these crowded settlements, intermixture of residence and workplace proved to be the rule rather than the exception. With the absence of feasible modes of intracity transportation, few other living and work alternatives existed, and residents found it difficult to segregate themselves from one another. These communities seemed to contemporaries, as indeed they seem to us, to be "integrated masses without sharply differentiated social or economic sectors."[24] The structure and image of wholeness appeared consonant with one another.

Between 1840 and 1880, however, a series of transportation innovations offered the elites and later, when less costly, the middling classes the opportunity to leave the crowded conditions of the walking city. First the omnibus and the horsecar provided a few urbanites with residential options. With the electrification of the horsecar in the 1880s, the process of residential sorting accelerated. At the same time these advances stimulated industrial mobility. By the 1890s, transportation innovations combined with increased immigration and internal migration to transform the American cityscape. Late nineteenth century cities ballooned, and many grew to cover an area of more than fifty miles.[25]

During this process of expansion, cities were poised in a tenuous balance between centripetal and centrifugal forces. The electric streetcar opened up new areas for settlement along the urban fringe and, consequently, set in motion a process of decentralization. At the same time, the new modes of mass transit exerted a centralizing effect, creating the central business district (CBD) as the economic focal point of the new metropolitan structure. Motivated by the desire to insure that the dynamics of the decentralizing forces did not overwhelm the centralizing forces, cities embarked upon a vigorous annexation program to keep the expanding peripheral areas within the municipality.[26] Annexations, acceptable to the fringe areas largely because of suburbanites' desires for superior central city services, restrained the separatist tendencies inherent in the centrifugal forces pulling at the city and served as a "countervailing force for unity."[27]

But municipal unity based on "unified urban rule"[28] did not eliminate the internal fragmentation of the metropolitan unit. The process of specialization of land use and socioeconomic segregation set in motion by the various transportation innovations intensified by the turn of the twentieth century. The city seemed to contain a spatially segregated "hodge-podge of people of widely divergent economic, social and cultural interests." Each segment possessed its own needs, desires, and place. In this context, "divergent groups demanded divergent actions." With a political structure that "maximized opportunity for local self-rule"[29] grafted upon a cityscape marked by economic and social particularism, it was possible by reference to the organic analogy to conceptualize a new type of urban form—one that seemed "composed of differentiated parts which could work together to form a larger viable whole."[30] As a result, this unique mixture of the centripetal and centrifugal forces between roughly 1870 and 1920 created conditions that made it possible for those interested in the city and imbued with notions of social organisms to see the city as an interdependent unit.

Visualizing the city as an organism encouraged those studying the city to discover the constituent parts of this interdependent unit and to understand the dynamics of the different parts that composed the city as a whole. Just as the city was seen as a distinct unit within a larger organic society, it was viewed as a "bunch of communities" and territorial units. And many students of the city identified the neighborhood, which they saw as the local unit of citizen identification and participation, as a critical component of the organic city. Earlier conceptions of the city had blurred the emergence of the neighborhood as an institution. The structure of the walking city, described as an undifferentiated whole, did not allow for segmentation.[31] But the "new city" that emerged after the Civil War, with its concomitant specialized land use pattern and system of socioeconomic segregation, encouraged an image of neighborhood.

Robert A. Woods, the head of Boston's South End House, was one of the first to recognize the importance of the neighborhood in the organic city. He expressed clearly and systematically the belief shared by numerous reformers and settlement workers, and later described by Arthur C. Holden in his review of the settlement movement, that "city life could never be understood nor its problems met unless the process began in the neighborhood."[32] As early as 1893, Woods stressed the importance of the neighborhood in city life and contended that the neighborhood represented the "microcosm of all social problems."[33] The neighborhood, Woods argued, was the

only unit of society which included essentially "every kind of community need and the resources to meet it." Because of the compact
nature of the city neighborhood, Woods believed, it could be "understood and handled" by residents of the area. As the fundamental
social unit, the neighborhood was the very "pith and core and kernel
of organic democracy."[34]

For Woods, the neighborhood in the organic city was more than
just a vital organ of the city; it was the "ultimate testing place of all
social reforms."[35] Sufficiently small to be comprehensible to and
manageable for the average citizen, it was at the same time large
enough "to include, in essence, practically all the problems of the
city, state and nation." The neighborhood, Woods argued, "is con-
cretely conceivable. The city, state, or nation is not and will not be,
except as it is organically related through the neighborhood."[36] As far
as Woods was concerned, the neighborhood not only served as an
important place for understanding local needs, but also as a "place
where the structural rebuilding of society had to begin," a place
where citizens could be "equipped for life in the broader sphere."[37]
The neighborhood, for Woods and for many of his contemporaries,
was the place where an "all-round, timely and locally-wise, cooperative electorate" could be made to blossom and set the stage for a
strong and vital society—from the neighborhood, to the city, and
then to the nation.[38]

Woods and others conceded, however, that not all neighborhoods
functioned according to the organic ideal. Instead, the city seemed to
many contemporaries to be an "organism with an imperfectly developed nervous system" because of defects internal to some neighborhoods.[39] Since they saw the city as a "central feature in modern
civilization" and thus the "arena where the social and political forces
that were coming to fore would play," Woods and his contemporaries
felt that the situation demanded immediate attention. And because,
given the nature of the organism, "all influences were transmitted
from one part to any other part,"[40] it was deemed necessary to
strengthen the neighborhood to insure a healthy, well-formed whole.

Imbued with the spirit of the "neighborhood in nation-building," a
variety of groups joined Woods in the effort to perfect the workings of
the neighborhood and therefore the organic city. Believing that, as an
organism, the city was capable of both healthy and unhealthy growth,

these groups placed a high premium on planning to nurture a healthy urban environment and a balanced pattern of growth.[41] Wise planning would counterbalance the forces of centralization and decentralization inherent in the organic city in such a way as to harmonize the multifaceted forces that affected the well-being of the metropolitan community. In general, planning in the organic city was either local or metropolitan in scope. While each approach stressed different procedures for integrating the urban community, the goal remained the same—to foster both neighborhood and citywide revitalization and facilitate the development of a nation of "well-constituted" urban communities.

The local approach to planning appears to have been the more popular, or at least the more studied, of the two. Reformers working in the neighborhoods—the units of the city—championed a wide variety of programs to develop the neighborhood as a vital part of the city. They believed neighborhood development would foster a high degree of concern for the entire city. "Community organization" programs represented attempts to effect the reconstruction, expansion, and integration of neighborhood and city life.[42] They all sought in some way to get neighborhood residents themselves to discover problems and to participate in the solutions to those problems.[43] The most popular locally oriented programs included the social settlements and the school/community centers.

One of the earliest programs to focus on organizing the neighborhood was the social settlement. Most historians argue that the social settlement, a celebrated community program of the late nineteenth and early twentieth centuries, originated in England in response to the suffering caused by the industrial revolution. It represented a unique type of community organization that stressed a combination of preventive social work and neighborhood reconstruction as the way to perfect city organization.[44] While most social work organizations provided minimal relief or bracing words in an attempt to cure the symptoms of urban distress, the settlement emphasized both rehabilitation and education for the general improvement of social and industrial conditions. Settlement workers, as an outgrowth of their activities, contributed to the shift from personal to environmental social work. They viewed individuals not merely as objects of charity and isolated beings who needed "moral" rehabilitation, but also as people caught in an environment that corrupted them. Because of the interdependent nature of the city, settlement workers argued, "problems were not confined to only one portion of the city." The city would not be healthy until all its parts were healthy. By working at the neighborhood level, settlement workers believed they could lay the groundwork for the rehabilitation of the environment and for the growth of a spirit of cooperation, which eventually would further the city's welfare and prosperity, and transform the lives of the "unfortunates."[45]

The settlement workers' commitment to the neighborhood expressed itself in a variety of forms.[46] Mary Simkhovitch of Greenwich House in New York City, for example, stressed the settlement's role as a guardian of a particular neighborhood's "interest." Because the settlement identified with the neighborhood's interest, she contended, it formed a "steadying and permanent element" in the area and helped foster the development of the neighborhood. By implication, it also served to invigorate the city as a whole.[47]

In a similar vein, Jane Addams of Hull House argued that because settlement workers "regarded the entire city as organic," they strove "to unify it" and to help guide it into the larger framework of city life.[48] Graham Taylor of Chicago Commons affirmed that because "neighborhoods are the source of civic strength and progress," by working on the neighborhood level it was possible to awaken residents to the existence of social needs and responsibilities. Such awareness, with the proper nourishment, Taylor argued, would both strengthen the neighborhood and the larger city of which it was a part.[49]

Finally, Robert A. Woods continually stressed the importance of neighborhood development for the benefit of civic health. In a very basic sense, Woods believed the settlement to be a "social organizer that opened the way for [neighborhood] intercourse with other parts of the city." As the essential social unit, the neighborhood contained in the "most manageable shape," Woods believed, "the whole variety of community problems." By fostering the "consciousness of common local needs," according to Woods, it was possible to develop a "realistic city loyalty." This, in turn, would foster a spirit that ultimately would transcend the city and tie neighborhood residents to the state and the nation as well.[50]

Two settlements in particular, the Neighborhood Guild and the Hudson Guild, adopted bold programs designed to involve local residents directly in building the neighborhood into a strong unit of the city. The Neighborhood Guild was established in 1886 by Stanton Coit in New York City.[51] Coit believed that social reform revolved around the conscious organization of neighborhood residents, who then directed their efforts toward building a "civic renaissance." The central ingredient for fashioning an organized neighborhood, Coit believed, was a system of block organizations.

According to Coit's plan, each block of the neighborhood was to set up its own council and elect delegates to represent it in a larger neighborhood guild with headquarters in the settlement house. Residents selected by the various blocks to serve on the neighborhood guild, Coit argued, represented the "natural leadership" of the community. These representatives, in their role as delegates, were to oversee all municipal services in the neighborhood and to raise sufficient money for a "variety of economic, educational and recreational activities" designed to effect "neighborhood reconstruction." Coit actually hoped to set up guilds throughout the city and eventually to federate them in a single city guild that would direct those activities transcending the neighborhood and touching the entire urban community. The Neighborhood Guild's metropolitan "machinery" never was set up as Coit had planned, and the guild ceased to operate along block lines once Coit left for England in 1890. But his was the earliest attempt to build a neighborhood organization that would ideally facilitate the development of a "well-constituted community."[52]

The Hudson Guild, another New York City settlement house, also stressed the need to organize the people of the neighborhood to involve the neighborhood in city building. Established in 1895 by John L. Elliott, an associate of Coit's, the Hudson Guild was modeled after the Neighborhood Guild. As in the case of Coit's organization, the Hudson Guild emphasized the importance of the participation of the neighborhood residents in community affairs to help themselves and to contribute to the well-being of the entire urban community. The Hudson Guild's district captains, similar in function to Coit's block representatives, were to work with the people in their respective blocks in cooperative ventures.

Although the Hudson Guild, like the Neighborhood Guild, failed
to implement fully its organizational structure, Elliott echoed Coit's
belief in the necessity of neighborhood development. Elliott hoped
that rejuvenating the neighborhood by helping residents determine
priorities and work together on solutions to problems would stimulate the residents to look beyond community boundaries to the larger
city. Once they did so, Elliott believed, they would discover the
relationship between neighborhood welfare and that of the larger
community, the city.[53] Or, as Robert Woods contended, the guild or
the settlement should "initiate local cooperation," secure for the
district "its full share of the city's intellectual and moral progress,"
and ultimately bring "people throughout the city to join with them" in
the pursuit of such progress.[54]

Many settlement workers, like their counterparts in the Neighborhood and Hudson guilds, hoped that the settlement could facilitate neighborhood development and evoke a strong sense of local
cooperation. Most settlements, however, experienced only limited
success in their attempts at community organization. While they
promoted the ideal that programs for social change should grow out of
the felt needs of the people, the largely institutional nature of the
settlements seemed to discourage the active participation of many
local residents. In the long run, settlement house workers found it
difficult to build their organizations around local interests, as veteran
community organizer Jesse Steiner pointed out in a review of the first
twenty-five years of neighborhood organization. Outside leaders
could be brought into the community, according to Steiner, but they
were to be no more than facilitators of action. Because they were
unable to serve such a function, for whatever reasons, the settlement
houses developed into institutions that served a few community
needs rather than into "levers for social change."[55]

Other organizations followed the settlements' lead in focusing on
the neighborhood as the central unit of city life. Like the settlements,
these organizations sought to help develop a sense of common enter-
prise among neighborhood residents. Leaders of these groups also
believed that "America was made up of the sum total of thousands of
neighborhoods," and that neither the city nor the "nation could be
understood nor their problems met" unless the process of problem
solving began in the neighborhood. Based on these beliefs, these

proponents of community organization hoped to encourage neighborhood residents "to assume their own responsibilities and to guide their own destinies."[56] Of these organizations, the school or community center programs were among the most popular.

According to settlement historian Allen Davis, as settlement workers realized the impossibility of the settlement as a community facilitator, they "discovered that every large city neighborhood had a ready-made neighborhood center—the public school—only waiting to be utilized and put to work."[57] Interest in the school as a community center also grew out of the recreational activities of the last decade of the nineteenth century. Neighborhood activists began to argue that the public school provided an excellent spot to multiply points of contact between neighborhood residents, to foster neighborhood unity, and to promote the recognition of common interests on the neighborhood *and* the city level.[58]

The school or community center movement first took form in Rochester, New York, under the direction of Edward Ward in 1907. Ward and his supporters hoped to fashion the school as the focus "for the educational, recreational, sociable and discussional life" of the neighborhood residents. School center organizers hoped to establish cooperation among neighborhood residents and stimulate participation in local affairs. Such activity, they believed, would ultimately lead to an understanding of the relationship between neighborhood needs and the needs of the larger community of which the school was but a part.

Following Ward's lead in Rochester, reformers in other cities began to set up school centers. After securing permission from local school officials, a trained organizer would be invited to the community to help facilitate the development of the school as a community center. By 1916 the movement had grown large enough to warrant a national organization, and in that year the promoters of the school center movement established the National Community Center Association. Following the creation of the national body, members of the association intensified their efforts to get more citizens involved in local affairs and, at the same time, to illustrate the relationship between the life of the neighborhood and that of the city as a whole.[59]

Although immensely popular, school centers failed to facilitate the identification of common needs among neighborhood residents or encourage residents to assume actual responsibility for their own affairs. The centers served mainly as social centers for the neighborhood, sponsoring recreational events in the evenings rather than serving as dynamic organizations for the revitalization of the neighborhood and the city. And even when these organizations did stimulate local consciousness and activity, they were not able to translate this recognition into a larger civic understanding.[60] Nonetheless, the school centers represented an important attempt to organize neighborhoods to "release their energies" in the "interest of both themselves and the city as a whole," as Ida Clarke pointed out in her study of community organization theory and practice.[61]

Although we know less about the metropolitan activities than we do about neighborhood-oriented programs such as the settlements and school centers, metropolitan activities perhaps more boldly advertised the ethos of the organic city. Concentrating on citywide issues rather than local issues, metropolitan groups based their operation on the proposition that not only did the health of the city depend on the well-being of its various parts, but also the health of the parts "depended upon centralized, coordinated management to determine priorities, to distribute the public goods equitably for the maximum benefit of all, and to establish mores to which all citizens must adhere for the promotion of the civic welfare."[62] This cohesion for civic progress, ideally occurring simultaneously with work in the neighborhoods, was believed to ensure that localism did not inadvertently separate and segregate the parts of the city from the larger civic structure.

Early twentieth century improvement associations are an excellent example of how proponents of the organic city sought to insure central loyalty and vision among the various parts of the city. In Cincinnati, Ohio, for example, the movement toward improvement associations began in the late nineteenth century. At first, these associations fought for local issues. Founded earliest in the peripheral districts of the city, these groups devoted themselves to securing local improvements such as better sewers, lighting, police and fire protection, and schools. Feeling slighted by the older wards of the inner city, these associations attempted to effect a balance of power between the fringe areas and the more central, older sections of the metropolis.

In 1907 these associations joined together into the Federated Improvement Association of Cincinnati. According to a spokesman of the federation in 1911, members of the different groups realized that they possessed "interests common to all."[63] By 1913 the federation boasted thirty-six affiliates with a total membership of 8,000 members. In its deliberations it consciously concentrated on citywide rather than local issues and stressed the importance of the joining of those common interests for the promotion of the larger civic welfare.[64]

In Baltimore, Maryland, a similar drive toward federated civic action occurred. During the last two decades of the nineteenth century, neighborhood improvement associations began to appear in Baltimore, and by 1900 over thirty organizations existed across the city. As in Cincinnati, these groups emerged to secure an equal distribution of city funds and to fight for local public improvements in their particular part of the city. During the early years of the twentieth century there were attempts to bring these associations together into a citywide alliance. In 1911 success came with the formation of the Baltimore City-Wide Congress. It was an organization composed of representatives from forty-one local improvement and protective associations in Baltimore. At the first congress meeting in 1911, member Alexander Johnson stressed the importance of guarding against associational parochialism and urged his fellow delegates "not to isolate themselves from the city-at-large."[65] As in Cincinnati, the Baltimore City-Wide Congress attempted to coordinate efforts of the different areas to solve common problems in such a way as to promote the civic welfare of the entire metropolitan community.

While most organizations focused on either local or metropolitan efforts at city integration, the social unit organization attempted to combine the local and civic thrusts. Based on the belief that each neighborhood represented a "nation in miniature" and on the notion of a "wholeness of the environment," the social unit organization operated from the basic premise that the neighborhood was a unitary and integrated structure that operated in a complementary manner to form a larger whole—ultimately a "nation of well-constituted communities."[66] Proponents of the social unit plan argued that, by studying the neighborhood and working closely with neighborhood residents, it was possible to further neighborhood betterment and, by constructing systems to facilitate communication between the various neighborhoods, ensure the revitalization of America's urban centers.[67]

Building on his experiences in the early twentieth century child health crusade, Wilbur C. Phillips devised the social unit plan of organization. From 1917 to 1920, Phillips sought to demonstrate, in the Mohawk-Brighton district of Cincinnati, Ohio, the feasibility of organizing neighborhood residents into occupational and citizen groups that would meet regularly, ascertain needs, and allocate community resources to make the neighborhood into a properly functioning unit of the city. Such a demonstration, Phillips believed, would spark similar organizational efforts in other Cincinnati neighborhoods, making the city into a well-constituted community. Inspired by Cincinnati's transformation, Phillips reasoned, other cities would follow suit. Of all the attempts to perfect the organization of the organic city, Phillips's social unit organization represents the quintessential example of the translation of the organic city into action.

2

Infant Health and Neighborhood Organization

Just as the notion of interdependence manifested itself in the definition of urban structure, it also influenced the nature of the attack on urban problems. This was particularly true in the field of public health. During the first decade of the twentieth century, many public health workers tended to view the human as an organism—a unitary and integrated structure that operated in a complementary manner with the total environment.[1] Viewing the human as an organism was not new in these early twentieth century discussions, but seeing it in relation to the environment was.

Prior to the twentieth century, the human organism and the environment were thought to exist as separate and distinct entities, each having little impact on the other. But by the turn of the century, public health workers began to find such a view unsatisfactory. They found that exclusive emphasis on either physical, environmental conditions or human, biological conditions failed to produce a healthy society. Concentration on the interrelationship between human and environment, on the other hand, seemed to promote the general health of both the individual and the community. By building on these notions, public health workers not only took important steps toward combating particular diseases, but also recognized and advertised the importance of mobilizing the entire community in the pursuit of health.

In his work with the New York Milk Committee and the Milwaukee Child Welfare Commission, Wilbur C. Phillips played an
important role in the creation of programs to mobilize communities
for fuller health services. By working with individuals within a community context, Phillips found that it was possible to provide good
medical care for needy individuals while encouraging the community
to attack health problems. As far as Phillips was concerned, once a
community saw the interrelationship between individual health and
community health, it was possible to think about community health
in relation to city health and to unite all citizens in a quest for the
health of the larger urban entity. On the basis of that experience,
Philips moved beyond community health organization to thoughts of
organizing neighborhoods and creating a structure to facilitate intracity interaction between neighborhoods. Like so many of his contemporaries, he hoped to develop the neighborhood as a vital part of the
city and to foster the creation of a "well-constituted" urban community.

The New York Association for Improving the Condition of the Poor
(AICP), Phillips's new employer, had been active in public health
activities since the mid-nineteenth century. Because private charities
were unable to combat the distress caused by the Panic of 1837, the
AICP was formed in 1843 to make New York City's charitable efforts
more effective. Robert M. Hartley, corresponding secretary and
general agent of the New York City Temperance Society, became the
first corresponding secretary and general agent of the AICP. It was
under Hartley's direction that the AICP launched a major campaign
against infant mortality—a public health crusade that eventually
would prove pivotal in Phillips's career.[2]

Robert M. Hartley had become interested in infant mortality
during his years as a temperance worker. During a campaign to
persuade distillery owners to enter a new line of business, Hartley
discovered that cows housed inside city limits were being fed mash,
or distillery slop.[3] When pasturage shrank in urban areas during the
first two decades of the nineteenth century, distillers had offered
dairymen cheap and easily produced fodder in the form of mash.
Dairymen found that cows could be induced, if semistarved, to eat
distillery waste and that these cows initially gave large amounts of
milk. To maximize profits, herdsmen housed up to 2,000 cows in a
single dairy. Under extremely unsanitary conditions, the cows were

milked. Dairymen then watered the milk to increase its quantity and added chalk, magnesium, and plaster of paris to improve its color and texture. By 1835, according to Hartley's estimates, over 18,000 cows in New York City and Brooklyn were fed on distillery slop. Aghast at this practice, Hartley commenced his lifelong crusade against swill milk.[4]

Hartley continued his investigation of the swill milk industry when he assumed the direction of the AICP. What made his discoveries so appalling to many who read his swill milk accounts was the coincidence of the identification of an adulterated milk supply with an increasing interest in the problem of infant mortality. To Hartley and many of his contemporaries, infant mortality appeared directly linked to lack of a pure milk supply in antebellum cities where continued population growth shrank the amount of pasturage available to urban dairymen.[5]

Hartley's tireless efforts drew attention to the AICP's crusade against milk-related infant mortality and resulted in the passage of legislation. Daily newspapers, *Frank Leslie's Illustrated Newspaper*, and members of New York City's Academy of Medicine joined Hartley's attack on the swill milk industry. Under mounting public pressure the Common Council of Manhattan appointed an aldermanic committee in 1858 to investigate the issue. Despite ample evidence that the milk produced in swill dairies was unsanitary, devoid of nutritive value, and a perfect medium for diseases such as *cholera infantum*,[6] the distillers won the day, and the council shelved the swill milk issue.[7] Undaunted, Hartley and his supporters continued their attack on the swill dairies, and in 1862 the State of New York enacted its first milk law. The law levied a fifty-dollar fine for the selling of "impure, adulterated, or unwholesome milk." The measure also fined those keeping cows in crowded and unhealthy conditions, and penalized dairymen who fed swill to cows. In addition, milk wagon drivers faced a hundred-dollar penalty for not displaying the source of their milk clearly on their wagons. While this was an advance over no law at all, the relatively imprecise nature of what constituted "impure, adulterated, or unwholesome milk" left a loophole that necessitated an amendment in 1864 specifically forbidding the sale of milk from swill-fed cows and the adulteration of milk with water.[8]

Although the 1864 law legally ended the swill milk industry in

Manhattan, enforcement proved difficult. Between 1864 and 1900, improvement of the milk supply of New York City was marginal at best. A description of the dairy environment in 1892 by W. T. Sedgewick of the Massachusetts Association of Boards of Health pointed to a common situation in large cities that left much to be desired. "Milk," Sedgwick wrote, "is usually drawn from animals in stables which will not bear description in good society, from cows which often have flaking excrement all over their flanks, by milkmen who are anything but clean."[9] As a result, despite efforts of the mid-nineteenth century reformers, milk remained unsanitary. Infants consuming this milk continued to run a high risk of suffering from infantile diarrhea, and many met death at a very tender age.

The campaign against impure milk and infant mortality took on new life with the advent of the bacteriological era in the mid-1880s. Armed with germ theory, scientists confirmed the belief of mid-nineteenth century crusaders that milk was responsible for a high percentage of infant deaths. Research sponsored by New York Health Commissioner Herman Biggs in the early 1890s indicated that milk provided an ideal culture medium for bacteria, the dangerous disease-producing organisms fostered by the two "great perils" of the milk supply—bovine and human filth. A report published in 1903 by Dr. William Park, one of Biggs's assistants, and Dr. L. Emmett Holt, an eminent pediatrician, further delineated the close relationship between infantile diarrhea and the quality of the milk consumed.[10] These and other studies strengthened the resolve of infant health workers, who intensified their efforts to ensure that clean milk would reach the greatest number of newborn babies.

The activities of these late nineteenth century infant health crusaders shared a basic orientation. Almost all health workers viewed infant mortality as unicausal. One group focused on sanitary engineering, inspecting the conditions under which milk was produced and transported. By 1906, the two most popular plans for securing clean milk from cow to baby bottle were the medical milk commission program of Dr. Henry L. Coit of Newark, New Jersey,[11] and the municipal regulation and inspection procedures of Dr. George Goler, the health officer of Rochester, New York.[12]

The other major group of infant health workers focused on providing affordable milk for the poor through the establishment of milk stations in urban areas.[13] Dr. Henry Koplik, a physician at the Good Samaritan Dispensary in New York City, opened the first milk depot in 1889.[14] Nathan Straus, a philanthropic New York City merchant, established the nation's first chain of infant milk depots.[15] Both the milk production and milk distribution orientations were adopted by numerous communities across the nation, and all crusaders hoped that their activities would reduce significantly milk-related sickness and death.[16]

Although infant health workers knew that they had not eradicated the infant mortality problem, they were aghast when the Census Bureau's first major compilation of mortality statistics, covering the years 1900 through 1904, came out in 1906. Despite all their efforts, the infant mortality rate was still high.[17] Local communities had published vital statistics prior to the Census Bureau's publication, but few of these local censuses provided detailed analyses of infant mortality. In addition, statistical methods varied to such a degree that the data collected in these community studies often were not comparable. The Census Bureau's 1906 publication, notwithstanding inaccuracies and uncorrected death rates, presented the first large-scale treatment of American infant mortality.[18]

For those working so hard to reduce infant mortality, the statistics were depressing. For the 1900-1904 period, out of a national total of 2,642,555 deaths, 507,467, or 19 percent, occurred before the first year of age. As Josephine Baker, soon to be the first director of the New York Department of Health's Bureau of Child Hygiene, observed, "It was the babies who never really had a chance to live that swelled the death rate." Since patterns of mortality generally have served as indicators of the level of health at any given period, infant health workers felt understandably discouraged when they studied the national statistics.[19]

When the workers turned from the national figures to the New York City tabulations, they found similar patterns. Although the overall death rate for infants dropped between 1898 and 1910, as indicated in Figure 1, from approximately 200 to 120 deaths per thousand infants, New York City experienced a sharp increase in the mortality rate in 1904—an increase that persisted with less intensity until 1908.[20]

Central in this climb in the infant mortality rate were the deaths

Figure 1. Death Rate per Thousand under One Year of Age, New York City, 1898-1911

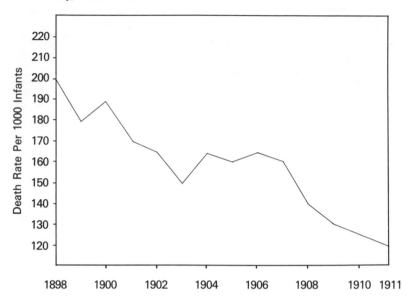

Source: S. Josephine Baker, "Reduction of Infant Mortality in New York City," *American Journal of Diseases of Children* 5 (1913): 159.

caused by infantile diarrhea. For the years 1902 through 1905, deaths from diarrheal diseases claimed 17,530—28 percent of all deaths reported for infants under one year of age in New York City.[21] As Table 1 indicates, the rise in the total number of deaths in 1904 and 1905 was matched with a corresponding increase in the number of deaths from diarrheal diseases. Not only were diarrhea-related deaths a significant proportion of the number of total deaths, but as infant health workers had maintained, *cholera infantum* was more likely to occur during the summer months because milk spoiled more easily in the warmer weather. Studies by William Park, L. Emmett Holt, and others between 1890 and 1906 substantiated the observations of the infant health workers. According to the studies, not only did the infant death rate mount during the summer months, as can be seen in Figure 2, but much of the increase was related directly to diarrheal

Table 1. Deaths of Children under One Year of Age, New York City, 1902-1911

Year	Deaths	
	All Causes	Diarrhea Diseases
1902	15,526	4,090
1903	14,413	3,769
1904	16,125	4,769
1905	16,522	4,945
1906	17,188	4,943
1907	17,437	5,314
1908	16,231	5,118
1909	15,976	4,254
1910	16,212	5,807
1911	15,030	3,843

Source: S. Josephine Baker, "Reduction of Infant Mortality in New York City," American Journal of Diseases of Children 5 (1913): 155.

deaths caused primarily by milk.[22] As the 1906 mortality tabulations indicated, the situation persisted. The total number of infant deaths in 1906 reached 17,188, and of that number deaths from diarrheal diseases represented 29 percent in the very category that pure milk crusaders had been working for over fifty years.[23]

Not surprisingly, the AICP was among those concerned about the mortality reports. Its response was to sponsor a conference to discuss the reports, evaluate existing programs to retain what had worked and to modify what had not, and then launch a fresh attack on the persistent infant mortality problem. Accordingly, on November 20, 1906, at the New York Academy of Medicine, the AICP in conjunction with the New York Department of Health sponsored a conference entitled "Clean Milk for New York City." The AICP hoped that the conference would encourage efforts among all interested in the milk question and foster "enlightened public understanding and opinion in support of all efforts to provide clean milk for New York City infants."[24]

Figure 2. Infant Deaths from Diarrhea, New York City, 1904-1912

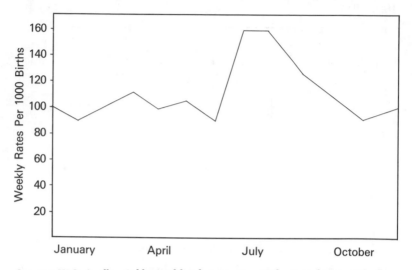

Sources: W.G. Smillie, *Public Health Administration in the United States*, 3d ed. (New York: Macmillan, 1947), 271; New York Association for Improving the Condition of the Poor, *Annual Report* #65 (30 Sept. 1908): 18.

Altogether, forty-one prominent physicians, sanitary experts, and philanthropic individuals attended the AICP conference. The participants came mainly from institutions and organizations in New York City whose activities touched on infant welfare. Twenty-two participants were city physicians connected with children's hospitals, asylums, and local medical societies. Twelve members were health officials from New York and adjoining states. Three participants specialized in animal husbandry, and three were well known for their philanthropic activities.[25]

The chairman of the conference committee, George Wickersham of the AICP, New York City Health Commissioner Thomas Darlington, and R. Fulton Cutting, president of the AICP, opened the conference. The general topics included pasteurization, infant milk depots, model milk shops, inspection of dairies, legislation, and education. The participants agreed that for milk to be safe from "cow to consumer," all dairy cows should be healthy; all personnel involved in the dairying process should be clean; all implements, such as dairying utensils, cans, and bottles, should be sterilized; all milk should be heated; and all shops that sold milk should be clean. The conference members also recommended an increase in the number of municipal inspectors so that all dairy operations would fall more fully under the "eye of the state." Furthermore, to guarantee that clean milk would reach the public, the conference participants suggested tightening regulations to aid inspectors searching for diseased cows and contaminated milk. And, since much of the milk was sold at creameries operated by the dairy companies, conference members hoped to encourage clean facilities and healthy employees by setting up "model milk shops" as examples to dairymen.

If all the conference's suggestions were enacted, all urban consumers would have access to clean and wholesome milk. But conference participants recognized that this milk probably would be above the purchasing power of the poor. To make this milk available to the needy, participants recommended that more infant milk depots be established. As the sessions drew to a close, members of the conference urged the formation of a permanent committee within the AICP to experiment with techniques designed to reduce the high number of milk-related deaths among infants and to show the city, by example, the benefits of "healthful milk practices."[26]

The New York Milk Committee (NYMC) of the AICP grew out of the 1906 conference. Formed early in 1907, the NYMC was charged by the AICP with the development of programs to reduce the rate of infant mortality and improve the milk supply of New York City. Robert Bruère, general agent of the AICP in 1907, appointed George Wickersham head of the NYMC and selected interested physicians, philanthropists, and social reformers active in the crusade against infant mortality as members of the committee. As stipulated by the AICP guidelines, members of the NYMC were to provide general direction and support to the secretary of the committee, paid to devote his or her time to the NYMC's programs. As the "working" member of the committee, the secretary was to oversee data compilation, help formulate policy, and implement the selected programs. It was to this position that Phillips came in 1907.

With Phillips's appointment, the work of the NYMC commenced. His first assignment was to compile a file on the various measures currently undertaken in milk depot work in the United States and

abroad.[27] Phillips began his research with a review of milk station
activities as of 1906, the year of the Census Bureau's publication of
mortality statistics.

Phillips found that most milk stations did little more than dispense
milk. As a general rule, the depots modified all milk according to
formulas designated for different age groups. After visiting a number
of stations in New York City, Phillips found that most station workers
made little effort to instruct mothers in the proper use of the milk or
to chart the medical progress of the infants. Like those working in the
field, Phillips found that while milk stations reached an increasingly
larger sector of the population, merely dispensing clean milk was not
the hoped-for panacea. A good milk supply barely helped if mothers
kept the milk improperly or if they failed to practice even basic good
child care.[28]

Phillips discovered that most European milk depots were organized along the same general lines as those in the United States. As
in America, these stations dispensed clean milk to needy infants.[29]
An important exception to this practice existed in France. Phillips
learned that during the early 1890s a physician attached to the
Charité Hospital in Paris, Dr. Pierre Budin, had grown concerned
about the high number of deaths among artificially fed babies. In
1892 he established the *Consultation de Nourrisons* where all mothers delivering children at Charité were to meet with him after giving
birth. In these conferences Dr. Budin stressed the importance of
breast-feeding and, for those mothers unable to nurse, the necessity
of sterilizing all cow's milk before use. Budin also encouraged mothers to bring their infants back to him for periodic examinations and to
attend short lectures on proper methods of child care. Based on his
work at Charité, Budin believed that only when good milk was
combined with proper methods of child care and periodic medical
examinations did infants have a good chance of survival.[30]

Following his discovery of Budin's work, Phillips looked for programs in the United States that provided either periodic infant
medical examinations or maternal instruction in child care methods.
He found that American examples, particularly in maternal instruction, did exist. One of the earliest programs had occurred in 1859.
During that year the New York Infirmary for Women and Children
appointed a "sanitary visitor" whose duty it was to provide poor
mothers with practical instruction on infant care and family health.[31]

Another program of maternal instruction grew out of the fresh air work of the AICP. Fresh air work, begun in 1883, was designed to remove mothers and children from city tenement districts during the summer. By 1900 these outings combined instructional sessions on family health with the pleasure of a day at the beach or in the mountains. In 1906, as a result of the mothers' interest in family health information, the AICP broadened its fresh air work with the establishment of Junior Sea Breeze, a day camp for sick babies. At the Junior Sea Breeze Center at 64th Street and the East River, the AICP provided shelter for mothers and sick children during the hot summer months. While at the center, the mothers received instruction in the proper techniques of infant care by physicians and nurses associated with the AICP. The AICP expanded its Sea Breeze activities further with the establishment of a field service program on the Lower East Side of Manhattan. The AICP sent nurses into the homes of infants under two years of age to follow up on the health of babies brought to the Junior Sea Breeze Center and to instruct the mothers in infant hygiene, when necessary.[32]

As a result of his research, Phillips grew to understand the multiplicity of "causes" that could touch a single issue. He learned that he could stress the importance of clean milk, for example, while recognizing that clean milk represented only part of the solution. This perception of the interdependent nature of the milk issue placed him squarely within the thrust of early twentieth century reform thought.

The notion of interdependence shaped Phillips's presentation to the leadership of the NYMC at the end of 1907. Phillips argued that infant mortality was not simply a milk problem. Emphasis on the dynamics of milk production only had failed to eradicate the problem. Phillips believed that, in addition to clean milk, medical supervision of each child and maternal instruction were necessary. He suggested that the NYMC establish a number of experimental milk stations designed not only to dispense milk, but also to provide mothers with instruction on the proper care of their infants. After some discussion, the members of the NYMC agreed to open seven experimental milk depots. Committee members directed Phillips to devise programs for these stations to test the comparable values of raw and pasteurized milk for infants and to evaluate the importance of maternal education in saving infant lives. Results from these experiments, committee members believed, would foster programs supported by municipal governments to prevent babies from dying and to give them the very best possible beginning in life.[33]

After deciding to establish the milk stations, the committee turned its attention to the selection of appropriate sites for the depots. Three concerns guided the committee in its decision—the density of the area's population, the nationality of the inhabitants, and the location of cooperating social and philanthropic agencies. The committee hoped to find areas that not only needed milk stations, but also allowed comparison.[34] To find appropriate areas, the committee sent letters to churches, settlements, and charitable organizations operating in the tenement sections of Manhattan. On the basis of information secured from these groups, the NYMC selected seven districts for the experimental depots in which it planned to study selected methods of depot operation.

Three stations were to sell modified pasteurized milk. The committee set up its first station in a mixed Jewish and Italian section at 262 East Broadway. At 160 Mott Street, in a predominantly Italian area, the Diet Kitchen Association shared its quarters with the NYMC. The third depot dispensing pasteurized milk was opened at 412 West 47th Street in a primarily Irish and American area. The remaining four stations dispensed modified raw milk: at 73 Cannon Street in a Jewish section; at 146 West 100th Street in a mixed Irish and American area where the NYMC shared space with the Bloomingdale Guild; at 434 East 73d Street in a Bohemian district; and at 246 East 82d Street in a predominantly Jewish section. So that all milk used in these depots came from one source, the NYMC arranged to have the Sheffield Farms–Slawson–Decker Company supply all seven stations.[35]

Following the selection of the depots, the committee hired nurses to staff them. Committee members regarded the nurses as the "soul" of the depot. Accordingly, the NYMC directed Phillips to select nurses who not only had a knowledge of infant care, but also possessed a "personality capable of holding the mothers to the depot."[36] In addition to the station nurses, the NYMC hired two "floating" nurses. Not connected with any particular depot, these nurses were to devote their entire time to home visitations. During their rounds, these nurses were to stress the importance of breast-feeding, teach mothers with young infants proper milk care, and provide general information on the basic principles of infant hygiene. For those nurses not fluent in the languages spoken by their clients, the committee hired interpreters to assist them in the station and in the homes.[37]

After the selection of the nurses, the NYMC mobilized a corps of volunteer physicians to work in the depots. The committee looked for doctors familiar with the selected districts and able to speak the predominant language in the area they offered to serve. Altogether, twenty-nine physicians agreed to work with the NYMC. Doctors attached to each depot selected a senior physician to assist the nurses in the general direction of the station's activities. The duties of the other physicians included providing medical examinations for all infants under each depot's care, prescribing feeding schedules for each infant, and holding weekly classes on the proper care of infants for area mothers.

Although the depots were not scheduled to open until June 17, 1908, the nurses and physicians began work on June 1. During the two-week period prior to the opening of the stations, the doctors and nurses outfitted the depots and familiarized themselves with their districts. The nurses took a preliminary census of each district to secure a rough idea of the number of families with young babies, and collected ideas for topics to be covered in the weekly child care lectures. Churches in the areas served by the stations provided lists of their parishioners with babies under one year of age, announced the opening of the depots, and encouraged their members to take their babies to the NYMC's stations. Neighborhood settlements cooperated by advertising the depots and contacting all families with infants involved in the various settlement programs.[38]

On June 17, 1908, the stations opened to the public. The physicians and nurses greeted the mothers and explained the operations of the NYMC's program. All mothers who entered the stations on June 17, and subsequently each new mother, first met with the physicians. At these sessions the doctors checked the mothers to ascertain their ability to nurse. Following consultation with the mothers, the physicians examined each infant. For those mothers unable to nurse, the physicians prescribed a suitable formula based on the condition of each baby. The nurses supervised the milk distribution and kept detailed records on each infant's progress. The nurses recorded all

Table 2. Deaths of Babies in the New York Milk Committee Experimental Program, June 17–August 31, 1908

Service	Total Number in Program	Number of Deaths	Percentage of Deaths
Raw milk depots	446	18	4.03
Pasteurized milk depots	338	15	4.43
Floating nurse supervision	205	4	1.95
Overall totals	989	37	3.74

Source: New York Association for Improving the Condition of the Poor, *Annual Report* 65 (30 Sept. 1908): 71.

changes in the feeding schedules, weekly weight reports, all instances of intestinal disturbances, and all other reported illnesses. On these charts progress curves illustrated graphically the change in each child's condition from the first visit to the last. From these charts the NYMC hoped to gather sufficient information to compare the value of raw and pasteurized millk and to assess the value of the examinations and the instructional services offered at the depots.[39]

During each consultation the physicians also encouraged the mothers to attend weekly sessions on the proper methods of infant care and hygiene. In these lectures the doctors talked about the importance of breast-feeding, procedures for preparing cow's milk in the home, feeding schedules, the necessity of regular feeding patterns, and other issues pertaining to the proper care of newborn babies. The nurses assisted the physicians during the lectures and reiterated the basics of proper care when the mothers came to pick up their daily milk allotments. The nurses followed up the work in the stations with home visits to each of the families in the program. During these visits the nurses checked to see that the physicians' instructions were being carried out and answered any additional questions the mothers raised about their babies.[40]

Although the stations had been in operation only three months,

Table 3. Babies Weighed at Consultations, Week Ending August 31, 1908, New York Milk Committee Experimental Program

Service	Gained	Stationary	Lost	Total
Raw milk depots	120	23	20	163
Pasteurized milk depots	127	8	21	156
Total modified milk	247	31	41	319
Floating nurse supervision	95	19	23	137

Source: New York Association for Improving the Condition of the Poor, *Annual Report* 65 (30 Sept. 1908): 71.

the NYMC issued a progress report in September 1908. According to the report, from June 17 to August 31 the physicians and nurses cared for a total of 784 babies. Of the 784 infants, 446 had gone to the raw milk depots while 338 were taken care of at the pasteurized milk stations. Another 205 infants were under the supervision of the floating nurses. As indicated in Table 2, the percentage of deaths among infants fed either raw or pasteurized milk was roughly equal at 4.03 percent and 4.43 percent respectively, while only 1.95 percent of babies under the care of the floating nurses died.

The low incidence of death among the infants under the supervision of the floating nurses illustrated, according to the NYMC physicians, the superiority of mother's milk for babies under one year of age. Overall, the floating nurses had far more breast-feeding babies under their care than did the nurses and doctors at the depots. The important finding, according to the physicians, rested not in the difference between the babies under the stations' care and those under the floating nurses' care, but, as shown in Table 3, rather in the fact that there was little difference from a nutritional standpoint between raw milk and pasteurized milk.[41]

Although nutritionally similar, raw and pasteurized milk differed in digestibility. Both the station personnel and the floating nurses found that babies fed on raw milk suffered a greater incidence of upset stomachs. When such upsets occurred, the doctors and the nurses instructed the mothers to boil all raw milk, whether modified or not. This led the NYMC to recommend that all raw milk, however excellent its quality or careful its preparation, be pasteurized.[42]

The committee believed it could see positive results from its instructional experiment as well. Overall, the NYMC found that, regardless of the milk supply, infant mortality could be reduced through maternal instruction in the proper feeding and care of infants. Station personnel and floating nurses alike discovered that babies nourished on the best milk still died because their mothers, while very exacting with the formula, fed their infants pork, pickles, or other highly indigestible foods at home. Other mothers failed to bathe or clothe their babies properly, thus materially contributing to their deaths. The home visits, in particular, helped reveal unhealthy practices, and such discoveries influenced the topics covered in the weekly lectures on child care. The mothers' enthusiastic response to the lectures and the information gathered during the home visits led the NYMC to recommend that the staff of each depot be enlarged so that the stations could expand both the instructional sessions and the follow-up home visitations.[43]

The committee also decided, after its review of the summer's work, that the depots should dispense whole milk as well as modified milk. In the first place, the physicians and nurses felt that the exclusive sale of modified milk placed an undue emphasis on hand-feeding and tended to discourage breast-feeding. Station personnel believed that the exclusive sale of modified milk also deprived mothers of the opportunity to learn how to prepare formula milk in the home, for it was too easy to pick up the prepared milk at the station. Once the mothers learned to modify milk themselves, the doctors and nurses contended, the mothers could design feeding schedules to fit more precisely the changing needs of their babies. And, finally, modified milk cost more than whole milk. Whenever possible the NYMC encouraged families to pay for the milk dispensed at the station. For those families too poor to pay, the United Hebrew Charities, the Saint Vincent de Paul Society, the Charity Organization Society, and the AICP underwrote the price of the milk. By providing whole milk and instructing mothers in its use, the NYMC could dispense milk that poor tenement families could afford to buy. Subsidized milk then would be provided only for mothers unable, because of employment or illness, to make the formula in their own homes.[44]

Despite the short observation period, the NYMC's experiment represented a watershed in the crusade for infant health and welfare. Since the 1880s, for example, a controversy had raged over the use of pasteurization in the production of milk. Scientific research notwithstanding, many doctors insisted that the heating process, in addition to killing harmful germs, also destroyed necessary enzymes. Others believed that pasteurization impaired the digestibility of the milk. Despite these claims, little comparative testing had been done, hence the importance of the NYMC experiment. It became easier for the proponents of pasteurization to attract supporters and influence municipal health officials after the NYMC tests.[45]

The other important issue addressed by the NYMC stations, that of maternal instruction, convinced many contemporaries that infant mortality was indeed more than a milk problem. If babies were to stay well, workers in the NYMC stations found they needed the supervision of an informed mother, not just clean milk. The NYMC illustrated that programs combining milk dispensation and instruction helped reduce the likelihood of infant death. With proper supervision, all mothers could learn rudimentary infant hygiene, thus not only helping their children escape possible death, but also giving them a strong beginning in life. As nascent centers for well-child care, the NYMC depots helped improve infant care in the home by promoting breast-feeding, providing properly modified milk along with instructions for its use, and visiting in the home.[46]

Despite the success of the NYMC's milk stations during the summer of 1908, by January 1909 the depots stood in financial jeopardy and their future appeared uncertain. During the second half of 1908, New York City suffered an economic slump. The AICP, to help alleviate the hardships caused by the recession, channeled a large part of its yearly resources into relief payments to stricken tenement dwellers and homeless men. As a result, it was unable to give the NYMC the necessary funds to keep the stations in operation.

On Monday, January 18, 1909, Phillips issued a statement to the press on behalf of the NYMC. According to Phillips, unless the committee could raise $25,000, all seven of the milk depots would be closed.[47] Following the release of Phillips's statement, leading New York physicians such as Drs. Abraham Jacobi, L. Emmett Holt, Henry V. Chapin, and William Park spoke out in support of the

NYMC, stressed the importance of the NYMC's work, and urged the public to respond positively to the NYMC's appeal for aid. These NYMC supporters also voiced an increasingly popular argument about the relationship between health and citizenship. Healthy babies, they reminded the readers of the *New York Times*, produced healthy citizens. Finally, as a result of such pleas and an intensive financial campaign waged by Phillips, the NYMC secured sufficient funds to keep four of the seven depots in operation.[48]

For the remainder of 1909 the NYMC concentrated its resources on the maintenance of its four depots, but in 1910 the committee expanded its operations to assist the newly established Division of Child Hygiene's drive for municipally funded milk depots. Created in 1908 by the New York City Department of Health to coordinate all Health Department programs touching on child welfare, the Division of Child Hygiene had been placed under the dynamic leadership of Dr. S. Josephine Baker. Dr. Baker, like the physicians and nurses attached to the NYMC, believed in the importance of maternal education in the fight for infant health and welfare. She wanted the city to fund annually a number of milk distribution centers so that she could design instructional programs for all mothers with infants under two years of age. But to secure long-term support, Dr. Baker had to illustrate the utility of the program. During 1910 and 1911 the NYMC provided invaluable aid to Dr. Baker through its milk station demonstrations,[49] which ultimately led to the municipal assumption of responsibility for providing New York City residents with the basics of well-child services.

Despite the success of the NYMC's milk depot program, Phillips became restive working within the confines of the NYMC. The milk depot activity represented only one part of the NYMC's overall attack on the milk issue. The committee also directed Phillips to devise programs for securing a pure and inexpensive milk supply for New York City and for regularizing milk standards.[50] Both projects reflected the interests of NYMC members in programs to improve the milk supply and the continuing strength of the nineteenth century emphasis on a clean environment.

Once the NYMC shifted its focus in the milk depots from the interplay of individual and environment to programs aimed at cleaning up dairy environment, Phillips found that the NYMC's work fell short of his growing expectations. Phillips felt that although the NYMC's depots cared for those infants whose mothers sought help or were brought accidentally to the attention of the depot workers, little effort was made to seek and reach every mother and every baby in the areas served by the stations. Phillips wanted depot personnel to contact every mother and infant in each area and then attack infant health problems on the basis of community rather than individual action. If personnel could establish a close and continuing relationship with the mothers, Phillips believed, the depot would grow into a social center. As he told members of the Child Welfare Conference for Research and Development in 1909, each depot would "radiate the influences of education and social betterment," thus improving the whole environment of the child. Furthermore, Phillips felt, if duplicated in neighborhoods across the city, not just in the neighborhoods of the poor, such work would provide the base for a thorough, citywide child welfare program. Each part of the city would contribute to the well-being of the larger whole.[51]

In the spring of 1911, when an opportunity came to organize a child welfare program in Milwaukee, Phillips left the NYMC. Milwaukee's mayor, Emil Seidel, was interested in Phillips's ideas about the possibility of total neighborhood mobilization for infant health and welfare. As Milwaukee's first socialist mayor, Seidel hoped to launch a vigorous program of public education to illustrate the need for expanded public services as a reflection of the government's commitment to the general welfare of the city. A successful child welfare program, Seidel believed, would not only improve health, but also illustrate the importance of citywide planning.[52] Nonetheless, despite Seidel's interest in Phillips's work, Seidel lacked the necessary councilmanic majority to give Phillips a job. So, Seidel offered Phillips a campaign instead, and because Phillips believed that once people understood the need for and the benefits of a particular program they would support it at any price, he felt confident that the Milwaukee venture would prove a success.[53]

Following his arrival in Milwaukee, Phillips launched a vigorous publicity campaign designed to drum up support for a child health demonstration. After an initial survey, he found that all existing child health activities in Milwaukee fell far short of the city's overall need in this area.[54] He gave a series of lectures at the Milwaukee Maternity

Hospital. He solicited the aid of Milwaukee's leading philanthropic
and medical societies. He capped his campaign with an open "baby
welfare" meeting to illustrate community interest in child welfare
work.

At a meeting organized by Sara Boyd, a leading member of Milwaukee society and president of the Visiting Nurse Association,
representatives of fourteen organizations assembled at the Hotel
Pfister to consider the most effective means of reducing the city's
infant mortality rate. Dr. John Beffel, a vocal supporter of child
welfare work, opened the meeting with a discussion of the infant
mortality problem and stressed the preventable nature of a large
number of infant diarrheal deaths. Phillips then spoke enthusiastically about the possibilities of a crusade against infant mortality.
He outlined briefly his work with the New York Milk Committee and
discussed the importance of maternal instruction in the reduction of
infant deaths. Phillips concluded his remarks with a proposal to help
reduce infant mortality in Milwaukee. He wanted to survey Milwaukee to determine which section of the city had the highest infant
death rate. He suggested the creation of an organization of city
officials and philanthropic agencies to sponsor a demonstration of
infant-saving techniques in the worst section of the city. And, finally,
he hoped the organization would use the experiment to instruct the
public in proper child hygiene procedures and encourage the gradual
extension of similar demonstrations across the city.

Following remarks supportive of Phillips's position from Dr.
Lorenzo Boorse, a physician at the Infant's Home and Hospital; Dr.
A.J. Patek, president of the Milwaukee County Medical Society;
Health Commissioner Kraft; and Kathryn Van Wyck, secretary of the
Central Council of Philanthropists, the participants passed a resolution asking the mayor to appoint a commission. This commission, to
consist of no more than five members, was to serve for three years. It
was to study all the conditions relating to infant mortality and child
welfare and then recommend to the city's Common Council the most
practical, economic, and efficient method of dealing with the problems. It could raise money and engage help in sponsoring an effective
and convincing demonstration. The participants petitioned the Common Council to grant immediately a large appropriation of city funds
to supplement the funds raised privately by the commission. Finally,

those attending the meeting selected a committee consisting of Mrs. Boyd, Dr. Beffel, and Nathan Perels, a local businessman, to secure the introduction of the resolutions at the Common Council meeting. Dr. Beffel closed the meeting, urging that all party affiliations be set aside "to make Milwaukee famous as the best place for a child to be born."[55]

Subsequent editorials in Milwaukee newspapers urged the Common Council to stand above party lines for "common humanity." They stressed the importance of a competent department of infant welfare. Because the city stood to gain by having healthy citizens who, according to the editorials, could contribute to the further development of Milwaukee, the majority of the newspaper editorials stressed that the city had a responsibility to support the work materially and morally. The editorials urged the public, "as citizens, mothers and fathers," to demand the creation of an infant welfare commission under the Health Department and, once established, to cooperate with it willingly. Milwaukee, the editorials contended, could not afford to lose potential citizens, for "the future needed more than stunted and sickly boys and girls."[56]

After such a public display of interest and some careful politicking by the mayor and Socialist members of the Common Council, the council voted to establish the Child Welfare Commission (CWC). Supported by both municipal and private funds, the commission was charged with the responsibility of investigating all conditions relating to infant mortality and child welfare in Milwaukee and of advising city officials on the most practical, economic, and efficient methods of dealing with infant mortality. Following his appointment as secretary of the Child Welfare Commission, Phillips encouraged his fellow commission members to establish a trial child welfare station to "ascertain the difficulties involved in extending expert medical and nursing care to all babies under one year of age in a single neighborhood before devising a city-wide plan for infant health and welfare."[57] And the plan of organization Phillips had in mind for this demonstration station centered around his interest in a total, community-oriented health program.

Accordingly, the CWC directed its first efforts toward securing an appropriate area for the trial station. Commission members decided to locate that section of Milwaukee where the death rate was the

Figure 3. City of Milwaukee and Ward Locations

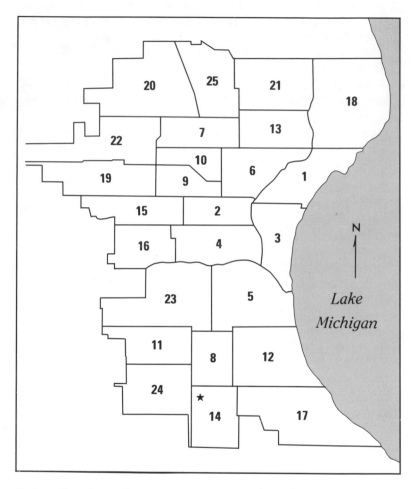

Redrawn from the *Wright Directory*, 1911, Iconographic Collection, State Historical Society of Wisconsin.

Note: ★ indicates location of St. Cyril's parish.

greatest in proportion to the birthrate. In this section of the city, determined after an analysis of Health Department records, a "station district" would be established to serve as the CWC's demonstration unit.[58]

The South Side, the poorest and most ethnically diverse area of the city, had grown rapidly with the expansion of industrial establishments into the Menomonee Valley during the 1870s and 1880s. The industrial plants attracted unskilled workers, and during the latter part of the nineteenth century large numbers of Poles, Germans, and Irish in search of work settled in the Menomonee Valley. The new wards soon had the highest population density in the city. Not surprisingly, this section led the city in the number of infant births and deaths each year. And of the new wards carved out of this area, the Fourteenth, with 870 acres and 32,542 people, led the entire South Side.[59]

Of the 9,797 babies born in Milwaukee in 1910, 1,451 or one-seventh were born in the Fourteenth Ward. The estimated birthrate in the ward was 44.3 per 1,000 population, while in the city as a whole it was only 26.1 per 1,000. In addition to this high birthrate, the Fourteenth Ward led the city in infant deaths. Given these conditions, the CWC felt that any change in the mortality rate would show up more dramatically in this area.[60] But funds for the CWC experimental station were not sufficient to serve the entire Fourteenth Ward. The section of the ward selected for service corresponded to the parish boundaries of St. Cyril's Church, a district of thirty-one blocks in the heart of the Polish-American community. The infant population in the area at the beginning of the experiment stood at approximately 360.[61]

After the selection of St. Cyril's Parish as the demonstration district, the CWC began setting up the neighborhood organization. Because the physicians occupied a central place in the fight against infant mortality, Phillips focused on them first. Rather than follow the usual practice of soliciting the aid of volunteer physicians who could afford to give a few hours "to charity," Phillips decided to draw upon the community doctors instead. He felt that an important part of the success of the station depended on securing the confidence, understanding, and help of the local practitioners. Phillips had found in the NYMC work that when a station's staff was drawn mainly from outside the area served, the local doctors resented the "interlopers." These neighborhood physicians feared the close contact between the mothers and the "foreign" doctors, and believed that when illness struck the mothers might seek the private services of the station's doctors. Phillips convinced the CWC to turn the baby station over to the local doctors, to pay them for their preventive services, and to provide a local eminent pediatrician to supervise them in their work. The twenty-two doctors who practiced in St. Cyril's Parish met together and selected seven of their colleagues to staff the station. Drs. F.S. Wasiolewski, Irene Tomkiewicz, K. Wagner, Alfred Schulz, D.J. Dronzniekewicz, John Rock, and H. Gramling agreed to work at the baby station. Their duties included holding weekly clinics for the mothers during which they would weigh and examine the babies and give the mothers formal instruction in the principles of child care.[62]

After organizing the doctors, Phillips and the CWC concentrated on the selection of a nursing staff to assist the physicians at the station and to follow up the station's work in the infants' homes. The nurses were to be in charge of establishing and sustaining contact between the station and the mothers. Their duties entailed visiting all babies each week and providing home instruction in the principles of infant hygiene. On the advice of various members of the medical community, the commission selected Jessie Bernoski of Maternity Hospital; Nina B. Zimmerman, a Visiting Nurse Association worker in the Fourteenth Ward; and Helen Hogan, a specialist in infant feeding problems. Under the supervision of Mrs. Price Davis, a former supervisor of the Visiting Nurse Association, each nurse surveyed a section of the baby district. Armed with cards of introduction from the local parish priest, Father Szukalski, the nurses canvassed the area to locate their charges. In the week before the opening of the station, the nurses acquainted themselves with the mothers of all the children under one year of age, explained the function of the station to the mothers, and began home instruction in the principles of infant care and feeding.[63]

The week before it opened, the newspapers publicized the station. Numerous articles encouraged the mothers to register at the baby center for instruction and to bring their babies under the care of the station's physicians. On the Sunday preceding the opening, the commission distributed handbills explaining the station's work and urging the mothers to take advantage of the preventive care and education offered to them. Finally, early Monday morning, July 24, 1911, the newly painted child welfare station opened its doors at 990 Eighth Avenue to the mothers and babies of St. Cyril's Parish. By the end of the first week, fifteen mothers had attended the daily clinic sessions. A week later the number had risen to twenty-eight.[64]

But not all the mothers came. Despite a general curiosity about the station in the early weeks of operation and the 100 percent visitation by the nurses to the homes of all infants under one year of age, only a handful of mothers actually brought their infants to the station for medical examinations. The nurses realized that they had not won the level of esteem, confidence, and friendship necessary to encourage the mothers' participation. Only one nurse spoke Polish. The others had to rely on German, which most residents understood to some degree, or use interpreters. This, of course, hampered communication between the station and the mothers. And the mothers apparently felt that the nurses were "blowing their own horns" by proclaiming the value of their services. The women in the parish had not requested the station; most did not realize the value of the instruction. The nurses discovered that it was easier to interest the mothers in coming to the station if they were urged by a person not attached to the health center—a "disinterested advocate."[65]

As a result of the nurses' problems, a new group joined the doctors and nurses in the baby station organization. To create a corps of disinterested advocates to promote the station and encourage the mothers to attend, Father Szukalski helped the CWC select eight of the most popular and influential women in his parish. Once convinced of the value of the work undertaken by the station, they served as the selling agency for the CWC demonstration. The women informally contacted a majority of the parish mothers and sponsored regular meetings in the basement hall of the parochial school. Only part of each meeting was instructive; the remainder of each session consisted of entertainment by different groups of residents. In these congenial settings the families got to know the station's staff and hear about its work. By stirring up interest and by securing goodwill for the station, this Committee of Eight helped station attendance grow.[66]

During the remainder of 1911 the baby station in St. Cyril's Parish absorbed the work of numerous child-oriented public and private agencies active in the area. Each organization sent agents into the neighborhood, asked residents similar questions, duplicated many actions, and frequently antagonized residents with continuous demands on their time. Such a situation was inefficient in terms of time and money spent to secure information. For instance, in St. Cyril's Parish, the registration of births, the education and control of local midwives, the prevention of infant blindness, the placing-out of babies, and foster home supervision involved not only the Health Department, but several other agencies as well. Baby station personnel found that they could perform the same tasks more completely, inexpensively, and efficiently than all the other organizations combined. The station was growing into a one-stop center for infant welfare for the residents of St. Cyril's Parish.[67]

To supplement the station's activities, the Child Welfare Commission investigated conditions of child welfare in Milwaukee and disseminated information about it to the city at large. The major investigatory project was a comprehensive survey of all conditions affecting child life in Milwaukee. The survey included a statistical study of infant mortality, and examination of the work of all individuals and institutions caring for babies, and a study of the problem of securing a clean and safe milk supply at a low cost for Milwaukee's infant population. The educational activities included lectures on infant care, exhibits, and a daily welfare column in the local newspapers that supplied information on infant and child health care.

Both the survey and the educational activities emphasized that child welfare meant the whole child and that a multiplicity of factors affected the solution of health problems. One exhibit for example, was held in conjunction with the International Dairy Show, October 10-18, 1911. In this show, where, according to a local newspaper, "Babe and Bovine Reigned as Co-Regents," members of the CWC provided information on the importance of clean milk and the most approved methods of child care. Special emphasis was placed on the relationship between good milk and good care for the promotion of the general welfare of Milwaukee's babies.[68] Furthermore, all supplementary activities stressed the relationship between the life of the child as a whole and the life of the community as a whole.[69] The theme of interdependence, which Phillips had pursued with the NYMC, underlay all of the CWC projects.

In January 1912 the Child Welfare Commission submitted a report on six months' work to the Common Council. As a result of constant and watchful supervision by the station's staff and the program of maternal instruction, the death rate for the months of September, October, November, and December in 1911 was 4.4 per 100 births, as compared with 12.5 per 100 births for the corresponding period in 1910. Only seven babies died during the test period, as opposed to twelve during the same period the year before. The commission believed that the decline in the death rate indicated a positive step toward the promotion of infant welfare and advocated the expansion of the program to other neighborhoods of the city. To cover this expansion, the commission requested a larger appropriation from the council and urged full municipal status for the CWC as part of the Health Department.[70]

Unfortunately for the commission, however, a change in municipal administration dashed these hopes. In the earlier 1910 election, the Socialists had won a plurality of votes, which enabled them to exercise a fair degree of control over the Common Council. Traditional Socialist support had combined with a voter reaction against the traditional parties whose leaders were tainted by a number of grand jury indictments. However, in 1912, the voters, satisfied that good government had been restored by turning the rascals out, returned to the chastised parties. The parties, caught up in a wave of nonpartisanship and determined not to lose again to the Socialists, entered into a coalition. Together, Milwaukee Democrats and Republicans backed former health commissioner Dr. Gerald Bading for mayor.

Bading, a firm believer in streamlined government and budget cutting, opposed any party that viewed government as expansive or activist. He viewed government as a necessary evil, whose purpose was regulation rather than public service. During his campaign he chided the Socialists for going beyond regulation and promised, if elected, to "sweep away Socialist programs" that cost money and resulted in the unnecessary expansion of government. Evidently, Milwaukee voters agreed with him, decided they had had their fill of reform, and swept Bading into office. On April 2, 1912, Bading defeated incumbent mayor Emil Seidel by 43,179 to 30,273.[71]

Bading's election proved significant for the fate of the Child Welfare Commission. As health commissioner, Bading supported only sanitary engineering; he did not back programs designed to promote activities for good health. During his tenure in office, the Health Department concentrated on cleaning up the physical environment to eliminate disease in Milwaukee. To combat infant mortality, he supported only those programs designed to secure a clean milk supply. Like many other health officers during this period, Bading failed to recognize how a social specialist could aid the medical specialist in the solution of health problems. Not surprisingly, Bading did not appreciate the purpose of the Child Welfare Commission's project. Once in office he took up the question of the CWC's future and labored to secure its dissolution.[72]

In his inaugural address to the Common Council, Bading stated that he wanted the Health Department to assume child welfare work. He also outlined his version of a child welfare program. He wanted a drastic reduction of the scope and orientation of the work. Headed by a physician, the city's child welfare program as envisioned by Bading would regulate the purity of the milk supply, oversee periodic dispensation of clean milk to needy areas of the city, and provide, at best, very rudimentary care only for those sick infants who happened to come to the attention of the Health Department. When Bading's supporters proposed the act providing for this type of work, the supporters of the Child Welfare Commission launched what turned out to be a last-ditch effort to save the commission's program.[73]

The ensuing debate centered on the question of the relationship between medical and social specialists. Supporters of the CWC insisted that good child welfare work depended on securing the most competent man available for the work, whether he was a doctor or not. In fact, they suggested that perhaps the Health Department had "enough medical men" and could use an "organizer" as the child welfare director. CWC supporters believed in the necessity of an attack on the entire infant health and welfare problem and felt that such work demanded the leadership of a sociologist, or social expert, to collect and analyze data on infant mortality and educate the public about the department's role in the prevention of disease and the promotion of good health.[74] But Bading supporters on the council stood firm and voted against what they considered the "mysterious abracadabra" of the sociologist.[75] On June 17, 1912, the Common Council delivered the deathblow to the Child Welfare Commission. The passage of Bading's act relieved Phillips of his duties with the commission and created a Division of Child Welfare, under the direction of a physician, in the Health Department. Dr. E.T. Lodedan, a Bading supporter, took over the administration of child welfare work in Milwaukee.[76]

Despite the failure of Phillips and the Child Welfare Commission to extend the work begun in St. Cyril's Parish, the commission's experimental station represented the first major example of a new form of health organization—the urban health center. By 1912, many health workers across the country, unlike Bading and his supporters, began to realize that it was virtually impossible to formulate from one office health programs suitable for neighborhoods of different occupational and educational levels, diverse ethnic or racial backgrounds, and varying health needs. Health workers started to look for ways to decentralize some functions of municipal health departments and devise programs that more nearly fit the particular needs of different groups of city residents. As Phillips told the participants of the International Congress on Hygiene and Demography later that year, the CWC not only pioneered in the design of practical methods for providing 100 percent contact between the public and a health care program, it also fashioned a plan tailored specifically to the needs of a particular segment of the community.[77] By 1915, child health workers had opened neighborhood health centers in Philadelphia, New York City, Cleveland, Buffalo, and Boston. While not exact copies of the CWC program, they all were designed to coordinate functions, shape administration in accordance with local needs, and foster community spirit.[78]

Thus, for many health workers the CWC demonstration, although abortive, provided a base from which to develop their own neighborhood health programs. For Phillips, the CWC experience proved to be an important stimulant for future activities as well. As Phillips stressed in his paper presented at the International Congress on Hygiene and Demography shortly after his departure from Milwaukee, he believed that at the very least the CWC had demonstrated the principle that geographic localization and administrative coordination, complemented by the social organization of a neighborhood, produced efficient and practically 100 percent health care and interest. On the basis of this experience and his work with the New York Milk Committee, Phillips suggested to his audience that, because conserving child life necessitated attention to every condition that affected the life of the family, a thorough child welfare program was really synonymous with a social program. Considered in this light, because a multiplicity of factors needed to be taken into consideration, a complete child welfare program demanded a "comprehensive thoroughgoing knowledge of the community." Once sufficient data about community needs was collected through research and investigation, Phillips argued, "social organizers" could construct a "social program fitted to the needs of each given community." He concluded by asking his audience to imagine each city as a "collection of small areas" rather than a "hodgepodge of conflicting forces," with each small area organized to further the conservation and proper development of all children. If each small area, under "expert leadership" supplemented by resident participation, solved the child welfare problems of its particular district, then the entire city, or the sum total of the small areas, would achieve social progress.[79]

When Phillips resettled himself in New York City, he reflected on his experiences with the NYMC and the CWC. As he reviewed the weaknesses and strengths of each program, Phillips found himself focusing less on health organization per se and more on the notion of social program that he had pointed to in his talk at the international congress. He began to dwell on the possibilities of planning, neighborhood experiments, and citywide neighborhood interaction. These reflections soon led him to conclude that "the needs of infants and children were the needs of parents and the entire community of which they were members, so the satisfaction of needs required a unified effort on the part of all. Now, the neighborhoods were the basic units of national life. If people in the neighborhood could convincingly prove that through the better coordination of community forces in the neighborhood, they could meet the needs of the entire community,"[80] then American democracy would be revitalized.[81] To create such a situation, Phillips strove to devise a complete social plan of organization. And he looked to the neighborhood, as did so many of his contemporaries, as the crucible in which to fashion a reconstructed society.[82] These conclusions led to schemes for neighborhood planning and resident participation that eventually resulted in an elaborate plan to perfect the interaction of, as Robert Woods so aptly put it, the "cluster of interlacing communities" that composed the organic city.[83]

3

The Social Unit
Theory of
Organization

After his departure from Milwaukee in 1912, Phillips reflected on his experiences with the New York Milk Committee and the Milwaukee Child Welfare Commission. During the next two years, supported largely by the generosity of numerous friends, Phillips shifted the focus of his concern from the development of neighborhood child health programs to the dynamics of social organization built on a well-developed neighborhood base. In his 1914 treatise on the social unit theory of organization Phillips laid out his grand scheme. His social unit plan, as it was called, manifested his acceptance and conception of the notion of interdependence. Centered on a structure through which citizens could participate directly in the control of community affairs while making use of the highest technical skill available, his plan assumed that the health of an entity depended on the well-being of its constituent parts. By 1916 Phillips had interested a number of prominent people in backing his scheme and financing a demonstration of his social unit theory. Following the formation of the National Social Unit Organization in November 1916, Phillips selected a laboratory in which to test his theory of organization—an experiment that ultimately would represent the quintessential application of organic thought to neighborhood organization.

Although the organization Phillips proposed was more developed than those planned by many of his contemporaries, the thrust of his proposal places him squarely in the mainstream of early twentieth century thought. And like many other schemes devised by social, economic, and political theorists informed by the organic analogy at the turn of the century, Phillips's plan would create a "cooperative society." Theorists argued that the American political system failed to meet the particular needs of American citizens while remaining responsive to their collective wishes. Most people had only sporadic and superficial contact with their chosen leaders, so the argument ran, and there existed little meaningful interaction between elected representatives and their constituents.[1]

Because, as Robert A. Woods pointed out, the "coordination of government with the developing needs of the people" had proved "imperfect and incomplete,"[2] the nation needed a new mechanism through which a full democracy could develop. In a similar vein, Mary Follett suggested in *The New State: Group Organization, the Solution of Popular Government* that America needed a new civic machinery. Ideally, according to Follett, such machinery would make it possible for the "fundamental ideas of people" to be discovered and then embodied "in public policies."[3] Under such a system, Americans would not possess merely "nominal representation" in the nation's political life, but instead would live in a democracy in which the government would "continuously represent all the people," because it would be based on "continuous mass involvement" of all citizens in the decisions affecting their lives.[4]

While citizens lacked full participation in the political life of the nation, proponents of a cooperative society argued, they also lacked access to the expert knowledge necessary to confront the problems of modern life. Just as theorists stressed the need for greater interaction between citizens and leaders, they also believed in the need to bring expert information into the life of the nation. As a result, creating appropriate structures to build a partnership between experts and citizens was an essential ingredient in formulas for good government during the first two decades of the twentieth century as well.[5] Seeing little reason to assume a basic conflict between democracy and expertise, proponents of a cooperative society championed the role of the expert in the creation of a well-constituted national community. Although these theorists recognized that many Americans distrusted experts because of the "general practice of imposing expert advice on Americans" rather than assimilating the expert into the "stuff of American social organization,"[6] they nonetheless believed that experts and citizens could effect a cooperative alliance that would result in overall social progress.[7] The public would define the ends while the experts would devise the means, and together they would shape the direction of the nation so that it addressed not only the needs of individuals, but also the collective wishes of the larger public.[8]

Herbert Croly's arguments in *Progressive Democracy* capture the essence of the cooperative society. His general theme in this 1915 treatise was cooperation and participation. "Democracy," he wrote, "implies and needs some method of representation which will be efficient and responsible enough a . . . policy but which does not imply the delegation of its ultimate discretionary power to any (fixed) body of men or law."[9] Active participation created responsible and creative citizens, who then relayed their needs to experts capable of devising suitable programs. Such interaction between citizens and experts, Croly contended, constituted a "fundamentally whole and sound society."[10]

In the social unit of theory of organization Phillips, too, stressed the importance of cooperative action and expertise. His organizational scheme rested on the belief that through cooperative action—which he termed democracy—people came together for the purpose of satisfying their common needs and interests.[11] According to Phillips, democracy was "an organization of US—of all of us—through which we ourselves can come together to study for ourselves our common needs; to decide for ourselves which of these needs comes first; to employ the highest technical skill the nation affords in formulating plans for meeting those needs; to study such plans in advance of operation, and finally to carry out those plans ourselves, not only because we desire them for ourselves but because their nature is such that they cannot be carried out by anyone except ourselves."[12] And because he saw democracy as something larger than a political system based on representative government, he wanted his theory of organization to embody democracy in its "fullest form." Accordingly, Phillips attempted to develop in the social unit theory the machinery that would enable the American people to plan and execute cooperative programs that touched their lives. In such a way, Phillips argued, all activities would further both the good of the whole and the good of each individual within that whole. [13]

Phillips believed in the importance of the expert as well. On the basis of his experiences in Milwaukee, Phillips identified two groups essential to the life of any community—citizens and experts. [14] He found that if he generalized about the people he worked with, he was dealing with two groups in the social structure—the group that supplied human service, such as the doctors and nurses, and the group that sought such service, such as the consumers of health and social programs. The social unit plan attempted to formulate a method of relating these "two separate but complimentary [sic] forces of supply and demand." Because Phillips believed that everybody was "inextricably related to and dependent upon each other," he wanted his system to provide for the expression of all people, be they producers or consumers. [15] Complete and continuous contact between both groups was needed to effect such interaction. Cooperation, he argued, demanded some mechanism that encouraged the collection of all necessary information concerning consumer needs and then provided for their transmission to the experts, or producers, for resolution. [16]

The neighborhood, Phillips believed, represented the ideal arena in which to begin this interchange between producers and consumers, [17] for it comprised the "most important unit of our national life." He visualized the nation as a grand union of neighborhoods which, when linked together, comprised cities, counties, states, and ultimately the nation as a whole. Learning to function intelligently and democratically within the confines of the neighborhood, he contended, would allow Americans to understand society, to participate more fully in its operation, and to enjoy the "fruits of living in a democracy." [18] Believing that the neighborhood was small enough to be manageable and comprehensible, yet large enough to reflect the needs of the entire community, [19] Phillips devised a system that used the neighborhood as a "laboratory unit" to coordinate needs and resources for all. [20] In short, Phillips's plan rested on the premise that citizen participation combined with expert analysis in the neighborhood setting would produce a "working democracy." [21]

Based on neighborhood units, the social unit plan depended on four instruments to stimulate popular definition and resolution of

Figure 4. Phillip's Social Unit Plan

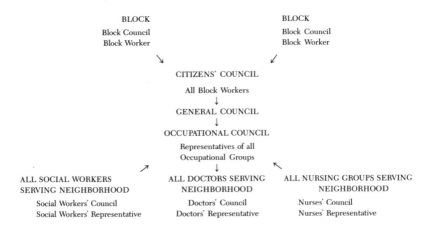

Source: Patricia Mooney Melvin, "A Cluster of Interlacing Communities: The Cincinnati Social Unit Plan and Neighborhood Organization, 1900-1920," in *Community Organization for Urban Social Change: A Historical Perspective*, ed. Robert Fisher and Peter Romanofsky (Westport, Conn.: Greenwood Press, 1981). Copyright 1981 by Robert Fisher and Peter Romanofsky. Used by permission of the publisher.

needs and to promote the interaction of people in their respective roles as consumers and producers. These integral components were block councils, the citizens' council, the occupational council, and the general council. In essence, his plan called for subdividing the neighborhood into block associations to promote face-to-face contact among residents. Then, to provide vehicles for the expression of block ideas, needs, and aspirations, Phillips set up a citizens' council and an occupational council. Representatives from each block council sat on the citizens' council to advance the needs of the locale, and representatives of the area's service sector sat on the occupational council to suggest ways to meet the needs. Phillips wanted both groups to meet regularly in a general council to seek consensus on practical resolutions of neighborhood needs. (See Figure 4.)

Phillips believed that the formulation of any sound program for social organization necessitated a well-grounded knowledge of each neighborhood and its needs. Such knowledge, he argued, rested upon the collection of full and accurate data. Once collected the information could be used by the neighborhood to determine what particular needs demanded immediate attention. Phillips felt that it was essential to reach all neighborhood residents and solicit their ideas and demands. His Milwaukee experience had convinced him that an organization like the Committee of Eight in St. Cyril's Parish could be expanded to secure information about neighborhood needs. And, instead of being merely adjuncts to a professional staff, neighborhood residents under the social unit plan actually would be part of the work. They would be the representatives of the people. Thus, Phillips reasoned, "nothing could be done in their block that they (the residents) didn't want."[22]

Phillips selected the block as the unit to represent neighborhood residents. Those over eighteen years of age in each block were to meet together and select members of a block council and then a block worker. After some instruction by the directors of the plan, each worker would then educate block residents about the work and principles of the social unit organization. Phillips wanted each worker to establish a friendly acquaintance with all the residents of the block. Each block worker would solicit the concerns of constituents and, after neighborly discussion, compile information on the needs of the area. Phillips believed that one fact collector, known to the residents of each block, could secure information and explain its importance far better than all the volunteers and paid agents from the numerous organizations who combed the city making intimate inquiries and duplicating both questions and services.[23] As Courtenay Dinwiddie, a National Social Unit Organization executive, said later, the block worker "was in the best sense of the word, a neighbor, familiar with the conditions and needs and responsive and responsible to the wishes of other residents."[24]

The block worker represented his or her block in the citizens' council. At regular meetings the block workers presented the problems and needs of their respective blocks. The council studied the data presented by the various block workers. From this information the council then prepared complete and accurate statements outlining the needs of the neighborhood residents.[25] Phillips, in a 1919 outline of the social unit plan, likened the relationship between block workers and the council to the nervous system of the human body.

Just as the "body had a system which notified every part of it as to what the needs of the body were," the block workers were to serve as the nerves of the district, knowing when a need existed and transmitting that need to the central node of the system—the citizens' council—making the need felt until it was satisfied.[26]

The third component of the social unit plan was the occupational council. Composed of representatives of the skilled groups or experts, such as doctors, nurses, and social workers who served the neighborhood, the members of the occupational council were charged with the formulation of "sound and efficient" programs for meeting the needs discerned by the citizens' council. In theory, members of each skilled group living in or serving the neighborhood organized and elected from their number a representative to serve in the occupational council. If the citizens' council desired a plan to meet a need identified by the block workers, the council contacted the occupational council. Once the question was presented to the occupational council, all service groups able to provide support collaborated on the plan, which was then sent back to the citizens' council for consideration. Phillips believed that collaboration among experts would produce a well-rounded program that covered all aspects of any particular need. By studying new opportunities for better and wider service to meet needs disclosed by the citizens' council, the neighborhood would be able to have at its disposal the "skill, judgement and experience of the service sector of the population."[27]

To ensure a close relationship between those possessing specialized knowledge and those needing expert service, Phillips capped his plan with a general council. Based on the premise that citizen participation combined with expert analysis to produce a "working democracy," the general council represented the union of the people—the citizens' council—and the experts—the occupational council. In the general council, Phillips argued, "the people can at all times tell the specialists exactly what they want done and can withdraw their support if they do not like what the specialists are doing. Similarly, the specialists must be able at all times to state and discuss their reasons for recommending any particular action, to answer questions, doubts, objections and be ready to see their proposals rejected, or modified to suit the feelings, wishes, opinions, desires, and needs of the people."[28] With individuals separated according to their special functions into occupational and citizen groups, the general council provided the arena in which the experts and the people worked together to develop practical plans for meeting neighborhood needs. In such a way, Phillips reasoned, all groups would work together to solve the problems of the neighborhood and to promote, by implication, a healthy society.[29] Phillips intuitively understood that expert knowledge and methods were not inherently impartial and that a group such as the citizens' council could temper expert advice, thereby reducing the potential for expert coercion.

Once general councils were functioning in neighborhoods throughout the city, Phillips hoped to achieve intracity cooperation. He wanted each neighborhood to send delegates to a citywide citizens' council and a citywide occupational council. These groups were to articulate city needs and strategies for action, the actual programs to be decided on in joint meetings of the two bodies—the city general council. Eventually, Phillips envisioned the reproduction of this organizational form at the county, state, and federal levels. He felt that such a structure permitted more group participation in the decision-making process, provided a sense of order throughout the designated social unit, and trained Americans to be responsible citizens.[30] In short, Phillips's social unit plan provided a total plan for community betterment.

In the summer of 1914 Phillips finished his treatise on social unit organization. He immediately sent copies of his manuscript, along with a discussion of his work with the New York Milk Commitee and the Milwaukee Child Welfare Commission, to "various social and medical workers" for criticism. Among those selected by Phillips to review his work was Dr. Richard C. Cabot, the founder of medical social service at Massachusetts General Hospital.[31] Dr. Cabot expressed particular interest in the medical roots of Phillips's work. He invited Phillips to come to Boston and talk with him about the social unit plan and its relationship to neighborhood organization for health care.[32]

During the meeting Dr. Cabot suggested that Phillips develop a neighborhood health program based on the principles set out in his study. At the close of their meeting Cabot extended an invitation to Phillips and his wife, Elsie, to visit with the Cabots for a week at their summer camp near Saranac Lake after Phillips had outlined a program for intensive neighborhood health care. According to a letter written in 1964 by Phillips to Ethel Pew, a close friend and one of Phillips's benefactors, Phillips and Dr. Cabot discussed Phillips's experiences and ideas each morning and then devoted the afternoons to relaxation. At the end of the week Dr. Cabot, who later said he was interested in Phillips's plan because it embodied a belief "in the principle of intensive medical social work within a small area to develop sound methods,"[33] volunteered to help finance Phillips's proposals for neighborhood health care.[34] Phillips agreed to test a health plan based on social unit principles as a demonstration of the feasibility of his method. Cabot's response to Phillips's plan, while supportive, foreshadowed the problems that would beset Phillips in the future. Despite the fact that Phillips's plan was a broad organizational scheme, the decision to focus on health care as a test of the plan's feasibility resulted in an almost overwhelming identification of the social unit theory of organization with neighborhood health programs. The outbreak of World War I in the summer of 1914, however, compelled Dr. Cabot to withdraw his offer, forcing Phillips to continue his search for supporters for his social unit method of organization.[35]

After Dr. Cabot rescinded his offer, Phillips went to Washington, D.C., to work for the Children's Bureau.[36] Organized in the summer of 1912, the Children's Bureau was established "to investigate and report upon all matters pertaining to the welfare of children and child life among all classes of our people and shall especially investigate the question of infant mortality, the birth rate, orphanage, juvenile courts, desertion, dangerous occupations, accidents and diseases of children, employment, (and) legislation affecting children in the several states and territories."[37] Under the direction of Julia Lathrop, a prominent crusader for social justice appointed by President William Howard Taft to serve as the bureau's first chief, the fifteen-member staff established the bureau as a national research agency responsible for the collection of all available information concerning the treatment and condition of children. The bureau's staff believed that such information would enlighten the American public about the needs of children and about the best methods with which to satisfy those needs. Julia Lathrop selected infant mortality for the bureau's first inquiry.[38] Although no records exist concerning Phillips's duties

during his self-described "brief job"[39] with the bureau, very likely he
shared his experiences in the fight against infant mortality with the
members of the Children's Bureau staff.

In any case, while in Washington, Phillips was able to interest a
number of people in the social unit plan. His wife's cousin, Jean D.
Cole, headmistress of Mt. Vernon Seminary, presented Phillips to
Judge and Mrs. William Hitz. They, in turn, introduced Phillips to a
number of Washington area residents such as Mr. and Mrs. William F.
Cochran of Baltimore, President Woodrow Wilson's daughter Margaret, Oliver P. Newman, the president of the Board of Commissioners of the District of Columbia, and John Joy Edson, president of
the Washington Loan and Trust Company, whom they believed
would be interested in Phillips's work. This core of interested people
circulated information about Phillips's social unit plan, and on February 23, 1915, they called a meeting of those curious to hear more
about Phillips's ideas. After some discussion, this group decided to
establish a committee to encourage the demonstration of Phillips's
theory of organization and to secure a large number of supporters[40] to
provide both technical experience and financial backing for the proposed venture.

This booster committee consisted of seven members. Oliver P.
Newman, John Joy Edson, and Mrs. J. Borden Harriman, a former
supporter of Phillips's New York Milk Committee work, headed the
group. The remaining members included Frederick L. Siddons,
associate justice of the Supreme Court of the District of Columbia;
Dr. Joseph P. Wall, supervising physician of the infant welfare stations
maintained by the Washington Diet Kitchen Association; Edith
Westcott, principal of Washington's Western High School; and Margaret Wilson. Once organized, the committee began to devise its
strategy to publicize and attract a wide base of support for a demonstration of the theory.[41]

The committee's advertising message depicted the social unit plan
as "essentially an experiment in democracy, with public health work
as the point of attack."[42] To aid the committee in its activities, Phillips
drew up a shortened version of the social unit theory in which he
incorporated the health care plan outlined earlier for Dr. Cabot as an
illustration. The committee also drew up several objectives to provide
a focus for the advertising campaign. First, it decided that the plan

should be tested in a community that had demonstrated a desire to host such an experiment. Second, the committee hoped to secure the endorsement of leading social and medical workers throughout the country. Third, committee members wanted to raise a substantial amount of money to assist the host city in financing a unit plan demonstration. And, finally, the committee wished to obtain the services of nationally recognized experts to serve as advisors to the host community. The committee submitted the plan for review to a select number of people, while Phillips traveled from city to city explaining the social unit plan and attempting to raise money to finance the projected social unit experiment.[43]

By late 1915 the efforts of Phillips and the committee began to bear fruit. After a period of uncertainty, a break came. Dr. Cabot, still a supporter of the plan, provided an introduction to Dr. Felix Adler, founder of the Ethical Culture Society, who in turn introduced Phillips to Herbert Croly, editor of the *New Republic*. Through Croly, Phillips became acquainted with Dorothy Whitney Straight, the financial backer of the *New Republic*. Then, wrote Phillips, "how the snowball grew!" According to his recollection, Mrs. Thomas Lamont, wife of financier T. W. Lamont, pledged $1,000 a year for three years. This donation was followed by "five thousand dollars a year for three years from Mr. and Mrs. Guggenheim. And another five thousand dollars a year from Albert J. Mellbank, on behalf of his cousin, Mrs. A. A. Anderson. Luncheon with Mrs. Gifford Pinchot at the Colony Club. Tea with her husband and her at the Bryce home on Fifth Avenue. Yes, the future Governor of Pennsylvania would serve as the president of our national body."[44] As interest and support broadened, the Washington committee decided to establish a national social unit organization.[45]

On February 9, 1916, at the home of Mrs. Straight in New York City, seventeen interested people came together to discuss the feasibility of sponsoring a demonstration of Phillips's plan. Beatrice Bend; Herbert Croly; John Elliot, the head worker of the Hudson Guild; Mrs. Daniel Guggenheim, active in the neighborhood work of the Emanuel Sisterhood; Mrs. J. Borden Harriman; Helen Hartley Jenkins, a member of the Hartley House board; Paul U. Kellogg, editor of *The Survey* magazine; Mrs. Alexander Kohut, a member of the Emanuel Sisterhood; Adolph Lewisohn, philanthropist for vari-

ous educational and humanitarian ventures; Mrs. Henry Ollesheimer; Virginia Potter; Charles Stelzle, former head of the New York
Labor Temple; Dr. John Vaughan; and Morris Waldman joined Mrs.
Straight and Phillips. By the end of the evening the group decided to
create a permanent organization to sponsor the unit plan. Such an
organization, they believed, was necessary to raise enough money to
finance the demonstration. In addition, they felt that only a permanent organization could interest a large number of cities in the
demonstration. Finally, they expected that participation in a national
body would give all supporters of the unit plan a "permanent and
organic connection" with the experiment.[46]

Under the chairmanship of Mrs. J. Borden Harriman, this group,
calling itself the National Temporary Organizing Committee
(NTOC), contacted various people about the projected social unit
experiment and invited them to become formal supporters of the unit
plan. By February 15, 1916, the committee had received affirmative
replies from twenty-two prominent individuals, including members
of the Washington committee, men and women active in the promotion of child health, editors of *New Republic* and *The Survey* maga-
zines, important industrialists, and leading social workers. The
NTOC welcomed the new members at its meeting on February 15
and voted to meet again in March to discuss the form of the permanent organization.[47]

On March 9, 1916, the NTOC gathered for its final meeting. The
members formally agreed to work toward the establishment of an
organization designed to "focus the brains of the country on the
development of an efficient manner of handling social and health
work." To this end, the NTOC voted to select a city for the demonstration which offered suitable conditions and exhibited a strong desire
for the program. In a small area of the city NTOC members hoped to
develop a model public health program with medical work for children as its pilot project. The NTOC members believed that this
experience in neighborhood planning for health would foster the
"creation of an efficient mechanism for wise social planning—one
whereby expert intelligence from many groups" could be made to
work for "community purposes."[48] The members closed the meeting
after a decision to call another meeting in early April to establish a
permanent social unit organization. Except for a temporary Ways and

Means Committee, headed by Miss Potter and consisting of Mrs. Pinchot, Mrs. Charles Tiffany, Mrs. Mowbray Clark, Harry Monasmith, William Loeb, Jr., Mr. Stelzle, and Mr. Waldman to oversee the transition, the NTOC voted itself out of existence.[49]

The Ways and Means Committee called a meeting of all those interested in Phillips's plan for April 11, 1916, at the home of Mrs. Straight. That night, according to Phillips's account, Mrs. Straight's long library filled with people in evening dress. John Elliott, who had agreed to serve as chairman, opened the meeting. He was followed by John Kingsbury, the commissioner of charities of New York City, who delivered a "rattling speech"[50] and moved to create an organization committed to encouraging the development of a "model program for community organization" in an American community.[51] Those present voted to sponsor a three-year demonstration of Phillips's social unit scheme, focusing on a preventive health program for young children to illustrate the plan's feasibility. Miss Potter announced that numerous pledges of money toward the cost of a demonstration had already been secured. According to her report, the new organization—the National Social Unit Organization (NSUO)—had received pledges totaling $63,000.[52]

The assembly then elected a governing body to direct the activities of the NSUO. This body was divided into a citizens' council, an occupational council, and an executive council. The citizens' council was to consist of members-at-large from the various cities expressing interest in the plan. The occupational council was to be composed of specialists interested in offering counsel and advice to the selected demonstration city. The executive council was to oversee the entire organization.[53]

Gifford Pinchot, prominent conservationist of Milford, Pennsylvania, was elected president of the executive council and of the NSUO. The members of the meeting then selected Mr. Edson to be treasurer. Oliver P. Newman and George W. Coleman agreed to hold the posts of first and second vice-presidents respectively. Phillips and his wife, Elsie, were made executive secretaries of the NSUO.[54]

Mrs. Harriman and Mrs. Tiffany of New York cochaired the citizens' council. The membership of the council included those present as well as those persons from the various cities in which interest in the plan had been expressed. From New York came Robert S. Brinkerd,

Herbert Croly, Helen Hartley Jenkins, Mrs. Daniel Guggenheim, Mrs. Alexander Kohut, William Loeb, Jr., Charles Stelzle, Rev. Howard J. Melish, Virginia Potter, Adolph Lewisohn, Mrs. Henry Ollesheimer, Professor E.R.A. Seligman, Dorothy Straight, and Helen Phelps Stokes. Dr. John Beffel of Milwaukee, a former member of the Milwaukee Child Welfare Commission, represented his city. The representatives from Washington, D.C., consisted of Mrs. Whitman Cross, Mrs. Henry C. Perkins, and Mary Gwynn. Mrs. James Storrow, Mrs. William Lowell Putnam, and R.G. Valentine spoke for Boston. Also included on the council were Professor Felix Frankfurter, Cambridge, Massachusetts; Mrs. George Rainey, Carrollton, Illinois; John Spargo, Bennington, Vermont; Arthur M. Allen, Providence, Rhode Island; Mrs. Henry Adsit Bull, Buffalo, New York; Charles Edison, South Orange, New Jersey; William F. Cochran, Baltimore; Mary Converse, Philadelphia; Isabel Hymans, Dorchester, Massachusetts; Edmund Huyck, Albany, New York; Alice Lee, San Diego; E.W. Williams, Cleveland; and Mrs. H. Wittpenn, Jersey City, New Jersey.

Henry Bruère, former director of the New York City Bureau of Municipal Research and former city chamberlain, chaired the occupational council. Dr. George M. Kober, former president of the American Association for the Study and Prevention of Tuberculosis, occupied the position of vice-chairman. The council set up areas of endeavor to provide assistance to the local demonstration unit. C.C. Carsten, secretary of the Massachusetts Society for the Prevention of Cruelty to Children, was appointed to direct those services dealing with children. Dr. S.S. Goldwater, former health commissioner of New York City, led the public health work. John Ihlder of the National Housing Association was to oversee work done in that area. Lillian Wald, head worker of the Nurses' Settlement in New York City, and later Ella Phillips Crandall, executive secretary of the National Organization of Public Health Nursing, were designated to direct the nursing services. Rowland G. Haynes, secretary of the National Organization of Recreation of the Board of Estimate and Apportionment of New York City, provided direction for recreational organization. Porter R. Lee headed relief activities, and Dr. Cressey L. Wilbur, New York State registrar of vital statistics, was to provide assistance to those involved in the collection of statistics for the unit demonstration.[55]

In the days following the creation of the National Social Unit Organization, announcements about its proposed demonstration began to appear in the press. In a statement released to the *New York Times* on April 12, 1916, the NSUO described its intention to "finance, organize and advise" a "model program for community organization with the counsel and advice of national social experts." The release further stated that the NSUO planned to begin "arousing interest in the experiment all over the country by enlisting the attention of persons in all parts of the United States in the workings of the plan." The announcement concluded by indicating that child welfare work would serve as the initial program undertaken in whatever city eventually was chosen to host the three-year demonstration.[56]

Phillips further elaborated on the social unit plan and the projected demonstration in an article in *The Survey*. Here Phillips stressed that the plan "grows out of the conviction which has been increasing among social experts within the past few years that no social problem—so called—can be solved in isolation—that a merging of effort is necessary, and that this can best be accomplished through intensive and democratic organization on a district basis."[57] Phillips also indicated that once a city was selected to host the demonstration, the NSUO would "serve in an advisory capacity, making available for the work the best of the nation's social experience . . . through the creation of national advisory committees."[58]

All publicity stressed that the NSUO planned to select for the demonstration the city that showed the most interest in the plan. Spokespersons for the NSUO stated that, due to the "democratic nature of the plan contemplated" and to the fact that the "enthusiastic cooperation of the social workers in the city was essential to its success," the NSUO planned to wait until interested groups in various cities expressed their desire for the plan and applied for the aid of the national organization.[59]

Within a few weeks NSUO officials received numerous letters from public officials, social workers, and private individuals across the United States.[60] Presumably, these individuals, like the members of the national organization, were attracted to the proposed demonstration for a variety of reasons. As Martin Duberman points out in *The Uncompleted Past*, we really know very little about human motivation in general, let alone why men and women do something very specific such as expressing interest in and support for a novel method of arousing community participation in local affairs.[61] Despite this admonition, it is possible to discern, albeit imprecisely, several reasons for the interest among the NSUO founders and individuals or groups seeking the demonstration for their communities.

In the first place, Phillips's plan attracted numerous supporters because of the NSUO's decision to establish a child welfare program as the demonstration's first area of concern. A central theme of humanitarian progressivism concerned the conservation of the child. For many, programs to better the condition of the child in society represented positive work toward the "physical, intellectual and spiritual development . . . of the whole race."[62] The child was seen as the "carrier of tomorrow's hope." One way to conserve children and to give them a good start in life, many believed, was to improve child health care delivery. For NSUO supporters, such as Dr. Richard Cabot, Dr. James Mason-Knox, Dr. Charles E. North, John Spargo, Mrs. J. Borden Harriman, Mrs. William Lowell Putnam, and C.C. Carsten, all of whom had been active in the campaign against infant mortality and the crusade for clean milk for babies during the first decade of the twentieth century, the selection of child welfare work by the NSUO as its demonstration program sparked their interest and support.[63]

For other supporters, such as Herbert Croly, Mrs. Willard Straight, and Felix Frankfurter, Phillips's plan, with its emphasis on "national social experts," seemed to offer a way to combine mass participation in community affairs with scientific management. The social unit plan, stressing the interchange between the citizens' council and the occupational council wedded the experts to the people. A demonstration of Phillips's social unit principles of organization appeared to those interested in fostering a symbiotic relationship between citizen and expert as an excellent opportunity to test in microcosm the feasibility of the expert-citizen combination.[64]

Still others found the social unit plan a step toward the reduction of duplication and waste in social welfare activities. A rise in the number, and a broadening of the scope, of relief schemes to aid depressed urbanites in the late nineteenth century resulted in overlapping and competing activities and agencies. Religious relief agencies, private charities, and fledgling public welfare services invaded urban communities, utilizing different and often conflicting methods to provide for the needs of their constituents. Proponents of centralizing and coordinating social welfare activities on a "scientific and businesslike basis," such as R.G. Valentine, Gifford Pinchot, and John Joy Edson, welcomed an opportunity to illustrate the benefits of cooperative and coordinated social welfare activity.[65]

Finally, others supported Phillips's plan because they believed that it offered an excellent opportunity to demonstrate the value of neighborhood organization for health care. For instance, Dr. John Beffel, Michael M. Davis, and Dr. S.S. Goldwater had been attracted to Phillips's work in Milwaukee and in New York City. They each had supported similar schemes following Phillips's experiment in St. Cyril's Parish. By grouping together closely related health and welfare activities, these proponents of neighborhood health care hoped to supply every family with the knowledge, medical attention, and nursing supervision necessary to prevent ill health. These supporters believed that the proposed experiment would demonstrate the effectiveness of community health programs.[66]

Surely a mixture of the founders' concerns, combined with various local reasons, accounted for the response of numerous individuals to the announcement of the NSUO's intention to select a city to host the social unit demonstration. Shortly following the NSUO's announcement, fifteen cities emerged as strong contenders for the experiment. Groups from Washington, D.C., Baltimore, Cincinnati, Akron, Denver, St. Paul, Minneapolis, Newark, New Haven, Kansas City, Providence, Syracuse, Poughkeepsie, Worcester, and Santa Barbara petitioned the NSUO to consider their city for the demonstration. The city boosters followed their initial requests for consideration with speaking invitations and arrangements for local leaders to meet with the NSUO representatives. Phillips later recalled that, in each city, the local boosters "royally hailed me when I spoke at meetings (and) extolled the unique advantages their cities presented."[67] By the fall of 1916, Washington, D.C., and Cincinnati remained as the two major contenders for the NSUO's demonstration.[68]

Oliver P. Newman, president of the Board of Commissioners of the District of Columbia and the first vice-president of the NSUO, championed the selection of Washington, D.C., as the host city. Supporters circulated a pamphlet, entitled "A Plan for Making the City of Washington a National Social Laboratory," that described the intent of the NSUO's experiment. The pamphlet presented the social unit plan as an attempt to extend gradually preventive medical and nursing care to all mothers and babies in the Washington area. It indicated that the plan contained a mechanism for eventually "bettering the total environment" and for "providing a civic activity in which the whole citizenship could participate." Newman and the Washington supporters urged the NSUO to consider Washington, D.C., because "being the capitol of the United States, a demonstration there would, if successful, have a publicity value probably not found in any other city in the country."[69]

Courtenay Dinwiddie, superintendent of the Cincinnati Tuberculosis League,[70] and Dr. John Landis, health officer of Cincinnati, organized Cincinnati's campaign to secure the NSUO's demonstration. Prior to the announcement of the NSUO's demonstration, the Municipal Tuberculosis Committee,[71] a special group formed by the Anti-Tuberculosis League, had developed a plan for an intensive experiment in neighborhood health care that involved the close cooperation of all public and private agencies whose work touched on the tuberculosis problem. The committee hoped to establish health centers in two neighborhoods having a high incidence of tuberculosis. In these health centers the committee hoped to reduce the white plague through early diagnosis and treatment, while at the same time research the causes and spread of the dread disease.[72] The publicity surrounding the committee's project had aroused considerable interest in the idea of a neighborhood-based health program. Dinwiddie and Landis, under the auspices of the Municipal Tuberculosis Committee, channeled this enthusiasm into a campaign for the NSUO's experiment in neighborhood health care.

During the months of May and June 1916, Dinwiddie and Dr. Landis presented the NSUO's projected demonstration to a number of important groups in Cincinnati, including the Cincinnati Men's Club, the Federation of Churches, officials of the school system, and local medical organizations. In mid-June, a committee composed of Dr. Landis, Dinwiddie, W.J. Norton, Judge Benton S. Oppenheimer, Dr. Arthur Bachmeyer, Max Senior, Miss Cooke, and C.M. Bodman contacted the NSUO. Because Washington was a creature of Congress, the committee argued that Cincinnati was a "more typical city than Washington in which to try out the national social service laboratory plan."[73] In addition, they asked the national organization to consider a donation of $15,000 per year for three years as a token of Cincinnati's interest in securing the social unit demonstration.[74]

In October 1916 Phillips decided to go to Cincinnati to meet with those promoting the Queen City and assess its desirability for selection as host city.[75] Accordingly, the Phillipses arrived in Cincinnati in mid-October. On October 21, after meeting with several different groups, Phillips spoke before the City Club at the Hotel Sinton on "A Social Unit Plan for Community Organization." In his talk, he outlined briefly his work in New York and Milwaukee and discussed how this led to his social unit theory of organization. Mrs. Phillips followed her husband's remarks with an elaboration on the work carried out in St. Cyril's Parish. She stressed that the baby station in the parish, because of its efficiency, "its democratic form of organization," and its familiarity with every home in the neighborhood, absorbed the activities of sixteen charitable organizations operating in that section of Milwaukee and raised the level of health care available to every home.[76] Impressed by the enthusiasm of numerous groups in Cincinnati for the unit demonstration, on November 9, 1916, Phillips recommended to the NSUO that Cincinnati be selected as the host city.[77]

On November 20, 1916, the NSUO announced its selection of Cincinnati as the host city for the social unit demonstration. In the announcement the NSUO outlined the reasons for choosing Cincinnati over Washington, D.C. Essentially, the NSUO voted against Washington, D.C., because Washington was not a "typical American city." The NSUO believed that because Washington residents were not franchised and were governed by Congress, they had a less developed interest in civic affairs than did residents in other urban areas. In addition, according to the literature put out by the NSUO, Washington lacked "the industrial base and distinct city sections" believed to exist in other American cities. These things, the NSUO felt, overshadowed the publicity value that a successful demonstration in the capital would have.[78]

Cincinnati, on the other hand, possessed the best facilities of all the interested cities for carrying out the social unit demonstration. The city had the cooperation of the mayor, a high degree of enthusiasm for the plan among the general public, and the promise of Cincinnati's social and public health agencies to support the experiment and relinquish their own work within the section selected for the demonstration. Also, the NSUO found that members of the medical profession in Cincinnati were "accustomed to working together on health problems." Both the Health Department and the municipal hospital promised to cooperate with the NSUO in a model neighborhood health center in the selected district. In addition, the NSUO saw Cincinnati as a typical American city because it lay near the center of the United States and no single industry dominated its economic base. The NSUO also argued that, as a "city of neighborhoods," Cincinnati lent itself to district organization. And, finally, the pledge of fifteen thousand dollars per year for three years to help finance the social unit demonstration represented a tangible demonstration of city interest in the experiment.[79]

Following the formal announcement of Cincinnati as the demonstration site, Phillips indicated that actual work would begin after the beginning of the new year. At the end of December, Phillips and his wife left New York City. On January 2, 1917, the Phillipses "set down our suitcases in the Hotel Sinton, wiped the soot from our noses and set to work."[80]

4

The Social Unit
Comes to
Cincinnati

The arrival of Mr. and Mrs. Wilbur C. Phillips in Cincinnati on January 2, 1917, launched the first year of the social unit demonstration. Immediately after checking in at the Hotel Sinton, the Phillipses began laying the groundwork for the social unit demonstration. After opening an office in the Bodman Building at 621 Main Street, they called their first meeting with the Cincinnati sponsors of the unit plan for January 4 at the headquarters of the Anti-Tuberculosis League. At this meeting the Phillipses sketched out what needed to be done in the months ahead. For the next three months the Phillipses explained the plan to the public and created the nucleus of a city social unit organization to oversee the experiment, to advise the unit laboratory, and to assist the National Social Unit Organization in the evaluation of the demonstration at the conclusion of the experiment.[1] By the end of 1917 the neighborhood of Mohawk-Brighton had been selected as the social unit laboratory, and a neighborhood social unit organization had been established to direct the experiment. On December 17, practical services commenced under the direction of the Mohawk-Brighton Social Unit Organization. The experiment was on its way.

Prior to their arrival in Cincinnati the Phillipses had decided to create a citywide social unit organization before selecting a laboratory district and beginning the actual work. At the January 4 meeting they outlined their reasons for favoring the creation of a city organization to supervise the launching of the demonstration. The Phillipses contended that a city social unit organization composed of representative Cincinnatians would stimulate competition among the various neighborhoods and result in a "healthy demand for the program." In addition, if the plan were to be extended throughout the city, a strong city organization would enable those not involved in the original experiment to familiarize themselves with the general principles of social unit organization. The city organization could relate the progress of the experiment to the nonparticipating neighborhoods and could serve as an educational medium for the general public. Finally, the Phillipses argued that the identification of the city residents with the social unit experiment would prove essential to the ultimate success or failure of the demonstration.[2]

With the help of the Cincinnati Municipal Tuberculosis Committee, Phillips formed the Temporary Organizing Committee to lay the groundwork for a permanent city organization modeled on the National Social Unit Organization. Described enthusiastically by Dr. John Landis, Cincinnati's health officer, as the "most representative group ever gathered together in Cincinnati,"[3] the committee drew from the city's major civic, professional, educational, and social welfare organizations and institutions; it did not represent the city's population as a whole.[4] Nonetheless, like its counterparts in other cities, this group saw itself as speaking for the general welfare of the urban community.

At the temporary committee's first meeting, Dr. Landis called for a public meeting to create an organization consisting of a citizen's council and an occupational council drawn from the city as a whole to oversee the neighborhood experiment. With this decision made, the committee decided to offer the position of honorary executive of the Cincinnati organization to George Putcha, the mayor of Cincinnati. In addition, the committee voted to invite Cincinnati's city council and the heads of the various city departments to send representatives to the city occupational council. By bringing members of the local government directly into the structure of the city organization, the committee hoped to foster a close and continuing relationship between the social unit experiment and the municipal government.[5]

In preparation for the meeting to create a permanent city organization, the Temporary Organizing Committee sponsored several mini-conferences to familiarize Cincinnatians with the social unit plan and to stress that the demonstration represented "a municipal laboratory for the development of an idea which had significance, value and importance to the entire citizenship." During the final days of February 1917 the committee secured pledges of support from leading businessmen and labor leaders, reaffirmed with the city's various social service agencies the agreement originally made with the NSUO to relinquish work in the experimental district, and received a promise of help from the Academy of Medicine in the development of the selected district's infant welfare plan. By March 1 the Temporary Organizing Committee felt the time had come to establish the permanent city organization. The committee appointed a nominating committee and arranged a meeting for March 22, 1917, to vote the Cincinnati Social Unit Organization formally into existence.[6]

Approximately six hundred people attended the meeting held in the Exchange Hall of the Chamber of Commerce. Like the Temporary Organizing Committee, this group was described by participants as "the most representative meeting of its kind ever held for the purpose of launching a social program in the Queen City, with practically every large professional, industrial and social group in the city having a representative or delegate in attendance." While this may have overstated the case, accounts of this meeting in the local newspapers pointed to a high degree of enthusiasm among those attending the meeting and included remarks attesting to the high level of interest displayed by leading Cincinnati social, economic, and political groups. In any case, the Phillipses and Dr. Randall Condon, a committee member and superintendent of the schools, opened the meeting. They were followed by Reverend Howard J. Melish, a former Cincinnatian and a member of the NSUO, who spoke "briefly but eloquently on the democratic aspects of the plan." Cincinnatians Dr. T.W. Gosling, Attorney Guy Mallon, Anti-Tuberculosis League President Benton S. Oppenheimer, Chamber of Commerce Secretary W.C. Culkins, and Cincinnati's Superintendent of Public Welfare J.O. White followed the Reverend Mr. Melish and delivered short speeches in support of the creation of a city social unit organization. Then John R. Frey, editor of the *Iron Moulders' Journal*, moved to create a Cincinnati Social Unit Organization (CSUO).[7]

Following the vote to create the CSUO, those attending the meeting approved the Temporary Organizing Committee's choices for the Executive Council of the CSUO and confirmed its selections for the city Citizens' Council and Occupational Council. Mayor George Putcha became the honorary executive of the CSUO. The Phillipses were appointed executives; F.W. Galbraith, president of the Businessmen's Club, treasurer; J.C. Duncan, an accountant, controller; and Roe Eastman, a local newspaperman, secretary. The Citizens' Council of the CSUO, headed by Mrs. Guy Mallon, president of the Woman's City Club, and Mrs. Ben Lowenstein, active in the Jewish Settlement, was composed of representatives from the various neighborhoods of Cincinnati. Mrs. J.O. White, wife of the city superintendent of public welfare, was selected as the council's secretary, and Jessie Bogen, daughter of Boris Bogen, field secretary for the National Conference of Jewish Charities, became the council's organizer. Courtenay Dinwiddie was confirmed as executive of the city Occupational Council. Members of this council included representatives from the public schools, medical community, social welfare groups, local businesses, and city government. The meeting ended following the selection of a committee on constitution.[8]

Headed by Randall Condon, the committee on constitution convened soon after the meeting to formalize the machinery of the newly created Cincinnati Social Unit Organization and to set forth its goals and objectives. Opening membership to "any person who sympathizes with its general purpose," the CSUO constitution provided for neighborhood councils, which, when set up throughout the city, were to send representatives to a citywide citizens' council, and an occupational council containing selected members of various skilled groups.[9] The General Council consisted of a merger of the Citizens' and Occupational councils. According to Phillips, these councils would "formulate a community social program"[10] designed to further "the coming of a democracy both genuine and efficient by building upon a basis of geographical units an organization through which the people can get a clear idea of their common needs and can utilize the technical knowledge of skilled groups in formulating and carrying out programs to meet those needs."[11]

In addition to the organization of the different councils, the constitution provided for annual meetings of the CSUO to be held on the third Thursday of March and for petitions, signed by fifty members, to initiate the amendment process. By the end of March the CSUO began to organize the various occupational groups whose cooperation was believed essential to the success of the experiment and to intensify the activities to familiarize the general public with the experiment.[12]

While members of the Citizens' Council held several general informational meetings about the social unit experiment,[13] those appointed to the Occupational Council met with members of the various skilled groups that they represented. Although the social unit theory of organization provided for the formation of a council in each field of endeavor, only seven groups—the social workers, nurses, teachers, clergymen, businessmen, statisticians, and physicians—were organized. While these groups occasionally assisted the social unit district later, for the most part the relationship that developed between the neighborhood and the Occupational Council proved to be an extremely casual one.[14] The physicians' and the statisticians' councils were the only exceptions.

On April 23, 1917, Phillips spoke before members of the Cincinnati Academy of Medicine. He outlined the social unit plan briefly and stressed the importance of the anticipated health care program in conserving the health of the citizens of Cincinnati. Dr. Franklin Martin, a member of the Council of National Defense and head of the NSUO's advisory medical council, also spoke and urged the doctors to cooperate fully with the social unit work. At the conclusion of the meeting, those members of the academy present authorized Dr. Landis, president, to appoint a committee composed of the past six presidents of the academy[15] to consider the best way to cooperate with the neighborhood health care experiment.[16]

After a month of deliberation this committee recommended to the academy that it endorse the social unit plan and cooperate with the social unit medical council when it was established in the selected neighborhood. Academy members adopted a resolution drafted by the Committee of Presidents to establish a medical council to advise and assist "the Social Unit Organization in promoting within some neighborhood of Cincinnati a method through which the doctors who live and practice therein, can organize on a democratic self-governing basis for the conduct of such work as seems to them feasible and desirable, with the understanding that these physicians will be asked to serve as a subcommittee of the Academy of Medicine to report back to the Academy on the result of their work when such work has passed the experimental stage."[17] In addition, the academy decided to consider the establishment of similar citywide health units if the social unit experiment proved successful on the neighborhood level.[18]

Although it proved difficult to organize a broadly representative council of statisticians (the CSUO found that "there were not many who could be classified as such in the city"), the CSUO did form a small, yet active group. Consisting of E. Walter Evans from the Board of Health, Professors James Magee and Curtis Meyers from the University of Cincinnati, and E. E. Hardcastle of the Union Central Life Insurance Company, the Statistical Council assisted the CSUO, and, once the demonstration was under way, the neighborhood social unit organization in the evaluation of social unit programs. In particular, the Statistical Council studied the data collected by the block workers and then presented the block workers with charts, diagrams, and spot maps summarizing the main conclusions drawn from the data and emphasizing the most important lessons for both the block workers and the neighborhood occupational councils.[19]

After the CSUO had created citywide occupational councils, it concentrated on the selection of an experimental district. The Executive Council announced in the daily newspapers that it intended to choose the neighborhood that proved most eager for the plan. Circulars were distributed throughout the city explaining the social unit plan. The leading newspapers also advertised the plan. Articles in these papers briefly outlined the plan and stressed that the intended program for the selected neighborhood would include, among other things, the development of a "model child welfare program," the establishment of a "general preventive health program," and the "encouragement of social progress."[20] From May 14 to May 21, all the major newspapers carried a column, "What the Social Unit Experiment Means for You and Your Neighborhood," which carried a series of questions and answers about the plan, its significance, and the advantages it could offer the neighborhood chosen to host the experiment.[21]

At the suggestion of Randall Condon, an informational leaflet about the social unit organization and a ballot were distributed throughout the public school system to collect information concerning neighborhood interest in the demonstration. Parents of school-age children were asked the following questions: "(1) Do you wish your neighborhood to be selected? (2) Will you help to make the plan a success? and (3) Do you wish to know more about the plan?"[22] Approximately five thousand ballots were sent in to the CSUO by the parents of the schoolchildren during the last two weeks in May. By the beginning of June five neighborhoods—Mohawk-Brighton, Cumminsville, Camp Washington, North Fairmont, and the Central-North-Western District—emerged as the leading contenders. Each of these neighborhoods sent petitions to the CSUO urging its selection as the host district. The CSUO, in response to such a display of interest, announced that it would select the neighborhood at a public meeting on June 7.[23]

After a few opening remarks by members of the Executive Council at the June 7 meeting, Phillips introduced the representatives from each of the five neighborhoods competing for the unit demonstration. These representatives spoke on behalf of their respective neighborhoods. Following their presentations, Dr. Landis expressed pleasure on behalf of the CSUO for the high degree of interest demonstrated by Cincinnati residents for the unit demonstration. At that point, Mrs. Ben Lowenstein, co-executive of the Citizens' Council, took the chair and announced the CSUO's choice of Mohawk-Brighton as the demonstration district. Neighborhood organization in the selected district would begin at once, she concluded.[24]

The selection of Mohawk-Brighton came as a result of intensive organizational efforts led by Mary Hicks, librarian of the Dayton Street Public Library, and Ruth Gottlieb, a teacher in one of the neighborhood schools. Together they headed a special Committee of One Hundred and Forty-five formed by interested residents in Mohawk-Brighton. Members of this committee canvassed the neighborhood block by block to encourage residents to support the drive to secure the experiment for Mohawk-Brighton. The committee forwarded to the CSUO a petition with 1,862 signatures, and 113 residents sent in letters urging the selection of Mohawk-Brighton. In addition, twenty-five business, social, civic, and religious organizations promised their cooperation.[25] The neighborhood schools sent in a larger proportion of affirmative votes than any other area of the city.[26] The people of Mohawk-Brighton, according to Phillips, had

selected themselves as the experimental district. He later wrote that
"the development of the program from this time forth was no longer
the movement of a national group. It was . . . the neighborhood's own
plan."[27]

Mohawk-Brighton lay slightly west of the center of Cincinnati. It
was nestled between the fashionable hilltop suburbs and a belt of
land, surrounding the central business district, that contained the
city slums. By 1917 it represented that part of the city known as the
Zone of Emergence, a term used by Robert A. Woods and Albert J.
Kennedy for that area of the city inhabited by residents who "had
emerged from the slum into the mainstream of American life."[28]

Between 1850 and 1910 Cincinnati had undergone the transition
from the nineteenth century walking city to the metropolitan community of the twentieth century. A combination of technological
innovations in intracity transportation, population growth, industrial
expansion, and successful annexations enlarged city boundaries from
a mere 6 square miles in 1850 to 50.26 square miles by 1910.[29]
Central in this process of physical growth was the emergence of a
differentiated urban structure in which the expanded central business district of the new city appeared to be surrounded by zones that
exhibited distinct residential or industrial functions.[30] In Cincinnati
three discernible zones emerged: the Circle, the Zone of Emergence, and the Hilltops.[31]

The Circle occupied the area on the periphery of the old walking
city. Populated by diverse groups of recent arrivals, the slums of the
Circle were crowded and relatively unstable. Poverty was the common condition of the great variety of residents in this downtown area.
The Circle also had a reputation as Cincinnati's "center of illegal
activity and disorderly behavior."[32] All in all, it represented the least
desirable residential sector of the city.

Those with enough resources to commute to work and allot more of
their income to housing lived in the Zone of Emergence. This large
area lay between the Circle and the hilltop suburbs that dotted the
city's periphery.[33] Mohawk-Brighton, like most areas in the Zone,
developed into a residential and industrial neighborhood. By the late
nineteenth century it had grown into an "industrial beehive," containing perfumeries, brass foundries, machinist shops, and a flour
mill. A wide variety of small enterprises, such as tobacconists, gro-

Figure 5. Circle, Zone, and Hilltop Sections of Cincinnati, 1910

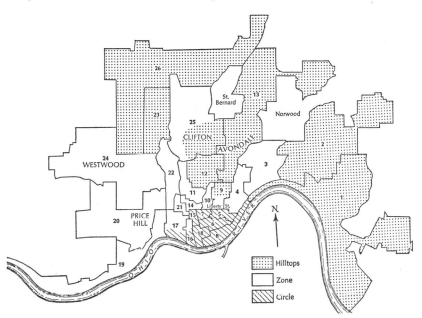

Source: Zane L. Miller, *Boss Cox's Cincinnati: Urban Politics in the Progressive Era*, Copyright © 1968 by Oxford University Press, Inc. Reprinted by permission.

Note: Mohawk-Brighton included parts of the Fourteenth, Eleventh, and Twenty-First Wards.

ceries, dry goods shops, and saloons, located primarily along Central Avenue—the main artery into Mohawk-Brighton—served the neighborhood residents.[34]

Residents in the Mohawk-Brighton area were predominantly second and third generation immigrants who had moved out of the Circle and were attempting to enter the mainstream of American life.[35] Despite the presence of recently arrived Rumanians, Germans, and Hungarians in the three wards of Mohawk-Brighton, 83 percent of the 39,835 residents in 1920 were native-born Americans of German or Irish extraction.[36] Most of the people living in Mohawk-

Brighton were not poverty-stricken and enjoyed "generally regular employment." Those nearest the Circle lived in brick tenements— aging buildings, but nonetheless superior to those found in the Circle. Residents of Mohawk-Brighton who lived closer to the Hill- tops owned their own homes, described by one contemporary as "red brick or weathered houses which clung to the bluff," or shared two or three-story homes with one or two other families. Overall, the people of Mohawk-Brighton lived in buildings less crowded and of higher quality than those in the Circle.[37]

Why Mohawk-Brighton residents sought the social unit plan so strenuously remains unclear, for the other neighborhoods in conten- tion were also part of the Zone of Emergence. One peculiarity of the Zone provides a partial explanation for their interest. The Zone of Emergence consisted of people of only marginal economic security who feared engulfment or re-engulfment by the slums. As a result, they exhibited a "penchant for organization." Contemporaries, as well as more recent students of the city, have argued that residents of zone neighborhoods tended to be joiners and organization builders. According to one contemporary description, Zone residents built up "many organizations, societies, associations, fraternities and clubs that bring people together who are striving upward, trying to lift themselves, and hence, human society."[38] By banding together, "Zone residents sought to realize their aspirations," however im- precisely defined, and to exert control over their communities. The other four neighborhoods in the social unit competition exhibited different levels of organization-making in their attempts to secure the unit demonstration. While Mohawk-Brighton residents set up a 145- member committee to canvass all blocks in their neighborhood and to sponsor public meetings about the unit plan, the other communities established relatively small and inactive committees.[39] Evidently the residents of Mohawk-Brighton, poised tenuously on the edge of the slums, responded more positively to neighborhood leaders' appeals for support in securing the unit demonstration—a demonstration they apparently viewed as an opportunity for both individual and neighborhood betterment.[40]

Contemporaries stressed two other reasons for Mohawk-Bright- on's interest in securing the social unit experiment. Some observers agreed with Ralph Diffendorfer, director of the Home Missions Survey Department of the Interchurch World Movement, who wrote that "the problems of the Mohawk-Brighton District are those of the average congested city community; namely, how to save the lives of babies, to prevent death from tuberculosis, to assimilate the foreign-born, to reduce poverty and unemployment, to improve housing conditions and sanitation, to increase public spirit, to promote recreation, to extend education, and to develop the moral and spiritual life of the people."[41] According to Diffendorfer, the residents of Mohawk-Brighton hoped to confront these problems with the social unit organization.[42]

Courtenay Dinwiddie, a CSUO executive and a tireless supporter of Phillips's plan, echoed Diffendorfer's remarks on the representative nature of Mohawk-Brighton, but also stressed that the residents' urge to confront the typical concerns of an urban civilization was combined in Mohawk-Brighton with an appreciation of the significance of the experiment. Dinwiddie suggested that an awareness of the possibilities for change offered by the social unit accounted for the keen interest of Mohawk-Brighton residents in securing the experiment. This awareness and interest, Dinwiddie argued, accounted for their readiness "to shoulder the responsibility for directing the social unit demonstration."[43] Recent research on other early twentieth century neighborhoods points to the interest of residents in joining together to combat local issues, as Diffendorfer and Dinwiddie suggest. This research indicates, as well, a willingness on the part of neighborhood leaders to participate in programs designed to benefit their areas.[44]

Once Mohawk-Brighton had been selected as the local experimental district, the committee in charge of the campaign to secure the unit met and voted to remain active as a temporary organizing committee for the district.[45] On June 15, 1917, sixty members of the committee assembled in the Dayton Street Public Library to discuss plans for commencing the organization of the neighborhood. Enthusiastic addresses by Ruth Gottlieb and Jessie Bogen, organizer of the CSUO, urged the residents "to act quickly in setting the unit work in motion." Under their direction two committees were appointed, one to write a constitution and the other to divide Mohawk-Brighton into blocks and promote the formation of block councils. G.H. Gaveling was elected chairman of the Constitution Committee and William

Figure 6. Boundaries and Block Divisions of the Mohawk-Brighton Social Unit Organization District

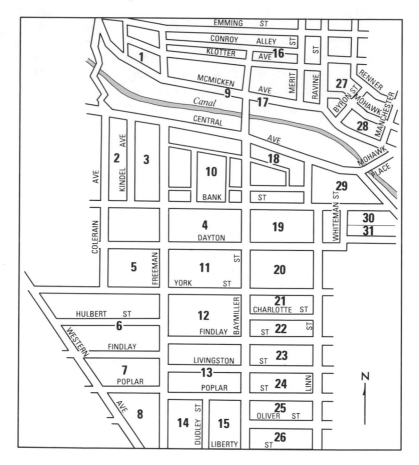

Redrawn from a map in the Wilbur C. Phillips Papers, Social Welfare History Archives Center, Univ. of Minnesota.

Evans was chosen head of the Committee on Block Organization.[46]

The Temporary Organizing Committee first established definite boundaries for the social unit area. Evans constructed a spot map showing the residences of all those who had signed petitions. The committee found that the area delineated by the spot map contained approximately twenty-five thousand people. Because the NSUO's budget allowed for a district of only fifteen thousand people, the committee reduced the size of the area by "fixing the geographical center and by eliminating those blocks around the border of the district which contained the smallest number of either petitioners or active workers."[47] Emming Street bounded the reduced area on the north, Liberty Street on the south, West and Colerain avenues on the west, and Linn, Renner, Manchester and Central streets on the east. The committee then divided this area into thirty-one blocks with approximately five hundred people per block.[48]

Once the district had been divided into blocks, the Committee on Block Organization began to set up block councils. The committee first separated all of the names of petition signers by blocks to identify those most actively interested in the social unit plan. Members of the committee visited all of these people to encourage their active participation in the formation of the block councils. Once the committee members found seven to twelve persons in a block ready to come together and discuss block organization, the committee set up a meeting to talk to residents about the social unit demonstration and about the importance of participating in the selection of a permanent block council. Following these informal sessions, the committee issued an invitation to all block residents to attend a meeting to elect the block council. Attendance at this meeting, which was usually held in the Dayton Street Public Library, averaged between one-fifth and one-fourth of the families in the block. Those present at the meeting elected a block council, which usually included five to nine block residents. This council, in turn, elected a block worker to represent the council in the neighborhood Citizens' Council and to serve as the disseminator of all information about block needs and neighborhood programs.[49]

Without exception, all the block workers elected at the beginning of the demonstration were women. According to Phillips, the Committee on Block Organization urged the selection of women for two reasons. First, the initial service tentatively planned for the social unit district, an infant health program, directly affected women as mothers. Second, Phillips, as well as the committee, believed that men would not have the time to devote the kind of attention necessary during the initial organizational phase of the social unit demonstration. Both Phillips and the committee encouraged the participation of men on the block councils and hoped that as work developed some men would become block workers.[50]

Following the selection of the block workers, the committee and Phillips, with the assistance of Mary Hicks and Jessie Bogen, worked tirelessly with the women to prepare them for their role as neighborhood educators and interpreters.[51] The block workers, Phillips stressed in these sessions, would be the "nerve center" of the organization. Their task was to "know every man, woman and child in their blocks, to study social needs, to interpret these needs to the experts, and to convey information concerning the solution of neighborhood needs to their neighbors."[52] Also, during these meetings, Phillips, Hicks, and Bogen acquainted the women with the social unit plan of organization and outlined the block workers' duties as block representatives in some detail. And because Phillips strongly believed in the importance of the block workers' role in the success of the demonstration, the block workers received eight dollars per week to compensate them for the time spent on social unit activities.[53]

Although subject to some modifications as the experiment progressed, the projected duties of the block workers, as explained during these instructional sessions, served as the nucleus of the block workers' activities for the life of the demonstration. First and foremost, the block worker was to be a real neighbor, "acquainted with the conditions and needs of those living near her and building up contacts with them and bringing them reports about the plan and programs and services that could be developed."[54] At weekly meetings the block workers were to discuss the problems and needs found in their blocks, and, when a question of policy arose, were to educate the block residents about the proposed activity. After consultation with their constituents, the block workers were to relay the neighborhood sentiment to the Citizens' Council. As spokespersons for the affairs of their own districts, the block workers were to serve as the link between the average citizen and the expert, and were to be responsible for the design and implementation of neighborhood programs.[55]

Phillips also worked with the Temporary Organizing Committee to organize the various groups destined for representation in the Mohawk-Brighton Occupational Council. Committee members approached the various occupational groups in the neighborhood and attempted to familiarize them with the plan. Because the NSUO recommended that the initial program focus on child health, Phillips and the committee members concentrated primarily on organizing the physicians, nurses, and social workers. They also spent time with teachers, businessmen, and clergymen, acquainting them with the plan and enlisting their help in the encouragement of neighborhood participation and the dissemination of information about the organization's activities. Once organized into a council, each occupational group elected an executive to serve on the neighborhood occupational council. In this way the different groups could contribute their special knowledge or skill to the community.[56]

The three most active councils for the life of the social unit demonstration were those of the physicians, nurses, and social workers. Of these groups, Phillips and the Temporary Organizing Committee approached the physicians first. Initially their organization proved more difficult than expected. Most physicians active in Mohawk-Brighton belonged to the West End Medical Society. The president of this group, Dr. C.C. Agin, known as "Pop" Agin, "was not in closest sympathy" with the Academy of Medicine, a strong backer of the social unit plan.[57] Because of the academy's support for the plan and out of a fear that the unit demonstration would interfere with private medical practice, Pop Agin, who had earlier supported the social unit demonstration, began to speak out "vehemently" against it. It was only after several talks with Phillips and members of the committee and repeated calls that Pop Agin finally agreed to hold a meeting to discuss the unit plan. After setting the date, however, he continued to insist that the meeting would not do any good because the "doctors down here don't want outsiders meddling with their practice."[58]

But much to his surprise, Pop Agin was overruled. Dr. John Grothaus, a supporter of the unit plan, brought with him to the meeting a contingent of physicians active in the Mohawk-Brighton area who were interested in setting up the Physicians' Council. According to Phillips, "discussion raged at that meeting until midnight. Then old Pop spat accurately into a cuspidor and drawled, 'Well, boys, you've heard the talk and you know how I feel about it.

I'm agin it. But I suppose we might as well have a vote.' "[59] When the votes were counted, the doctors supporting the unit won. At a subsequent meeting they elected a nine-man council with Dr. Grothaus as head to represent the twenty-six physicians active in Mohawk-Brighton. Upon the advice of Phillips, the Physicians' Council proposed to serve as a "board of health" for the neighborhood. It was to formulate and help carry out all medical programs approved by the neighborhood organization. With the formation of the council, the physicians began to prepare to take charge of the medical work of the Mohawk-Brighton social unit demonstration.[60]

Following the creation of the Physician's Council, members decided, because of the Academy of Medicine's support, to establish a formal relationship with the academy. On October 7, 1917, the Mohawk-Brighton Physicians' Council voted to accept a resolution passed earlier that year by the academy to appoint the local physicians' council as a subcommittee of the academy's Committee of Presidents, the group established by the academy to assist the social unit demonstration neighborhood. In this way, Phillips wrote, the Mohawk-Brighton Physicians' Council would be in touch with the best medical work in Cincinnati. Such a plan, Phillips believed, would also lift the plan "from the district and make it capable of extension to other cities and municipalities."[61]

Once they had secured the support of the doctors and had established the Physicians' Council, Phillips and the Temporary Organizing Committee turned their attention to the organization of the nurses and the social workers. First, they asked the four nursing organizations active in Mohawk-Brighton—the Visiting Nurse Association, the Children's Clinic, the Board of Health, and the Anti-Tuberculosis League—to assign specific nurses to the district. The seven nurses appointed by these groups served as the unit's initial Nurses' Council. The nurses met and elected an executive to represent them on the neighborhood Occupational Council. In a similar fashion, the social service agencies active in the neighborhood, such as the Associated Charities, the Episcopal Maternity Society, the Court of Domestic Relations, the Juvenile Court, the Social Service Department of General Hospital, the Salvation Army, and the Roman Catholic Home Service, designated certain workers to serve on the Social Workers' Council. These individuals met and together elected

William T. Jack, assistant superintendent of the Department of Public Welfare, to serve as their executive and representative on the Mohawk-Brighton Occupational Council.[62]

Although Phillips and the Temporary Organizing Committee focused their attention on the physicians, nurses, and social workers, other occupational councils were organized. Phillips and the Temporary Organizing Committee viewed these councils, which included teachers, businessmen, clergymen, and trade unionists, as support groups. In particular, Phillips and the committee wanted their help with the interpretation of programs to the neighborhood and with an evaluation of the unit's activities when the demonstration period ended. These groups were helpful but failed to function as fully as the physicians, nurses, and social workers in the unit's activities.[63]

The Teachers Council was the first of the auxiliary groups to be formed. Phillips and the Temporary Organizing Committee invited the principal of each of the three public schools in the district to appoint a six-member committee. Each committee consisted of the principal, a kindergarten teacher, one teacher representing the first three grades, another the fourth through sixth grades, a third the upper grades, and a representative-at-large. Each group then elected an executive who served as a member of the Teachers' Council for the neighborhood.[64]

The clergy of the neighborhood also organized a council. The Protestant clergy met and elected a nine-member Protestant Ministers' Organization. The Catholic priests, under the direction of Father Schoop, pastor of St. Augustine's Catholic Church, encouraged the formation of a Catholic association of lay men and women to cooperate with the social unit work. Both these groups pledged to spread information about the social unit's activities and support those activities among their parishioners.[65]

The last two groups organized during the summer were the local businessmen and the neighborhood trade unionists. The Mohawk-Brighton district's two businessmen's clubs, the Sands Business Men's Club and the Mohawk-Brighton Improvement Association, pledged their cooperation. The chairman of each organization arbitrarily selected five men to represent the neighborhood's business community on the Occupational Council. Because a neighborhood trade unionist organization did not exist, Cincinnati's Central Labor

Council appointed Kathryn Nordman, a Mohawk-Brighton resident, to organize a council to represent the local members of the Central Labor Council in the social unit's activities.[66]

By mid-September 1917, as a result of the organizational activities carried on by the Temporary Organizing Committee and Phillips, the residents of Mohawk-Brighton grew impatient for action.[67] In response to neighborhood demand, the committee held a meeting in the assembly hall of Lafayette-Bloom School on September 27 to discuss the neighborhood's progress. At this meeting, members of the fledgling block organizations and of the newly established occupational councils joined neighborhood residents in an "enthusiastic clamor" for the commencement of the social unit program. Mrs. G.B. Twitchell, wife of a Mohawk-Brighton physician, introduced a motion for the formal creation of the Mohawk-Brighton Social Unit Organization (MBSUO), which was promptly seconded by the Reverend Walter D. Harrell, pastor of the Poplar Street Presbyterian Church. After a report on the constitution, which was a virtual duplication of the CSUO's constitution, Charles Dittmar, a local businessman, called for the adoption of the constitution for the Mohawk-Brighton organization. Following the unanimous seconding of this motion, those attending the meeting formally approved the constitution drawn up by the constitution committee. Those at the meeting also voted for the creation of the Mohawk-Brighton Social Unit Organization, consisting of a neighborhood citizens' council, an occupational council, and a general council. At the close of the meeting, Phillips and his wife were elected Executives of the MBSUO General Council, Alexander Landesco treasurer, and S.W. Pandorf controller. The MBSUO, "created for the purpose of planning and controlling definite intensive services for the people of Mohawk-Brighton," was on its way.[68]

During the next three months the General Council of the MBSUO perfected the neighborhood organization and selected a headquarters for the district operation. The council focused on fleshing out the skeleton block and occupational councils. It also explained the NSUO's projected budget for the coming year to neighborhood residents and encouraged neighborhood cooperation in the determination of the final document. Phillips later described these last three months as "full of vivid experiences and changing viewpoints" as the residents of Mohawk-Brighton prepared themselves for the commencement of practical services.[69]

One of the first projects sponsored by the General Council was the establishment of a neighborhood bulletin to serve as a "medium for the expression of the community's thought"[70] and to assist in the exchange of information between the various groups active in the neighborhood organization. Set up by the General Council, the biweekly *Social Unit Bulletin* was under the control of an editorial board composed of a member of the Citizens' Council and a member from each of the occupational councils. The executive of the neighborhood Occupational Council served as the editor-in-chief. Each block worker was to act as a local reporter, responsible for gathering news items in her block. Each occupational council executive was in charge of keeping the citizens up-to-date on the activities of the occupational groups. From the very beginning the *Bulletin* served as a forum for community discussion of all policies and plans considered by the General Council prior to their adoption.[71]

Concurrently with the establishment of the neighborhood newspaper, the General Council attempted to secure permanent headquarters for the local organization. But the search for an appropriate place lasted longer than hoped, until the end of November. Finally, the General Council selected the Peale House, opposite the Hulbert Playground at 1820 Freeman Avenue, as MBSUO headquarters. According to a description in an early issue of the *Bulletin*, this three-story house "offered on the first floor two large rooms for meeting purposes, two rooms for the health center and a nurses' office; on the second floor six office rooms; and on the third floor a suite of rooms—kitchen, diningroom and parlor—for social purposes."[72] By December, this building had been renovated, painted, and stood ready for use.[73]

Also following the formal organization of the MBSUO, the General Council completed the organization of the Mohawk-Brighton Citizens' Council and Occupational Council. By the end of September only half of the blocks had elected full block councils and a block worker. With the help of Mary Hicks and Jessie Bogen, elected at the founding meeting of the MBSUO as executives of the neighborhood Citizens' Council, all but one of the thirty-one blocks in the social unit district had elected a block worker and all but two had set up a block council. Once elected, the block workers proceeded to acquaint themselves with all the families under their care.[74] Members of the various occupational councils elected representatives to serve on the neighborhood Occupational Council, which was under the leadership of William A. Evans who had been selected September 27 to serve as that group's executive.[75]

The other major task before the MBSUO General Council during the last three months of 1917 was the preparation of the budget for 1918. For the period beginning February 9, 1916, and ending in May 1917, the expenses incurred in selecting a city for the unit demonstration and for setting up the Cincinnati Social Unit Organization were paid directly by the treasurer of the NSUO. On June 1, 1917, the NSUO transferred approximately fifteen thousand dollars from the national organization's treasury to the treasurer of the Cincinnati Social Unit Organization. During the period from June 1, 1917, to December 31, 1917, the CSUO dispensed this money to the MBSUO, which operated under a budget drawn up by the NSUO. During the six-month period beginning June 1, 1917, the NSUO, to raise funds from private donations, had set up a tentative budget calling for an expenditure of approximately thirty-five thousand dollars for 1918. With this tentative budget as a guide, the General Council of the MBSUO drew up a budget for 1918. Members of the council presented this budget in great detail to all members of the Citizens' Council and the Occupational Council. Following the General Council's budget presentation, the block workers held meetings to discuss it with the members of their blocks.[76]

In addition to the budget presentations before the Citizens' Council, Occupational Council, and the block councils, the General Council discussed the proposed budget in the *Social Unit Bulletin*. According to the General Council, forty-nine thousand dollars was available for all phases of social unit work in 1918. The NSUO had divided this money, the General Council reported, into three different expenditure groups—one for national expenses, another for city expenses, and a third for neighborhood expenses. Within this tripartite division, the NSUO had allotted the largest share for the MBSUO. The national organization expected the funds to cover the rental of the headquarters, the health center physicians' fees, the salaries of the nurses employed directly by the MBSUO health center, the salaries of the executives and their assistants, the salaries of the block workers, all other operating expenses of the MBSUO, and a number of miscellaneous expenses.

The General Council also indicated in the *Bulletin* article that, following the distribution of copies of the tentative budget, a public meeting would be held "for the purpose of giving each citizen in the Mohawk-Brighton District an opportunity to express his opinion about it, to make criticisms or suggestions, to question any item of expenditure, and thus do his part in the task of working out a wise plan for the spending of the organization's funds."[77]

The General Council of the MBSUO held the public meeting on the proposed budget on December 4, 1917, in the Lafayette-Bloom School auditorium. At this meeting Phillips spoke briefly about the budget and fielded questions raised by the residents about expenditures. Following the discussion, the seventy residents present voted to accept the proposed budget for 1918. The General Council then submitted this budget to the NSUO for final approval.[78]

By early December the NSUO had spent six months organizing the Cincinnati Social Unit Organization and another six months establishing the Mohawk-Brighton Social Unit Organization. As 1917 drew to a close, the neighborhood residents called for action, and the MBSUO General Council held a neighborhood meeting to discuss the selection of the first project. Topics under discussion at this meeting included how to decrease infant mortality, how to prevent death from tuberculosis, how to improve housing conditions, and how to increase neighborhood cooperation. But the NSUO's suggestion of a public health program with emphasis on child health as the most effective way to test the organization undoubtedly influenced the final decision of those attending the meeting, who voted in favor of an infant health program for the unit's pilot program. On December 17, 1917, the MBSUO launched its infant welfare program,[79] and the Mohawk-Brighton Social Unit Organization commenced its test of the social unit theory of organization.

5

An Experiment
in Neighborhood
Health Care

After almost a full year of organizational activity, the practical services
sponsored by the Mohawk-Brighton Social Unit Organization commenced on December 17, 1917. In keeping with the National Social
Unit Organization's suggestion that a public health program would
provide an effective test of the efficiency of the organizational
scheme, the MBSUO selected an infant health campaign as its pilot
project. But as 1918 progressed, the social unit health station in
Mohawk-Brighton expanded the scope of its activity. By mid-1919
the health center offered, in addition to its postnatal services, prenatal and postpartum supervision of neighborhood mothers, and
preschool and adult physical examinations. The MBSUO cooperated
as well with a variety of organizations active in the neighborhood
whose work touched the lives of Mohawk-Brighton residents. In
addition, two unforeseen events—the Children's Year campaign and
the influenza epidemic of 1918—tested the efficiency of the MBSUO
structure. Overall, the work undertaken in 1918 and 1919 represented, according to medical historian George Rosen, "one of the
most seminal experiments in social organization for health embarked
upon in the United States."[1]

When the baby station opened its doors on December 17, 1917,
the four doctors elected by the Physicians' Council to serve at the

clinic for the first quarter of the year—Drs. R.E. Gaston, G.B. Twitchell, C.A. Stammel, and H.E. Schilling—greeted their first patient, seven-month-old Armilla Eickler.[2] Soon other babies were brought by their mothers to the station for examinations. The apparent ease with which the center operated from the beginning resulted in large part from the intensive preparatory activities of the physicians, nurses, and block workers during the three months prior to the opening of the station.

At their organizational meetings during the late summer and early fall, the members of the neighborhood Physicians' Council decided that they would serve in rotation at the clinic. They divided into groups of six, with four doctors selected as regulars and two as alternates, and decided that each group would work at the health station for three-month periods. The physicians voted to hold the station clinics from 10:00 to 11:00 a.m. four days a week. They also agreed to offer daily conferences on disease prevention for the mothers of the infants served at the clinic.[3]

During the late summer and fall the MBSUO Nurses' Council set up its organizational structure and planned for the infant campaign as well. Anticipating the selection of the MBSUO's proposed child health program, the nurses tailored their initial preparations toward that end. The Nurses' Council divided the social unit area into five nursing districts, one for each nurse on the council. Council Executive Abbie Roberts set up headquarters at the MBSUO center. A nursing assistant, hired to relieve the nurses of a variety of nonnursing duties, completed the staff of the Nurses' Council. In consultation with the Physicians' Council, the Nurses' Council drew up a nursing service record, an infant welfare record, and a registration card for babies under two years of age. The nursing service report sheet was to be used as a daily record, giving the name and address of the patient and a description of the type of service rendered. The infant welfare record provided for the child's vital statistics, a listing of any physical defects discovered during the examinations, a summary of illnesses, and a record of all the visits to the health station. The registration card included space for each infant's vital statistics, information about each baby's feeding schedule, and the name of the block worker.[4]

Once the official decision had been made to adopt an infant health campaign, the Nurses' Council and the Physicians' Council worked quickly to prepare the block workers for their role in the MBSUO health center program. The two councils wanted the block workers to locate all the homes with babies under two years of age, to register the babies, to stress the value of the supervisory care offered by the doctors and the nurses, and to encourage, when necessary, the neighborhood mothers to bring their infants to the station for the medical examinations. The Nurses' Council and the Physicians' Council met with the thirty-one block workers, explained their request for the block workers' aid, and formally asked the block workers to participate in the infant health program. The block workers agreed to cooperate and asked both councils to give them some instruction on the basics of preventive care before the block workers canvassed the neighborhood.

The instructional activities began shortly after the meeting. The executives of the Physicians' and the Nurses' councils presented short informational talks during a series of special meetings set up by the Citizens' Council. At these sessions the medical staff traced briefly the history of the child welfare movement, stressed the importance of infant medical supervision, discussed the types of service offered at the health center, and sketched the results the staff hoped to obtain as a result of the examinations. Whenever possible the executives drew their examples from known cases in Mohawk-Brighton. According to Phillips, when block workers saw the program in terms of their own families and friends, they began to appreciate the advantages of a preventive approach to the well-being of the neighborhood infants.[5] The block workers then carried the information back to the mothers in their respective blocks.[6]

Efforts to provide information about regisration and the preventive examinations were furthered in two other ways. The local MBSUO newspaper, the *Social Unit Bulletin*, carried numerous articles on the types of services to be rendered at the health center and the value of the preventive medical examinations. The clergymen of the district helped to disseminate information about the preventive services as well. They discussed the registration project from their pulpits and encouraged their parishioners to participate in the infant health program.[7]

The block workers held several informational meetings on the infant health campaign for the members of their blocks. The block workers then proceeded to canvass their blocks house by house to locate all homes with infants under two years of age. At each home with such a child the block workers explained the services offered at the health station and encouraged the mothers to come with their babies to the doctors' morning examination sessions. Unlike the nurses in Phillips's experience in Milwaukee, the nurses in Mohawk-Brighton found themselves welcome in the infants' homes. According to Phillips, "the hinges which creaked in St. Cyril's Parish, here seemed to be greased,"[8] in large part by the participation of the neighborhood residents in the operation of the health center. The center had been a neighborhood venture from the start. By the time the health center opened on December 17, 1917, the block workers had secured a complete registration of all infants under two years of age in the social unit district, and the nurses had secured introductory meetings with all the mothers involved.[9]

By the end of January 1918, the clinics began to fill up with babies brought in for checkups. After each complete examination, the physician on duty consulted with the mother and gave her a full report on the child's health. In cases requiring medical attention, the doctor referred the baby to either the family physician or the appropriate agency and gave the mother a copy of the medical report. These sessions were followed up promptly by the nurses who instructed the mother in the proper nursing techniques required for the child's condition and encouraged her to bring the child to the station for follow-up visits with the physicians. As new babies were born, they automatically came under the station's care.[10]

At the first annual meeting of the Cincinnati Social Unit Organization on March 21, 1918, at the Hotel Sinton, the executives of the MBSUO's Physicians' Council and Nurses' Council reported on the progress of the infant health campaign. They applauded the block workers' role in providing basic information to the mothers. Dr. Kreidler, who succeeded Dr. John Grothaus as head of the Physicians' Council, stressed that "at the present time mothers in the district come and eagerly seek information which will help them (and their families) to lead more healthful lives." He reported that 297 babies had visited the station and were under nursing supervision. "Over 70 percent of the children," Dr. Kreidler continued, "were returning to the center at regular intervals for checkups." Mrs. Reinhardt, a neighborhood mother elected as spokeswoman for the mothers in the district with babies under two years of age, then told how she and many other mothers had benefited from the instruction and examinations available at the station. All in all, the conference participants agreed that the initial service had proved to be a success.[11]

The service at the center continued to be popular. In her report for the year 1918, Abbie Roberts, executive of the Nurses' Council, focused on the station's accomplishments in infant health and welfare. In particular, she felt that the standards of infant care offered by the mothers "had been raised immeasurably" and that a "noticeable decrease in illness among babies had resulted" because of the periodic medical examinations and the close ties developed between the mothers and the medical staff at the baby station.[12] Mrs. C.E. Sibbert, a kindergarten teacher at Sands School, expressed a similar sentiment in 1919. According to Mrs. Sibbert, the result of the medical and nursing care "provided by the Social Unit Organization to the small children of the Mohawk-Brighton district (was) very apparent." There existed, Mrs. Sibbert wrote, "a markedly greater interest and intelligence about child care" in the neighborhood.[13]

The success of the postnatal medical service fostered an extension of the medical and nursing services offered at the health station. The enthusiasm of the MBSUO staff and the apparent success of the infant health campaign heightened the neighborhood mothers' receptiveness to the advantages of preventive health care. For example, the fact that their own children were involved in the program and the mothers could see the results firsthand sparked their interest in the doctors' informal discussions of prenatal care. The mothers began to understand that many of their babies' problems requiring medical attention sprang from inadequate health precautions during the early stages of pregnancy. Block workers' reports to the members of the Physicians' Council and the Nurses' Council confirmed this growing interest in maternal care. As a result of this interest, during February 1918 the number of informal prenatal discussions at the baby station was increased.[14]

After consultation with the Occupational Council and the Citizens' Council, the medical staff established a formal prenatal program on April 1, 1918. The block workers began to register expectant mothers as well as infants at the health station. The physicians held prenatal conferences at the center every Wednesday from 3:30 to 4:30 p.m. During these sessions the doctors examined the mothers, monitored their condition, and gave brief lectures on proper prenatal care. The conferences were well attended, and by September 1918 approximately 45 percent of all pregnant mothers were registered at the health station and under medical care. Nursing supervision in the home by members of the Nurses' Council supplemented the conference sessions. As in the case of infant services, the station's doctors referred all mothers with problems to the family physician or to the appropriate agency for treatment.[15]

Postpartum nursing supervision evolved in a similar fashion. The physicians and nurses noted an increasing number of questions from the mothers on the proper care following a pregnancy. A number of mothers interested in care after birth contacted their block workers, who then relayed the information to the station's medical staff. After meeting with the Physicians' Council and the Citizens' Council, the Nurses' Council decided to visit all maternity patients for a ten-day period after the women had given birth. By the end of 1918 the Nurses' Council reported that postpartum nursing had been provided to one-third of the 221 maternity cases in the neighborhood.[16]

At the same time that the health station expanded its activities to include prenatal supervision and postpartum care, the Citizens' Council decided to broaden the infant registration and examination program to include all preschool children in Mohawk-Brighton. This decision came as a result of neighborhood interest in a nationwide campaign to focus attention on the health of the American preschool population. According to Phillips, the block workers felt that this campaign, sponsored by the U.S. Children's Bureau, provided a ready-made project to illustrate the effectiveness and efficiency of the MBSUO operation and to promote the health of more neighborhood children.[17]

The 1918 campaign of the Children's Bureau for child welfare, called Children's Year, commenced on April 6, 1918, and was a direct result of six years of inquiries into the state of child health in America. Organized in 1912, the Children's Bureau began "to investigate and report upon 'all matters pertaining to the welfare of children . . . among all classes of our people; infant mortality; the birthrate; orphanages; dangerous occupations; accidents and diseases of children;

employment; and legislation affecting children in the several States and Territories.' "[18] Under the direction of Julia Lathrop, the bureau undertook numerous studies of infant mortality and health problems of preschool children.

The Children's Year campaign became one of the most publicized of the bureau's early efforts in the area of preschool health. With the entrance of America into the First World War in 1917, thousands of young men had their first complete physical examinations. Many of them suffered from a variety of defects, most of which could have been prevented if the adults had been examined periodically during their childhood. In light of these discoveries the Children's Bureau staff felt "that it could offer no more valuable contribution to the country during the war than to assist in stimulating and coordinating public and volunteer effort for child welfare."[19] In cooperation with the Women's Committee of the Council of National Defense, the Children's Bureau organized a campaign to weigh and measure as many of the nation's preschool children as possible to direct public attention to the problem of correctable defects and demonstrate the value of periodic physical examinations. Later the bureau hoped to broaden the program to include studies on the types of recreation available for children and youth, public protection of maternity and infancy, and child labor laws.[20]

Phillips first became aware of the proposed Children's Year campaign in late February 1918 while in New York City for meetings with members of the NSUO. During his stay in the city he unexpectedly met Miss Lathrop, with whom he had worked at the Children's Bureau in 1915. She told Phillips of the bureau's plans for the proposed children's health campaign. Although enthusiastic, according to Phillips, Miss Lathrop expressed a few reservations about the project. Phillips wrote that Miss Lathrop feared that the bureau would not be able to get a "very considerable percentage of these children even weighed and measured, (as) superficial a test that it was," because the bureau lacked the machinery for such a program. "Child welfare clinics, baby stations and the like can help," Miss Lathrop said, "but they cover only a small fraction of the children in our American communities." As a result, the bureau would have to "organize volunteer staffs of doctors and nurses and set up new machinery all over the country."

But the lack of machinery was not the only problem Miss Lathrop felt the bureau faced in the child health campaign. A second problem concerned the ability of the bureau and the volunteers to locate the children. She stressed that "although we have a complete . . . registration of the children already attending the public schools, when it comes to the little ones not yet in school, this great country doesn't even know how many of them there are, much less where they live." Program publicity and the tireless efforts of countless volunteers would unearth numerous names and addresses, but once the bureau located these children, she pointed out, it then faced the challenge of persuading the mothers to participate. At best, she felt, under these conditions only a fraction of the preschool population would be weighed and measured. At this point, Phillips recalled, Miss Lathrop paused and then concluded her remarks by asking Phillips to make use of the MBSUO machinery in the Children's Bureau's campaign. The MBSUO health center with its block worker organization, Miss Lathrop stressed, represented "the only place in the country ready to do a complete job."[21]

Without promising anything to Miss Lathrop, on his return to Cincinnati, Phillips discussed her request with the residents of Mohawk-Brighton at a special session of the MBSUO General Council. In his presentation Phillips outlined the essential elements of the Children's Year campaign and explained in more detail the proposed weight and measurement tests. Designed to provide "a rough index of the health of growing children," the tests would identify those children whose measurements deviated from the average weights and heights expected for this particular age group. In all those cases below average, the bureau would encourage parents to secure appropriate treatment for their children. Phillips concluded his remarks with the Children's Year timetable. The bureau hoped to kick off its first campaign for child health with a drive to weigh and measure all preschool children between April 6 and July 6, 1918.[22]

Following Phillips's presentation, members of the General Council discussed the Children's Year campaign and Miss Lathrop's request for help with the weight and measurement tests. Dr. Kreidler, executive of the Physicians' Council, urged immediate compliance. Other members of the Physicians' Council applauded the program but felt that the bureau's weight and measurement tests were not

extensive enough to provide a useful index of the health of the
district's preschool population. "Why not give every pre-schooler a
complete physical examination?" these physicians suggested. "We'll
gladly volunteer our services." At this point Dr. Kreidler interrupted
and reminded his fellow council members that the program would not
work—despite their willingness to give the examinations—if the
mothers were not interested in participating in the program. Were
the block workers willing, Dr. Kreidler asked, to assess neighborhood
interest in the examinations?[23]

Those members of the Citizens' Council attending the meeting
indicated their willingness to undertake the necessary canvass of
Mohawk-Brighton to locate neighborhood preschoolers. But before
they began their survey, they wanted to confer with their constituents. Accordingly, the block workers called block meetings and discussed the project with their neighbors. Articles about the proposed
Children's Year campaign appeared in the *Bulletin*. At a meeting of
the General Council held at the end of March, the block workers
announced that neighborhood residents supported the child health
crusade sponsored by the Children's Bureau and that the preschool
canvass would begin at once.[24]

The block workers embarked on their survey the next day and by
April 4 had secured 100 percent registration of all preschoolers in
Mohawk-Brighton. Mary Hicks, executive of the neighborhood Citizens' Council, sent Miss Lathrop a list of the 1,173 children.[25] On
receipt of this list, Miss Lathrop sent Miss Hicks a note commending
the work of the MBSUO's block workers. "The Mohawk-Brighton
Social Unit Organization's list," wrote Miss Lathrop, "was the first
notice of the complete registration of children in a district received by
the Children's Bureau." In addition, Miss Lathrop expressed her
interest in the social unit organization and stressed that she "felt
strongly that the social unit organization would make a special contribution to Children's Year." This contribution, according to Miss
Lathrop, lay "not only in the actual work which it (MBSUO) had
already undertaken which had made possible the prompt efficiency of
the registration, but because every effective piece of work should be
widely popularized as a part of the whole Children's Year Movement."[26] Miss Hicks, on behalf of the Citizens' Council, sent a letter
to Miss Lathrop thanking her for her kind remarks and agreed with

Miss Lathrop that the MBSUO "would contribute quite [a lot] to the Health of the neighborhood."[27]

Following the registration of the preschool children, the General Council decided to sponsor a Children's Year parade to generate even more enthusiasm for the weight and measurement program and to promote the goal of 100 percent examinations of the neighborhood's preschoolers. Approximately three thousand district children participated in the parade on April 29, 1918. According to accounts in the newspapers, Mayor Galvin sat on the reviewing stand and cheered. Four neighborhood fathers, designated by the block workers as parade marshals, were mounted on Shetland ponies and led the procession. School Superintendent Randall Condon followed the marshals in an automobile filled with toddlers whose fathers were serving in World War I. Next came students from St. Augustine's Parochial School. Eighty automobiles filled with mothers and youngsters too small to walk followed the St. Augustine delegation. Numerous neighborhood residents reported that they had never seen the people of the district so excited and touched "as they have been by these thousands of marching children."[28]

In May the physicians began conducting the physical examinations. They held daily preschool health conferences at the health center until the middle of July. In addition to the social unit preschool health reports, the physicians filled out a record card supplied by the Children's Bureau. On this form the doctors recorded the height and weight of each child. The figures were then compared with the national averages supplied by the Children's Bureau. By July 6, 1918, the Children's Bureau's target date, the physicians had given 994 children, or 85 percent of a possible 1,173, complete physical examinations. The doctors found that 471—nearly 50 percent of the children in the district—were underweight and that 236, or approximately 25 percent, were under the average height. A total of 640, or 64 percent of those examined, suffered some physical defect, such as enlarged tonsils or adenoids, malnutrition, or cardiac trouble. The Nurses' Council, assisted by the block workers, followed up these cases with home visits and encouraged the parents to have the defects corrected. Examinations continued at regular intervals throughout the year, and by December 1918, 90 percent of the 1,173 children registered had received full medical examinations.[29]

Phillips felt that the Children's Year campaign demonstrated the efficiency of the social unit organizational structure and resulted in "an increased interest in preventive health measures."[30] Because of the block workers' knowledge of the neighborhood, they were able to provide the names and addresses of all preschool children in their respective blocks. Once the examinations were under way and the defects began to show up, the neighborhood went into action. For example, one child had a heart leakage—a potentially fatal condition if neglected. Because it was discovered, however, steps were taken immediately to remedy the leakage. According to Phillips, this incident "hit the neighborhood between the eyes, for the child happened to be widely known and liked." Situations such as this, Phillips believed, helped neighborhood residents see the value of preventive examinations. All in all, Phillips felt, the Children's Year campaign in Mohawk-Brighton was an excellent example of the successful interplay between consumers and producers. In this case, neighborhood residents, the consumers, and the medical staff, the producers, together decided on a program and then worked to produce results.[31]

As the nursing staff assumed the new tasks—prenatal and postnatal care and preschool examinations—the manner in which the nurses executed their duties underwent a change. The nurses found that many of their new patients lived in homes already included in the nurses' regular baby rounds. As a result, specialized nursing services proved to be impractical, for such services brought a series of different nurses into the same home. Many MBSUO residents disliked the multiple intrusions, and after discussions in the Nurses' Council and the Citizens' Council, the MBSUO adopted a generalized nursing service program. Under guidelines drawn up by the General Council, each nurse assumed responsibility for all patients located in her original baby district. The five nursing districts established during the baby registration drive became permanent. Each nurse covered one district regardless of the types of services needed. Because the nurses did not possess sufficient training in the different types of services, each nurse took a series of short "working visits" to a variety of local public health agencies to acquaint herself with the different nursing specialties. In this way, the nurses were trained to serve their patients competently,[32] and they were ready to treat the individual, the family, and the district as a whole rather than as isolated units.

Critics of this approach, in particular the Visiting Nurse Association and the Department of Health, argued that generalized nursing required the visiting nurse to absorb too much varied knowledge. As a result, critics stressed, the nurse would not perform all types of work with equal competence. The social unit nurses contended that the benefits provided by the generalized nursing service overshadowed any initial lack of nursing expertise. Time and time again, Nurses' Council Executive Roberts noted in her report of nursing service for 1918, "a home visit in the interest of one service led to the discovery of cases that were covered by the other programs of the health center." With specialized nursing, all new cases would have been referred to specialists, and a number of different nurses would have been sent into the home to treat individual family members as isolated cases. Under a system of generalized nursing, the nurses could serve the family unit. With her knowledge of the family's health conditions, the nurse would be able "to more fully understand the relationship between health problems and environmental problems, leading to better service for the family." In addition, the Nurses' Council found that generalized nursing increased family cooperation, eliminated unnecessary duplication of services, and reduced interference between the various public agencies.[33]

While local critics continued to complain periodically about the form of the MBSUO's nursing service, on the national level members of the nursing profession applauded the work of the Nurses' Council. Ella Phillips Crandall, head of the National Organization of Public Health Nursing, congratulated the council "on the work done in the Mohawk-Brighton district of Cincinnati." Mary Lent, supervising nurse of the U.S. Public Health Service, expressed her "appreciation of the nursing work in Mohawk-Brighton" in a note to Council Executive Roberts, and wrote that "your report is so splendid . . . the entire profession must be very proud of it. I want you to know that I heartily agree with you on the unification (of services)."[34] In short, under the generalized nursing program the MBSUO brought a greater number of people than previously under some form of nursing care. The nurses helped to standardize nursing techniques and procedures in the homes and to foster the understanding and willing cooperation of the community—that element they believed so important in the determination of effective public health programs.[35]

The ease with which the nurses discovered medical problems and encouraged patients to seek care was illustrated in the relationship established between the MBSUO and the Anti-Tuberculosis League. The league and the Municipal Tuberculosis Committee had developed plans in 1915 for a neighborhood health center to care for the city's tuberculosis patients and to demonstrate the importance of intensive preventive work. When Courtenay Dinwiddie, then superintendent of the league, and Dr. John Landis, head of the Municipal Tuberculosis Committee, heard about the proposed social unit demonstration, they felt that the program would illustrate the value of intensive preventive care to the public. As a result, both Dinwiddie and Dr. Landis strongly supported the advertised plan and were largely responsible for the campaign waged by Cincinnati for the social unit experiment.

Although the budget adopted by the MBSUO for the first year of service did not provide for nursing supervision of tuberculosis cases in the district, the Anti-Tuberculosis League offered to meet the expense of such service and to assign one of its nurses to assist the MBSUO Nurses' Council. In addition, the league held special clinics to train all the unit's nurses in the proper nursing care for tuberculosis patients. As a consequence, on May 1, 1918, after a favorable vote in the MBSUO General Council, the Anti-Tuberculosis League turned over the twenty-nine reported tuberculosis cases in the neighborhood to the social unit's Nurses' Council.[36]

The nurses worked closely with the Anti-Tuberculosis League. They met with league officials weekly and gave them carbon copies of the unit's tuberculosis records. The nurses visited all bedridden patients in the district two to three times a week and saw all ambulatory patients at least once every other week. In their work the nurses discovered numerous cases of pulmonary tuberculosis that were still in the early stages and hence suitable for sanitorium treatment. All patients with arrested disease remained in their own homes under medical and nursing supervision.[37]

The cooperation between the Anti-Tuberculosis League and the MBSUO proved successful. When the health center opened, the league had given the MBSUO a list of all individuals in the district known to have suffered from tuberculosis since 1908, in addition to turning over to the Nurses' Council the twenty-nine cases reported since 1915. The block workers then checked to see which of the patients registered in 1908 still lived in the district. Those patients still living in the neighborhood and the twenty-nine active cases served as the core of the tuberculosis service.

By May 1919, the number of tuberculosis cases handled by the nursing staff had grown to 108. Of the 79 new cases reported, most were located by unit workers in the course of their daily work. N.A. Nelson, superintendent of the league, felt that the "gains in tuberculosis work were directly attributable to the neighborhood organization through which alone many of the cases have been discovered and through which helpful medical and social contacts could be made without misunderstanding and resentment."[38] In particular, Nelson emphasized that the comprehensive nature of the contacts between the nurses and the block workers on the one hand and the neighborhood on the other hand was responsible for bringing such a large number of cases under care in such a relatively short time.[39]

Nelson further stressed the efficiency of the MBSUO in handling tuberculosis cases in a report issued at the end of 1919. He reiterated that "unusual neighborhood cooperation" enabled the medical and nursing staffs to increase the total number of cases handled by 373 percent. In particular, Nelson noted that the greatest increase in cases represented the "groups with which the most preventive work could be done." Nelson recommended that the league take the social unit health care program under consideration when planning for future work.[40] Through a system of generalized nursing and block work, the MBSUO health station was able to render significant service in tuberculosis prevention, while illustrating the efficiency of its own organizational structure.

The outbreak of the influenza epidemic in the fall of 1918 interrupted many normal health care activities of the MBSUO. Influenza, a respiratory infection transmitted from person to person by infectious droplets, first appeared in a mild form during the spring of 1918. By the beginning of September 1918, Massachusetts health officials noted the existence of a few cases of "Spanish influenza," as it was called, in Boston. Very quickly after their observation, the virus began to spread throughout the country along the main east-west lines of transportation. By the end of September virtually the entire country had been affected. Young girls at schools across the nation were soon skipping rope to a catchy ditty: "I had a little bird / And its name was Enza / I opened the window / And in-flu-enza."[41]

In the social unit district the nurses began reporting to the General Council early in September 1918 an "alarming number of colds and sore throats." Although numerous health officials did not believe that influenza endangered the Midwest, the Nurses' Council felt that the virus had arrived. As the epidemic spread in the East, the Nurses' Council suggested that the MBSUO take immediate action in Mohawk-Brighton.

Accordingly, members of the MBSUO's General Council voted to disseminate information about the influenza virus and about the possibility of the epidemic striking Cincinnati. The General Council also decided to issue a simple set of instructions on how to avoid the flu and how to treat the flu. A committee appointed by the General Council drafted a handbill that alerted the neighborhood to the possible dangers of influenza and exhorted all residents to report any colds or sore throats in their families. The handbill also contained all available information about the best treatment for the virus and about the various methods of prevention. The day after the meeting of the General Council the MBSUO executives approved the handbill, and later that afternoon block workers were given printed copies to distribute to their constituents. Within twenty-four hours the block workers had delivered a handbill to every home in the district.[42]

Armed with this information, Mohawk-Brighton residents were better prepared than most Cincinnatians when the epidemic reached the Midwest in late September. The nurses and the block workers worked tirelessly from October to December, the peak months of the epidemic. The block workers canvassed the neighborhood for suspected cases of influenza. For the most part the nurses abandoned all regular nursing services and began nursing influenza victims in the social unit district and in areas bordering on the neighborhood. Together, the nurses and the block workers found neighborhood women who would serve as household helpers. These women entered the influenza victims' homes, performed general housekeeping duties, and cooked meals for the stricken families. By the end of December the nurses, block workers, and household helpers had taken care of 756 patients in the social unit district and had made 139 visits to families living outside of Mohawk-Brighton.[43]

After a study of all influenza cases reported to the Health Department, the social unit medical and nursing staffs found that the "percentage of cases per thousand population was [as] great, if not greater, in the Mohawk-Brighton District than in the city as a whole."[44] Even so, the area had a lower death rate than that of the city. The mortality rate from influenza and pneumonia per thousand population for the rest of the city for the months of October, November, and December stood at 4.10, as compared with 2.26 for the social unit district.[45] Although the medical and nursing staffs could not say with absolute certainty that the unit organization was responsible for the lower death rate, the fact that the district organization "proved to be more efficient in the prompter and more complete reporting of cases, in the quick dissemination of information about the epidemic, and in the care provided by the nurses, blockworkers and physicians, indicated that the neighborhood organization, if nothing else, certainly facilitated the saving of lives."[46]

Following the influenza epidemic the nursing and medical staffs entered into two new activities directly related to the influenza experience. The physicians began providing physical examinations for adults. What began as a monitoring activity for those adults recuperating from influenza soon broadened into a service for all interested adults. For conditions requiring treatment, the doctors referred patients to their family physicians or to the appropriate agency. The nurses followed up the examinations with home visits.[47]

The other venture arising from the epidemic involved the Red Cross campaign "to train one woman in every home in the elementaries of sickroom knowledge." During the influenza epidemic the Red Cross found that too few people knew how to nurse and care for the sick. After the peak of the epidemic had passed, the Red Cross launched a training program in sick care for the community. After discussion with the Physicians' Council the Nurses' Council, and the General Council, the Cincinnati chapter of the Red Cross granted the MBSUO "the privilege of conducting classes" in home care for the sick. These lessons, numbering fifteen in all, were taught by the MBSUO nurses. The topics included bacteria and their relationship to disease, the cause and transmission of disease, personal hygiene, care of the house, care of the sick in the home, sickroom appliances, and the household medicine chest. These lectures ran sporadically during the first six months of 1919 and attracted large audiences.[48]

As part of their work with the health programs during 1918, the block workers took a number of limited censuses. The block workers counted, for example, babies, preschoolers, and expectant mothers. Every time the block workers secured information about a particular neighborhood group, the Statistical Council of the CSUO studied the data and presented the block workers with charts, diagrams, and spot maps summarizing the main conclusions and emphasizing the most important findings for the block workers and the various occupational councils of the MBSUO. Through these statistical pictures of specific local conditions the block workers grew to appreciate the usefulness of collected data. The women began to see that information pertaining to the character of the population and the distribution of age groups, for instance, was important in the interpretation of the neighborhood's medical and social needs. At the same time, they found that launching a new census for each specific need was time-consuming and inefficient.[49]

According to Phillips, one evening, after block workers had conducted several limited censuses, plans were being considered for a new survey. During the discussion one block worker remarked that this was "about the sixth time we've talked with some of these families and everytime we've brought back information it's had to be written down on different cards." After a pause, she continued with a suggestion. "Why don't we get all the facts about everybody in the Unit down once and for all on one card." Others began to echo these same sentiments. Another block worker observed that "it would save . . . a lot of time and work" if all the basic information about each family were recorded at the social unit headquarters. In addition, this block worker stressed, each worker had accumulated "a stack of information" that was not recorded, but was nonetheless important in the block worker's overall task. As a result, the block worker continued, "the doctors and nurses keep running to us all the time with questions about this and that." If this knowledge of local family conditions were written down along with the basic family information, the block workers would not be "bothered with these incessant questions." The discussion continued in a similar vein, and by the end of the evening the block workers had voted to take a comprehensive neighborhood census.[50]

The block workers then discussed what questions should be asked. After many suggestions had been made, they began to quibble. "For heaven's sake. Let's hand this job to the Occupational Council! They're supposed to know all about these things. Let them make a list of questions, and send it back . . . for us to go over." And so, much to Phillips's delight, the block workers had seen how practical a comprehensive neighborhood census would be. But the block workers even went a step further; they decided to go to the Occupational Council—the experts—for help. When recounting this discussion, Phillips wrote that this decision on the part of the block workers represented "democracy turning spontaneously to skill! They'd caught the idea!"[51] He saw the event as an excellent example of the ability of the citizen and the expert to function together for the good of the entire community.

When the block workers' request for a census questionnaire reached the neighborhood Occupational Council, the members of that council decided to consult with the statistical councils of the CSUO and the NSUO. Both statistical councils had been organized early in the experiment to serve as consultants for the MBSUO and to evaluate at the end of the demonstration the possibility of "an interpretative statistical study of a progressive community experiment in which the neighborhood services would supply the basic data."[52]

The MBSUO Occupational Council first approached the NSUO. Members of the national Statistical Council—Mrs. Robert M. Woodbury, Charles V. Chapin, Frederick S. Crum, Louis I. Dublin, Irving Fisher, Joseph A. Hills, Wesley C. Mitchell, William F. Ogburn, I. M. Rubinow, Frank Steighthoff, and Robert Chaddock—all participated in the collection of social statistics for different organizations and projects. On receiving the MBSUO Occupational Council's request, the council members drew up a proposed questionnaire and submitted a draft to the CSUO Statistical Council. This council, composed of E. Walter Evans, James Magee, E. E. Hardcastle, and Curtis Meyers, made suggestions. Then, the proposed questionnaire, along with the amendments from the city Statistical Council, was sent to the MBSUO Occupational Council for consideration. After much discussion, this council drew up a form based on the drafts to be submitted to the Mohawk-Brighton Citizens' Council.

Members of the city Statistical Council and the MBSUO Occupational Council met with the MBSUO Citizens' Council when the questionnaire was ready for consideration. Members from the city

Statistical Council opened the meeting with a thorough explanation
of each item on the census questionnaire. They then answered questions posed by the block workers. After the meeting, the members of
the Citizens' Council took the form back to their block councils and
discussed it with their constituents. The Citizens' Council then re-
convened to discuss the questionnaire. At this meeting the block
workers decided to accept all the questions on the proposed form
except two, one relating to income, the other to place of occupation.
At a special meeting of the General Council, the MBSUO officially
adopted a neighborhood census questionnaire.[53]

This exercise in project determination, Phillips believed, was of
prime importance. On a practical level, the experience of the block
workers led them to find a more efficient way to secure background
information about their constituents. On an abstract level, their
decision to take a census and to enlist the aid of the experts on the
compilation of the questionnaire represented an example of the
essence of the social unit theory of organization. The census deliberation demonstrated Phillips's belief that the experts and the people
could cooperate and that their collaboration would result in the
creation of a well-rounded effort. In short, the experts and the people
worked together to meet the needs of the neighborhood.

The institution of the census during the latter half of 1918 attracted
the attention of a number of outside groups. These organizations,
which included the Ohio Health and Old Age Insurance Commission, the Cincinnati Americanization Committee, the Vocational Bureau of the Board of Education, and the Better Housing League, were
impressed with the centralized information cards of the MBSUO and
enlisted the aid of the Mohawk-Brighton organization in performing
their services within the social unit district. Information gathered by
the block workers during the census helped the Ohio Health and Old
Age Insurance Commission locate all people in the district over sixty
years of age and compile a picture of the average status of those
persons in the Mohawk-Brighton area. The Cincinnati Americanization Committee received, as a result of the MBSUO census, "more
complete information concerning the foreign-born in the district"
than it had for any other area of the city.[54] And, according to Helen T.
Wooley of the Vocational Bureau of the Board of Education, the
information gathered by the block workers for the census facilitated

the work of her bureau in issuing working papers, placing children leaving school, and giving mental tests to schoolchildren of all ages.[55]

Of the four agencies attracted to the work of the MBSUO, the Better Housing League (BHL) alone established a long-term relationship with the organization. From the beginning of the Mohawk-Brighton experiment, block workers had filed informal reports about the housing conditions in their blocks, particularly if the conditions materially contributed to poor health. At several meetings of the Citizens' Council, the block workers expressed an interest in surveying the neighborhood housing situation. Concurrently, the Better Housing League, according to Courtenay Dinwiddie, who was active in both the MBSUO and the BHL, "entirely independently of a suggestion from the MBSUO, from its own observation, became convinced that it offered a machinery through which the League could develop intensely its visiting housekeeping work."[56] Particularly impressed with the decision to centralize information about the neighborhood through the census, the BHL approached the MBSUO. After meeting with the neighborhood General Council, the league appointed a visiting housekeeper to the social unit district to survey all housing conditions in Mohawk-Brighton.[57]

The Better Housing League appointed Anna Loughman, a block worker, as visiting housekeeper for the social unit district. Her first task was to ascertain the conditions of all residential structures in the area. From this information, the BHL would devise an appropriate program designed to remedy defects such as bad toilets, poor garbage disposal, and inefficient drains that were discovered during the investigation. At the conclusion of the survey, Mrs. Loughman, with occasional assistance from Bleeker Marquette, executive secretary of the BHL, "worked closely with the blockworkers to foster better understanding between tenants and landlords, to teach tenants (when necessary) . . . the essentials of good housekeeping and to urge tenants to take proper care of the owner's property."[58] In addition, Mrs. Loughman kept the owners informed about the conditions of their property and encouraged them to make all necessary repairs and renovations.[59]

The Better Housing League was very pleased with its cooperation with the MBSUO. In particular, the league found that the social unit contributed greatly "to the success of the League's work in the district."[60] In other sections of the city the visiting housekeepers found it difficult to conduct the survey. Many tenants in the rest of Cincinnati failed to understand the purpose of the survey, and the housekeepers had to spend considerable time just gaining entrance into these homes. As a result, many of these surveys proved to be superficial. In the social unit neighborhood, the block workers explained the survey thoroughly to the residents. Subsequently, Bleeker Marquette found that not only "has a considerable amount been accomplished by way of improving housing conditions, but this has been done with a more cordial approval by landlords and tenants and with less friction than is possible in a section of the city where an intensive district organization such as the Social Unit does not exist."[61]

Overall, most of the activities undertaken by the MBSUO centered on neighborhood health. As a result, the other occupational councils established during 1917—the Social Workers' Council, the Teachers' Council, the Businessmen's Council, the Clergymen's Council, and the Labor Council—failed to develop into active organizations like the Physicians' and Nurses' councils. Of these five councils, the Social Workers' Council most resembled the Physicians' and Nurses' councils in its involvement with the neighborhood. For example, at the weekly Social Workers' Council meetings, representatives from all the social agencies handling cases in Mohawk-Brighton reported on their particular cases to the council as a whole. Following each report, council members discussed the case, pooled their experiences, and reached a policy decision based on a consensus of their professional opinions. Copies of each discussion were kept in a central file at the social unit headquarters. Included in this file were copies of the census information and the health records of those families or individuals under the care of the Social Workers' Council. In this way, the council functioned as a clearinghouse for all neighborhood social-welfare-related information.[62]

Most organizations represented in the Social Workers' Council found the relationship with the unit organization beneficial. For instance, the Associated Charities dealt with a number of families in the social unit district. It decided to cooperate with the MBSUO and redistribute its casework duties to assign one social worker to the Mohawk-Brighton district. According to Alice E. Richard, secretary of the Associated Charities, cooperation with the social unit organization resulted in a "much higher standard of casework" than elsewhere in the city.[63] During the first three months of collaboration, the Associated Charities reported that the social unit referred to the agency more families in need of attention than did any other group in the city. In addition, the Associated Charities found that the Social Workers' Council helped effect "more intelligent service" on the part of local workers. The weekly case discussions served to eliminate duplication of effort of the various agencies. At the same time, the close working relationship between the Occupational Council and the Citizens' Council encouraged families to see the social workers as helpers rather than intruders. As a result, neighborhood residents began to "appreciate the variety of social services available to them."[64]

During the duration of the social unit demonstration, several other agencies cooperated with the social unit. When the work of outside organizations, such as the Domestic Relations Court, the Juvenile Protection Agency, and the Humane Society, touched on individuals or families in the social unit district, representatives from those agencies consulted with the Social Workers' Council. At these meetings the representatives received information that allowed them to serve their charges more fully.[65]

The remaining four councils participated far less than did the Social Workers' Council in the MBSUO demonstration. Despite initial enthusiasm, the Clergymen's Council did little more than help disseminate information about social unit programs. The Teachers' Council also helped spread information about social unit activities. In addition, it sponsored a lecture series based on suggestions from the block workers. Under its aegis, local authorities spoke at neighborhood meetings on such topics as the importance of the family in the community, the problem of the "feeble-minded," the community's responsibility toward its children, and the industrial education program in the public schools. The Businessmen's Council and the Labor Council provided only casual assistance. For the most part both councils remained inactive during the life of the social unit experiment.[66]

No provision had been made for a recreation council during the organizational stage of the MBSUO, but during 1918 the block workers and the Social Workers' Council reported that residents were interested in a recreational program. At a meeting of the General Council, W.A. Evans, executive of the Occupational Council, was selected to chair a recreation organizing committee. This committee was to combine "the various recreational organizations of the Mohawk-Brighton community in an effort to secure greater cooperative community activity." Evans asked all community athletic clubs, social clubs, and neighborhood recreational societies to send representatives to an organizational meeting. He stressed that such action would help bring "the people of the community in closer touch and thereby engender true community spirit."[67]

On January 15, 1919, representatives from the public schools, the community centers, the YMCA, the Girl Scouts, the Boy Scouts, the churches, the playgrounds, and the War Camp Service voted to form a Recreation Council and to be part of the MBSUO Occupational Council for the purpose of drafting "intensive programs of community recreation designed to reach every man, woman, person and child in Mohawk-Brighton." Those present elected T.M. Meier, F.L. Reuter, C.E. Hiebaum, E.M. Sawyer, F.L. Remley, Mary Hicks, Miss M. Hussey, Mrs. Charles Dittmar, Anna Strochman, and the Reverend C.L. Atwater to serve on the council. W.A. Evans was elected council chairman.[68]

After it was formally admitted to the MBSUO, the Recreation Council decided to survey the neighborhood recreational situation. Such a survey "would determine what the leisure time interests of the people are, how they are spending their leisure time under existing circumstances, which community recreational facilities are being patronized and which are not, why and what the people want."[69] The members of the council planned to use this information to construct a program to meet the recreational needs of each resident. In addition, the council hoped to federate all existing neighborhood social and athletic clubs and to centralize their facilities.[70]

Some activities sponsored by the Recreation Council included block parties, community baseball games, community sings, and neighborhood suppers. It also supervised the neighborhood war gardens. In 1918 the General Council of the MBSUO turned a vacant lot at the corner of York and Freeman into a large garden in response to the government's call for foodstuffs during the war. Jacob Koch and

William Guethliem, codirectors of the project, divided the lot into two hundred plots. The *Bulletin* carried articles about the war garden program. Residents with gardening experience gave lectures. The librarian of the Dayton Street Public Library set up a garden reference shelf for neighborhood residents. One hundred families, "from parents to little tots,"[71] cultivated the plots. The Recreation Council found that the gardens were a great success, both in terms of food produced and demonstrable community spirit. Reported one observer after the appearance of the first beans and tomatoes, "Mrs. Wiggs' Cabbage Patch was never the scene of such neighborly good spirit," and the MBSUO war gardens represented a true example of "country neighborliness in city blocks."[72] Overall, during its existence, the Recreation Council facilitated "general sociability," and its programs were popular. At the end of 1919 one public school assumed the council's programs as an adjunct of its own activities.[73]

During 1918 and 1919 the Mohawk-Brighton Social Unit Organization established a fairly comprehensive neighborhood health care program. From its initial infant welfare campaign to the establishment of a generalized nursing service, the neighborhood social unit organization brought trained health personnel into a working relationship with the citizens of the district and stimulated a local health consciousness. The MBSUO's activities demonstrated that geographic localization and administrative coordination, complemented by the social organization of the neighborhood, resulted in a health care program that met the needs of a particular community. By focusing on the interaction between health experts and the people, the MBSUO fostered nearly 100 percent health care and demonstrated the importance of mobilizing the entire community in the pursuit of health and social welfare.[74]

By nourishing the interaction between medical and social welfare personnel and residents, the MBSUO helped improve significantly the overall health of the Mohawk-Brighton district. Courtenay Dinwiddie and Dr. A.G. Kreidler, head of the MBSUO's Physicians' Council, concluded that the unusual features of the social unit's health care operation were responsible for the improved level of neighborhood health care. According to Dinwiddie and Kreidler, the fact that the need for many services offered at the center were not determined by an outside group, but rather by neighborhood-based

medical and social welfare personnel in conjunction with neighborhood residents, increased local participation in the social unit's
programs. In addition, because nurses and physicians spent a great
deal of time explaining the services offered and the expected effect on
the health of the community, many residents grew to understand and
appreciate the importance of preventive health care.[75]

In his study of the health programs offered by the MBSUO, Haven
Emerson, a former health officer of New York City, found that the
neighborhood organization had produced a number of "tangible accomplishments." The MBSUO had provided necessary prenatal advice to a very high percentage of expectant mothers and had
supervised all babies born in the district. The physical examinations
of the neighborhood preschool population uncovered a number of
correctable defects, and many children with defects received correc-
tive treatment. Emerson reported that the "prompt and efficient
nursing service" of the MBSUO during the influenza epidemic helped reduce the number of deaths from the virus. In general, he
concluded that "the mothers and fathers of the district had become
educated to an alertness, an understanding, and an interest in the
relation of health and its maintenance to their children's welfare, and
that the medical needs of the district had been better met than
before."[76]

The MBSUO also achieved some intangible accomplishments
during 1918 and 1919. Mohawk-Brighton experienced a "noticeable
growth of initiative and community spirit." In his study of the social
unit experiment, Courtenay Dinwiddie found that the constant interchange of opinions between the citizens and the experts proved "to be
a worthwhile experience in community education." For almost every
service, after the discovery of a need, there commenced a neighborhood discussion of the various methods available to meet the
need. After the discussion, the residents worked together to devise
an appropriate plan of action. Once approved by the entire neighborhood, the plan devised by the Occupational and Citizens' councils
to resolve the discovered needs went into operation. This sequence of
events encouraged community participation and fostered a general
understanding of all neighborhood programs.[77]

As a result, once the MBSUO finished its first year of practical
service (1918) and entered its second (1919), many people believed

that it had begun to demonstrate the possibilities of cooperative action and to indicate the benefits that could be derived from such action. It appeared that the NSUO's social laboratory would run its three-year course and provide an unparalleled opportunity for social scientists to study the dynamics of Phillips's notion of neighborhood organization.

6

Politics and
the Social Unit,
1919-1920

The third year of the social unit experiment opened auspiciously. The MBSUO had carried out one of the most comprehensive neighborhood health care operations in the nation. Neighborhood interest and general participation in the MBSUO was high, and many observers of the experiment predicted further advances in neighborhood cooperative activity for the year ahead. Some even suggested that the organization would spread to other areas of Cincinnati by the end of 1919. But by the summer of that year these optimistic predictions lay shattered. As the contagion of suppression fostered by the aftermath of World War I spread across the nation, political leaders in Cincinnati openly challenged those groups and individuals believed to harbor radical tendencies. Denounced by Mayor John Galvin as "but one step away from Bolshevism," the MBSUO valiantly struggled to answer all the charges levied against it by Galvin and his supporters.

The MBSUO survived 1919, but its defense against the attack on the unit organization dissipated its energies, and the MBSUO limped dejectedly into 1920, a mere shell of its former self. Despite the heroic efforts of the neighborhood residents to keep the social unit's health programs operating, by the end of 1920 little remained of the nation's boldest attempt at neighborhood organization during the first two decades of the twentieth century.

The outbreak of the influenza epidemic in the fall of 1918 had post-poned two important administrative issues, the block elections for 1919 and the budget for that calendar year. Once the worst of the epidemic had passed, the Executive Council of the MBSUO called a special session of the General Council to decide which project to tackle first. As most of the interest of this body focused on the budget, the Executive Council set up meetings with all the occupational councils and the block councils to solicit their suggestions for the 1919 budget. The council also outlined the process of budget selection to each of the groups. According to the procedure drawn up by the Executive Council, once a proposed budget had been drafted, it was to be submitted to each block council for review and published for all residents to see in a special issue of the *Social Unit Bulletin*. Shortly after its dissemination, the proposed budget would come up for discussion, revision, and approval at a special meeting of the General Council.

As in 1918, the amount of money raised by the city and national social unit organizations predetermined the income of the organization. Each branch of the MBSUO and the NSUO submitted an estimate of its expenses for 1919. These estimates, in which 69.7 percent of the total budget went to the MBSUO and 30.3 percent went to the NSUO, were sent to the General Council of the MBSUO and provided the basis for the proposed budget drawn up by a coordinating committee appointed by the General Council.[1] After its completion, this budget went to all members of the MBSUO's Citizens' Council along with a progress report of all the MBSUO's 1918 activities. Once the budget and report were in their hands, the block workers held a series of meetings to review the report and discuss the proposed expenditures with their constituents.[2]

During January and February of 1919 the block councils studied the two documents. By late February general neighborhood consent had been secured and the MBSUO General Council sent the approved budget to the NSUO. Unlike the budget prepared for 1918, the 1919 document was shaped by the various councils themselves rather than by guidelines from the NSUO. The delay caused by the epidemic brought great pressure on the organization to complete a budget for work that was already under way—a situation that may have influenced the final document; even so, most MBSUO officials felt that the 1919 budget was a product of neighborhood needs and desires. As a result, members of the MBSUO staff, as well as all council chairpersons, suggested that the MBSUO budget was drawn up in a more democratic fashion and with greater public understanding than those of most organizations active in Cincinnati neighborhoods.[3]

As in the case of the budget discussion, block worker and block council elections for 1919 had been planned for the fall of 1918 but were delayed by the influenza epidemic. As a result, the General Council rescheduled elections for March 5, 1919. A total of 1,830 neighborhood residents cast their votes for the members of their block councils and for their representatives on the MBSUO's Citizens' Council.[4]

Following a plan devised by the General Council, every block supervised its own election. Each block nominated candidates for the block council and for block worker, selected the site for the block election headquarters, and elected three tellers to count the ballots. At the polling places voters placed their ballots in envelopes on which they wrote their names, addresses, and block numbers.[5] Before separating the ballots from the envelopes, the tellers checked each ballot against a master list to eliminate any illegal votes. The tellers then counted the votes "according to the proportional representation plan."[6]

As it turned out, the voters returned all the block workers to their posts. The composition of the block councils also remained essentially the same, with the exception that a few more men were selected to serve on the councils than before. While not all eligible voters participated in the elections, social unit officials felt heartened by the fairly sizable turnout. For every one hundred families on the average, sixty-seven families cast a vote in the election. Overall, voter turnout on a family basis averaged 71 percent, a figure "far in advance of voter participation in most local elections."[7] According to MBSUO officials, despite the fact that the 1919 election was the first general election held in the district, that "in many instances voters felt that one (vote) per family sufficiently expressed their opinions," that those between the ages of eighteen and twenty-one were unaccustomed to voting, and that no sharp issues were to be decided in the election, the level of participation demonstrated at the very least that neighborhood support for the MBSUO operation existed.[8] And so, by the beginning of March 1919, with the budget approval and the block elections behind them, social unit supporters looked ahead to another year of progress.

Although social unit officials, Mohawk-Brighton residents, and nationally prominent health and welfare supporters applauded the activities undertaken by the MBSUO during 1918, certain individuals in Cincinnati had spoken out against the social unit plan shortly after the demonstration was under way. These attacks, which commenced in June 1918, foreshadowed the antagonism toward the MBSUO that flared up in mid-March 1919. And while social unit officials fought the opposition in 1918, they viewed it as a singular event rather than a portent of what was to come. As a result, when hostility toward the social unit demonstration did erupt in 1919, it caught the organization unaware and off guard.

The first overt opposition to the social unit plan came from James O. White, superintendent of the city's Department of Public Welfare and an ex officio member of the Cincinnati Social Unit Organization. On June 22, 1918, White announced his resignation from the CSUO Occupational Council. He charged the social unit organization with hiding "socialistic tendencies" behind a facade of social service. He asserted that the organization served as a vehicle for the dissemination of dangerous political propaganda and that the social unit organization had changed its purpose from that of rendering social service to that of becoming "a national political party with socialistic tendencies." White further stated that with his resignation all funds for the unit promised by Mrs. and Mrs. Charles P. Taft would be withdrawn immediately. Resignations from C.R. Hebble, secretary of the Chamber of Commerce, and Michael Mullen, city councilman from the Eighth Ward and a crony of Taft's, followed shortly after White's announcement.[9]

These resignations prompted the CSUO Occupational Council, of which White, Hebble, and Mullen had been members, to discuss the issue of "socialistic tendencies" in the social unit organization. The council asked Dr. John Landis, who had been instrumental in bringing the social unit organization to Cincinnati, for his reaction to White's accusations. Dr. Landis replied that he found nothing amiss "as long as the experiment was conducted along the lines being followed."[10] Not fully satisfied, the CSUO then decided to invite the Helen S. Trounstine Foundation, an organization "devoted to the investigation of social problems, particularly those present within the city of Cincinnati," to investigate the work of the social unit organization in Cincinnati and to report its findings to the CSUO.[11]

The Trounstine Foundation asked William J. Norton, an eminent social worker and secretary of the Detroit Community Fund,[12] to carry out the investigation. They selected Norton because he had worked in Cincinnati in 1916 as director of the Council of Social Agencies and had helped Dr. Landis and Courtenay Dinwiddie secure the agreement that had brought the plan to Cincinnati. During the campaign to invite the social unit to Cincinnati, Norton had heard Phillips speak at numerous meetings and had read all of the material on the unit plan submitted at that time. The foundation believed that Norton's prior association would not bias him toward the unit, but rather would enable him to evaluate more fully the performance of the organization with reference to its originally stated purposes. Norton spent July 13 through 15 in Cincinnati reviewing the social unit organization. In accordance with the guidelines established by the foundation, he limited his inquiry "to studying what the original plan was that the promoters of the Social Unit Organization announced before they were asked to go to Cincinnati; whether any departure had been made from this plan; and, especially, whether its officers and employees had been using the organization for the dissemination of any political or economic theory."[13]

Norton reviewed all the literature issued by the NSUO and the CSUO and the minutes of both organizations, interviewed the staff of the MBSUO, and talked with the members of the CSUO. His report, issued on February 1, 1919, exonerated the unit organization and dismissed White's charges. Norton stressed that the social unit organization only appeared radical because it differed from traditional social work schemes in the application of an "intensive cultivation of the democratic principle" and in its insistence that the people of the locality should be involved directly in the operation of all programs.

Norton reported that the promoters presented their plan as an "attempt to bring efficiency to democracy." According to Norton, they proposed to demonstrate the possibility of creating an efficient democracy by organizing a neighborhood in such a way as "to make

100 percent contact with all the persons in the district in order to learn their social needs, to teach them how to determine those needs; to educate them in how to solve those needs and to get the local . . . specialists engaged in solving those needs." The neighborhood in question had been organized in such a way, Norton stressed, and he found that nothing was undertaken in the district "without the actual consent of the representatives of the residents of the district." It was this introduction of the self-governing principle, as opposed to an authoritative principle, that gave rise to the suspicion that a socialist dogma had been introduced. Under these circumstances, it was important not to confuse a departure from "old time methods of organization and administration" with socialism.

Norton concluded his report by stating unequivocally that he had discovered no evidence of "the preaching of any political or economic program," but instead had found "plenty of evidence of the preaching of democratic control of social work and democratic dissemination of social knowledge frankly promised in the original presentation of the plan to Cincinnati." If a misunderstanding existed, the fault lay not with the promoters of the plan but "with those who invited the unit organization" to Cincinnati. [14]

Norton submitted his report in February 1919 to the Helen S. Trounstine Foundation. It was approved by a committee consisting of Luke W. Smith, president of the Cincinnati Chamber of Commerce, Professor Guy A. Tawney of the University of Cincinnati, and Dr. E.W. Mitchell, a well-respected local physician, appointed by the foundation to review the report. The committee agreed with Norton's conclusions and recommended that the experiment continue. After carefully studying Norton's report and the Helen S. Trounstine Foundation's recommendation, the CSUO accepted the report and passed a resolution reaffirming its belief in the support of the social unit experiment. [15]

The MBSUO believed that the publication of Norton's report and the vote of confidence by the CSUO, coupled with an announcement on March 10, 1919, that Secretary of the Interior Franklin K. Lane had accepted the honorary headship of the NSUO, unequivocally exonerated the MBSUO from any further charges of radicalism. Gifford Pinchot, the first president of the NSUO, had resigned his post during the summer of 1917 because of "an inability to give anything like the proper time and consideration to the work of the NSUO." George W. Coleman, founder of the Ford Hall Movement,[16] became acting president, and the NSUO voted to give Pinchot the position of honorary president.[17] Pinchot held this post until the winter of 1918, at which time the NSUO voted to offer the position to Franklin K. Lane. On March 10, 1919, Mrs. Charles Tiffany, president of the NSUO's Citizens' Council, announced Lane's acceptance of the office. In a statement released to the press, Lane stated that he accepted the post because he was convinced that the social unit plan of organization, as tried out in Cincinnati, had far-reaching significance for solving the problems of community organization that faced the nation. In his acceptance speech Lane declared that he believed that "the NSUO had great potentialities for bringing government close to the lives of the people, for securing the cooperation of all classes in the most democratic way imaginable, [and] for developing the community as a unit of the nation to provide its people with the municipal and civic life fulfilling their desires."[18] With such support, the future of the MBSUO appeared secure.

Following so swiftly on the heels of the demonstrations of support for the social unit organization, the attack on the unit organization by the mayor of Cincinnati greatly shocked the supporters of the MBSUO. On March 11, 1919, Mayor John Galvin, caught up in the wave of post–World War I antiradical hysteria that swept the nation, announced that he found the social unit organization a "serious menace" to the city of Cincinnati. Galvin declared that the people of Cincinnati "had been misled by the beautiful theories propounded by the prime movers of the plan," who had portrayed it as a panacea for all ills and the "road to utopia." But, according to Galvin, Cincinnatians "had the wool pulled over their eyes." Rather than a utopia, Galvin told reporters, the social unit organization was in fact "the most insidious type of socialism . . . and but one step away from Bolshevism." As a result, Galvin said it was his duty as a good American citizen to stop the social unit from spreading and eventually "overthrowing the U.S. government!"[19]

Galvin based his accusations on two things, a letter from Dr. Landis to Wilbur Phillips in June 1918 and a meeting held in early March 1919 on the feasibility of extending social unit-style health programs throughout the city of Cincinnati. First of all, Galvin charged, Dr. Landis withdrew his support from the unit because "he had concluded that the movement was of a political nature." To support this statement, Galvin produced a letter given to him by Health Officer William Peters, written by Dr. Landis to Phillips following the charges levied against the unit by James White in June 1918. According to Galvin, the letter clearly indicated that Dr. Landis believed that the social unit "planned to develop a form of government antagonistic to our own."[20]

As Galvin reported, Dr. Landis had written a letter to Phillips on June 24, 1918. In the letter Landis expressed concern about Phillips's prior membership in the Socialist party, his pacifist beliefs, and his support of Herbert S. Bigelow, a Cincinnati social gospel minister who had been tarred and feathered by a "patriotic" mob during the war for his antimilitaristic views. In this same letter, however, Dr. Landis also wrote that despite his reservations about Phillips's political beliefs, he was "still heart and soul for the plan." In addition, Landis assured Phillips that he had "no intention of severing his connection with the social unit organization so long as the experiment was conducted along the lines then (mid-1918) being followed." Galvin did not release this part of Dr. Landis's letter to the press, and by not doing so, misrepresented the letter's intent to the public.[21]

The second basis for Galvin's attack on the social unit organization grew out of a plan to extend health programs modeled after the unit form of organization to other Cincinnati neighborhoods. During June 1918, Dr. Franklin Martin, chief of the Medical Division of the Council of National Defense and head of the NSUO's Physicians' Council, suggested to the CSUO and the Academy of Medicine that they appoint a committee to study the medical organization of the social unit organization and to consider the feasibility of extending it on a trial basis throughout the city of Cincinnati. In reponse to this request, the CSUO Physicians' Council, in conjunction with the Academy of Medicine, set up a committee consisting of Drs. J. Victor Greenbaum, W.D. Porter, E.O. Smith, John D. Miller, D.I. Wofstein, Robert C. Carothers, William Mithoeffer, Sidney Rauh, E.W. Mitchell, and W.B. Haines to investigate Dr. Martin's proposal and report back to the CSUO and the Academy of Medicine. To assist this committee in its work, the NSUO established a National Advisory Council, composed of highly respected members of the national medical community.[22] At the request of the Cincinnati committee, several members of the National Advisory Council came to Cincinnati and helped the Cincinnati committee work out "a plan for combining curative work of the city's hospitals with preventive programs reaching continuously to every home in the city along the lines laid down in the social unit district."

The Cincinnati committee presented this plan at a meeting of the Executive Council of the CSUO's Physicians' Council on March 1, 1919. At this meeting the CSUO's Physicians' Council and representatives from the Academy of Medicine asked the Cincinnati health officer, Dr. William Peters, for support. Peters grudgingly indicated that he would support a plan to draw up a citywide medical program, but stressed that he believed that such a program rightly should fall under the control of the Health Department. Evidently Peters impressed on Galvin the danger of any widespread health program not under the Health Department's jurisdiction, for Galvin used the proposed program as evidence of an attempt "to set up a government within a government."[23]

Phillips was in New York City when the mayor's attack broke in the local and New York papers. Since the beginning of October 1918, Phillips had been working at the request of Dr. Franklin Martin in New York City and Washington, D.C., as Martin's personal advisor and assisting him with his work with the Medical Division of the Council of National Defense.[24] When Galvin's accusations hit the press, Courtenay Dinwiddie, the acting executive of the MBSUO, issued an immediate rebuttal. Dinwiddie declared that Phillips was not "dangerous or Bolshevistic." He suggested that Cincinnatians examine the MBSUO's remarkable record in preventive health work during 1918 and stressed that the MBSUO "by its nature could not be a vehicle of personal propaganda." "In fact," Dinwiddlie wrote, "the social unit is the most sane and constructive effort in community service now going on in America and just such constructive measures to achieve the highest ideals of our Great Republic are the best answer to Bolshevism and class measures of all kinds." He concluded his remarks by demanding that the social unit organization be judged on the basis of its record and nothing else.[25]

Immediately on learning of the mayor's charges, Phillips also issued a rebuttal and sent the mayor a letter outlining the development of the social unit theory of organization. Phillips described the evolution of his work from the days of the New York Milk Committee. He stated that, although he had been a member of the Socialist party during his stay in Milwaukee, he had withdrawn his membership after the Child Welfare Commission was disbanded. He was interested, Phillips wrote, in building an organization which "would represent and express, not the opinions of any party or group or element, not only one political, social or economic belief, but the total thought of the community." He reminded the mayor that Cincinnati had asked to host the experiment and that during Cincinnati's campaign for the social unit, the citizens had ample opportunity to familiarize themselves with the social unit theory. Phillips stressed that he was not interested in "building a government within a government", as Galvin charged, but rather in developing a "sound and constructive democracy." And this, Phillips continued, "could not be done through cataclysmic changes but in a slow and ordered manner through a steady process of community self-education and practical demonstration." Phillips concluded his letter with a challenge to Galvin to submit his evidence to the people at a mass meeting, to answer all questions posed concerning his stand, and then to allow the people to vote on whether or not to keep the experiment in Cincinnati.[26]

Galvin announced, in response to Phillips's letter, that he "would not, under any circumstance, enter into any discussion" with Phillips about the social unit organization. Such a discussion, Galvin declared, "would be bunk."[27] He continued to denounce the unit as "the same type of Soviet government that disrupted Russia," and soon other groups began to join the attack. Health Officer Peters issued a statement supporting the mayor's stand, agreeing that the scheme was revolutionary and stressing that the Health Department would have nothing to do with the MBSUO. Those present at a joint meeting of the Sands Business Men's Club and the West End Medical Society—the one Mohawk-Brighton group opposed to the MBSUO from the beginning—voted twenty-two to eight to endorse the mayor and agreed that the social unit's "motive was to establish a Soviet in Cincinnati." Those in control of the meeting voted down a resolution offered by Dr. Kreidler to set up a committee to investigate the unit before the medical society took a stand.[28] Then, Professor William

Burris, dean of the Teachers College of the University of Cincinnati, jumped on the bandwagon, declaring that "the movement only wore the garb of democracy." Local minister Henry Meyer, who announced that "luckily someone discovered the snake in the grass before it bit," concurred.[29]

Others, however, rushed to the defense of the social unit demonstration. Members of the national organization offered their support of the social unit plan. Dorothy Thompson, publicity agent for the NSUO, declared that the unit plan was not bolshevistic but rather a scheme designed to help the people of a community "study their own needs and meet them through their own skill and experience." Mrs. Charles Tiffany, president of the NSUO's Citizens' Council, stressed that the social unit "did not seek to disrupt the present system of government but rather to help evolve a better government, one more responsive to the people." And, Mr. and Mrs. Guggenheim, financial backers of the NSUO, sent a letter to Phillips confirming their support for the social unit organization.[30]

Expression of support came from a variety of Cincinnati groups as well. The Cincinnati Federation of Churches and the Graduate Nurses Association endorsed the MBSUO. At a meeting to discuss the unit and its contribution to the health of Mohawk-Brighton, the Academy of Medicine passed a resolution supporting the MBSUO and calling for continuation of the experiment. And the CSUO issued a statement assuring the public of its support for the social unit work and for the social unit theory of organization.[31]

But by far the most vocal defense of the social unit experiment came from the residents of Mohawk-Brighton. Immediately following the mayor's accusations, the MBSUO Citizens' Council called a special meeting to discuss the mayor's charges. They invited him to attend a neighborhood meeting and asked him to produce convincing evidence for his statements. They also suggested that Galvin appoint an unbiased committee to investigate the unit organization in Mohawk-Brighton. They followed these initial requests with a letter drafted by the MBSUO's Citizens' Council which included several questions for the mayor to answer. The residents wanted to know if Galvin "opposed the organization of people in blocks for the purpose of studying their own needs and then meeting those needs not met by existing governmental agencies"; if he opposed allowing skilled groups to assist citizens; if Galvin considered the community councils established under the auspices of the Community Councils of National Defense "Bolshevistic"; if he could point to a "single Mohawk-Brighton resident wishing to replace the existing government"; and if he could produce convincing evidence "to warrant the statement that 'the social unit was tending to revolution.' " Galvin refused to attend any meeting sponsored by the MBSUO and ignored the questions posed to him by the Mohawk-Brighton residents.[32]

The MBSUO Occupational Council also issued a statement following the mayor's accusations. A spokesman for the council stated that the Occupational Council "resented the charge that its work was in any sense Bolshevistic," and stressed that the council organized "for the sole purpose of serving the community." In addition, according to the statement released by the MBSUO Occupational Council, that "we should be charged with bolshevism when we are merely endeavoring, in a neighborly way, to serve the needs of our own people, is an intolerable insult to the nurses, clergymen, physicians, social workers, dentists, laborers, businessmen and recreational workers composing the occupational groups of the social unit." And like the MBSUO Citizens' Council, the Occupational Council wanted the mayor to submit his evidence "to an impartial tribunal to determine if the charges were valid."[33]

Even though the mayor refused to attend any meetings sponsored by or about the social unit organization, the residents of Mohawk-Brighton voted to hold a meeting to consider the mayor's charges. They wanted to give Phillips an opportunity to explain his position and to answer the mayor's accusations. On March 18, 1919, Gustave C. Schneider, president of the Mohawk-Brighton Improvement Association, presided over the meeting on the mayor's charges held in the assembly hall at Bloom School. Over four hundred people came to hear Phillips's remarks and to discuss the controversy.

After a short statement in support of the MBSUO by the Reverend F. L. Flinchbaugh, Phillips spoke for approximately half an hour. He briefly explained the growth of the social unit idea. Phillips stressed that he was no longer a member of the Socialist party and that he did not intend for the social unit organization to represent the opinions of any particular party. When asked by Catherine Grace, a Mohawk-Brighton resident, if the American form of government was really subject to change through an extension of the social unit, Phillips replied that "the social unit is not a political organization and is not at this time working on forms of government. But it is possible that if the social unit grows and expands it could affect the form of government by registering the opinions of the majority. But it is so constituted as to avoid hasty change." Phillips concluded his talk by stressing that if Cincinnati did not want the social unit, the organization would leave.

After Phillips's speech the meeting was thrown open for general discussion. Dr. Randall Condon, superintendent of schools, stressed that no other community exhibited such a great interest in community affairs as the one organized into a social unit. Several women spoke about the beneficial impact that the unit had exerted on the health of the neighborhood. Mrs. L.C. Fillmore, former president of the Federated Mothers' Clubs of Cincinnati, and Mrs. A.L. Whitaker, president of the YWCA, moved to endorse the social unit organization. After a unanimous vote of confidence for the unit, the assembly decided to hold a neighborhood referendum so that all neighborhood residents could have the chance to express their opinion of the unit and to ascertain the strength of the desire to continue the experiment.[34]

Following the meeting at Bloom School, the General Council of the MBSUO stated that it failed to find evidence "to connect the activities of the Social Unit Organization with the Bolshevik movement." At the same time, the General Council announced the decision to hold a neighborhood referendum on the social unit organization. According to the statement issued by the General Council, a referendum committee, consisting of Mohawk-Brighton residents C. Edward Neibaum, John Brand, Mrs. Charles Harding, and Mrs. Frank Cole—none of whom held any office in the MBSUO—was in charge of drawing up the plans for the neighborhood referendum. In addition, the council appointed Mrs. A.L. Whitaker, another neighborhood resident, to head a special committee to direct the dissemination of information concerning the social unit both in the district and in the city at large. And finally, the council authorized both committees to use the *Social Unit Bulletin* to outline all the events surrounding the controversy and to serve as a forum for questions and answers about the social unit demonstration in Mohawk-Brighton.[35]

The General Council selected April 10, 1919, for the date of the referendum on the social unit demonstration. From March 28 through April 8, 1919, the Referendum Committee ran a series of articles in the *Social Unit Bulletin* about the social unit organization, the mayor's accusations, Dr. Landis's letter, Phillips's letter, and a variety of statements from residents both for and against the unit. Most of these statements either expressed the belief that the charges were not supported by convincing evidence or were commendations of the unit's health program. Very few residents spoke out against the unit. During this period the Referendum Committee chairman, C. Edward Neibaum, using the neighborhood census, compiled a list of all 7,225 voters eligible to participate in the Mohawk-Brighton social unit elections. Then Neibaum and his committee selected polling places for each block. The committee decided to open the polls at noon. At 9:00 p.m. the polls were to close, and the committee would pick up all the ballot boxes and take them to the social unit headquarters on Freeman Avenue to be counted by the members of the Referendum Committee. The committee decided to hold the ballots for thirty days so that all residents of the district or of the city would have ample time to inspect the outcome of vote. [36]

As planned, on April 9, 1919, the block workers distributed the ballots to all eligible voters in the district. At noon on April 10, "a rainy and miserable day," the polls opened. The Referendum Committee had selected the home of the block worker as the polling place for each block. As residents brought in their ballots, the block workers checked their names off the list of eligible voters. When the polls closed, the Referendum Committee counted the ballots at the social unit headquarters. Of the 7,225 eligible voters, 4,154 or 57 percent, cast ballots. Of the 4,154, a total of 4,034, or 97 percent, favored continuing the social unit experiment in Mohawk-Brighton. Only 120, or 3 percent, voted against the unit. According to an account of the election in the Cincinnati *Commercial Tribune*, "the block-workers were jubilant" over the high level of community support for the social unit demonstration. [37]

As soon as the referendum had been held, the special committee headed by Mrs. A.L. Whitaker to direct the dissemination of information about the social unit called a meeting at the Business Men's Club of all those interested in participating in the informational campaign. These citizens, approximately forty in all, voted to form a public education committee to explain both the purposes and the possibilities of the social unit to Cincinnati and to publicize the unit's achievements in Mohawk-Brighton. In this way, the committee members believed that the city as well as the participants in the MBSUO would understand the importance of the social unit organization for Cincinnati.

Those present at the meeting elected Dr. E.W. Mitchell chair of an executive committee of nine to head the educational campaign. Professor Guy A. Tawney, Mrs. A.L. Whitaker, and the Reverend F.L. Flinchbaugh joined together as the speakers' committee, and Mrs. Paul Wooley, Dr. Thomas Hart, and Dr. William B. Wherry composed the publicity committee. As its first project, the executive committee sent a letter to all groups and organizations active in Cincinnati requesting their opinion of the social unit and also announcing the availability of speakers on the social unit organization.[38]

After its formation, the public education committee sponsored a series of informational talks in various sections of the city. But before its programs really got under way, a new controversy arose that temporarily deflected its attention from the work at hand. On May 6, 1919, Attorney Ralph Clark, hired to audit the books of the Visiting Nurse Association, accused the Council of Social Agencies of mishandling funds given to the CSA by the War Chest.[39] Clark revealed that approximately $150 per month of the Visiting Nurse Association's allotment from the War Chest went to the social unit organization.

The Cincinnati War Chest was a centralized fund-raising scheme stimulated by World War I. All local social welfare agencies joined together in a council to centralize fund raising. At first it included only war-related groups, but by 1918 numerous other organizations, including the Council of Social Agencies, joined the War Chest operation. In addition to centralizing local fund-raising efforts, the War Chest also determined which agencies were to receive money from the central fund. Earlier in the year the War Chest had rejected the MBSUO's application for funds. Thus, Clark was aghast when he discovered that money had been transferred to the social unit organization by the Visiting Nurse Association without the knowledge of the War Chest.[40]

Immediately following Clark's charges, Walter Friedlander, executive secretary of the Cincinnati War Chest, demanded that the CSA cease all payments to the MBSUO and that the CSA submit an itemized list of all social-unit-related expenses incurred. C.M. Bookman, director of the Council of Social Agencies, countered this demand with a statement clarifying and explaining the CSA's position. Bookman said that when the committee under the direction of Dr. Landis and Courtenay Dinwiddie asked the social unit organization to come to Cincinnati, it promised to give the social unit organization five thousand dollars each year of the experiment to defray the cost of the nurses and social workers employed in the social unit district. Because of the nursing redistricting to accommodate the unit organization, Bookman believed that it was only fair to transfer the money that would have been spent in Mohawk-Brighton anyway to help the social unit organization.[41]

The executive committee of the Council of Social Agencies met on May 8, 1919, to discuss Clark's charges, the War Chest's attitude, and the decision to provide money for the social unit organization. The statement issued by the executive committee on May 9, 1919, declared that the CSA believed the "criticism was entirely unjustified." The CSA said that each agency cooperating with the CSA budget submitted an estimated budget at the beginning of the year, in which it outlined its projected income and expenditures. All these budgets were submitted to a special committee of the CSA for approval, and once the final version of each budget had been drawn up, the proposed agency budget was sent to the budget committee of the War Chest for review. The budgets, which included line items of expenditures for the social unit organization, were those of the "Children's Clinic—special fund, Social Unit, $800; the Visiting Nurse Association—special fund, Social Unit, $1800; the Associated Charities—special fund, Social Unit, $2500; the Anti-Tuberculosis League—special fund, Social Unit, $800. Total, $6900." Before going into operation, the CSA insisted, all these budgets had been approved by the War Chest budget committee.

As a result, the CSA statement continued, the War Chest council "either knew or had the opportunity of knowing" that a total of $6,900 was budgeted through certain organizations for work in the social unit district. While it was true that the War Chest finance committee had turned down the MBSUO's request for additional funding, as far as the CSA was concerned that decision did not affect the line items for the social unit organization already included in the budget. In fact, the CSA declared, a resolution to that effect had been passed on April 23, 1919, at a meeting of the War Chest finance committee. This resolution, the CSA said, read "that although the Cincinnati War Chest refused the application of the social unit organization for funds, it did not have the jurisdiction over the constituent organizations of the Council of Social Agencies to prevent them from rendering services or appropriating money from their own budgets to the Social Unit." Thus, the CSA contended, the attack by Clark on May 6, that the CSA used War Chest funds in an unauthorized fashion, was unjustified.

The CSA concluded its statement by making public a resolution passed by the executive committee of the CSA on March 20, 1919. The resolution stated that a committee of four, consisting of Maurice Freiberg, A. Clifford Shinkle, Eugene Buss, and Fred A. Geier, would "investigate and report whether the beliefs held by the Executives of the National Social Unit Organization are such as to justify the Council of Social Agencies in assuming that the National Social Unit Organization has failed to live up to its agreement, and, hence, that the Council of Social Agencies should refuse to finance in part social work in the Mohawk-Brighton District." On the basis of that report, the CSA statement ended, the Council of Social Agencies would decide whether or not to provide funds for the MBSUO in the future.[42]

The committee established by the CSA to investigate the social unit organization issued its report on June 25, 1919. In the report's preface, the committee wrote that it based its investigation on a study of all available records and publications of the social unit organization, on discussions with many individuals connected with the social unit organization, and on the replies of Wilbur and Elsie Phillips to questions concerning their personal beliefs. The committee reported that it was investigating not merely a local endeavor, but one of many ventures undertaken throughout the country to develop a more democratic form of organization. The committee stressed that it viewed the plan as *"an experiment in organization"*[43] with public health selected as the medium for demonstrating the soundness of the proposed organizational form. But, the committee emphasized, "the numbers dealt with were so small and the time period so short" that it believed all results to be only tentative. In addition, the committee stated that although it believed it necessary to delve into the personal beliefs of the Phillipses, it felt strongly that "neither the Phillipses or the organization they created should necessarily be upheld and supported or criticized and rejected because of the theories, economic or otherwise which the Phillipses or any other staff members held." The committee stressed that its conclusions were not infallible and that they only represented an attempt to provide sound information with which to formulate a decision on the future of the social unit organization.[44]

The committee divided its investigation into three general areas: the invitation to the social unit organization, the criticisms of the social unit organization, and the recommendations of the committee. First the committee discussed the efforts of Dr. Landis and Courtenay Dinwiddie to secure the unit demonstration for the city of Cincinnati. The committee analyzed the talks given by Phillips in Cincinnati prior to the selection of Cincinnati and found that throughout the discussion the Phillipses stressed that the social unit organization was primarily "an experiment of a *method of organization*" with health work selected as the program with which to demonstrate the democracy and efficiency of the organizational scheme. With the selection of Cincinnati, the committee reported, the NSUO secured a promise from Dr. Landis's committee to raise ten thousand dollars a year from direct private contributions and to provide five thousand dollars a year through the budget of the CSA. Following this financial arrangement, the report continued, Phillips arrived in Cincinnati on January 2, 1917.[45]

In the section entitled "Criticisms of the Social Unit Organization," the committee looked at the so-called radical tendencies of the plan, the democratic features of the plan, and the efficiency and economy of the social unit organization. It outlined the charges levied by the mayor concerning the "Bolshevistic" nature of the plan and then discussed Phillips's answers to the twenty or so questions submitted by the CSA concerning Phillips's beliefs and party affiliations. On the basis of its investigations, the committee exonerated Phillips. It concurred with the findings of the Helen S. Trounstine Foundation report earlier in 1919 that "there was no evidence of the spreading of any political or economic propaganda transmitted through the literature or in the meetings held by the social unit organization." The committee further stated that it felt that any move to make the social unit organization a tool through which "to effect the creation of an industrial democracy" could be undertaken, given the form of organization, "only if the people of the district so desired."[46]

In its study of the democracy of the social unit plan, the committee found that Phillips did not, as charged by Mayor Galvin, function as a "dictator." The committee believed that although the "founder of the social organization exerted the initiative at first, as time went on the indications were such that the unit program was coming less and less from those in charge and more from the people of Mohawk-Brighton." The committee concluded that, despite the favorable vote in the referendum, the crucial test would come when the experiment ended and the residents were asked to finance for themselves the work made possible by outside contributors.[47]

The final part of the criticisms section focused on the efficiency and economy of the social unit plan. The committee found that the social unit organization did foster a "general community health consciousness" not developed in any other section of the city, which resulted in a "general betterment of the health of the neighborhood." However, the committee stressed, the time period under consideration really was too short to analyze fully the outcome of all the programs, thus making the results inconclusive. While the committee acknowledged that the unit organization's health programs raised the number of birth registrations in the district, increased the number of tuberculosis patients under nursing care, and kept the death rate lower than the rest of the city during the influenza epidemic, it wondered "if the unit's program would have been equally successful under another less controversial method of organization." The committee noted as well that the unit failed to alter the infant mortality rate significantly for the district and that, overall, the work had been expensive. It reported, for instance, that the cost of nursing care provided by the unit stood at an average of sixty-three cents per visit as opposed to the fifty-five cents per visit by the Visiting Nurse Association. The committee did acknowledge that all pioneer efforts tended to be expensive, but still stressed that the Visiting Nurse Association provided comparable service for less money.[48]

The committee concluded that the overall work of the social unit organization "had been of an Excellent Character." The committee recommended that the CSA continue to channel money into the MBSUO up to an amount of five thousand dollars until the expiration of the unit laboratory in January 1920. It suggested that further analysis of the work after the expiration of the experiment be undertaken by an impartial city committee consisting of representatives from the Academy of Medicine, the Board of Education, the Board of Health, the Bureau of Catholic Charities, the Business Men's Club, the Central Labor Council, the Chamber of Commerce, the Cincinnati Woman's Club, the City Club, the Commercial Club, the Council of Social Agencies, the Federation of Mothers' Clubs, the Federation of Churches, the Graduate Nurses Association, the Social Unit Organization, the United Jewish Charities, and the Women's City Club to determine whether or not the social unit should receive CSA funds for 1920. In addition, the committee urged the CSA to take into account the "post-war attitude of fear of change in reviewing the unit's work."[49]

While most groups in Cincinnati applauded the CSA report, others—both friend and foe—expressed reservations. The mayor continued to be opposed to the unit. "Nothing," he said, "with even a tinge of socialism" would receive his support. Courtenay Dinwiddie also expressed dissatisfaction with the CSA report. He felt that the CSA's decision to launch another investigation before deciding whether or not it should continue to provide support for social unit programs made it virtually impossible for the unit to be eligible for CSA funds in 1920 because all cooperating agency budgets were drawn up in the fall for the next year. Thus, any decision to delay consideration of the unit until after the budgetary decisions, Dinwiddie believed, hindered any plans for the extension of social units throughout the city. It was, in effect, a de facto decision not to support the social unit organization.[50]

The MBSUO's public education committee also criticized the CSA report. This committee felt that the CSA placed too much emphasis on possible theories rather than on actual activities and accomplishments of the social unit plan. The committee also believed that the CSA downplayed the "wholesome and genuinely democratic checks of the plan," which would automatically halt implementation of "hasty and unwise policies." And, like Dinwiddie, the committee stressed that the decision of the CSA to delay judgment on social unit funding until January 1920 represented a definite attempt to force the unit out of existence.[51]

Following the release of the CSA report, the public education committee accelerated its efforts "to interpret the social unit to Cincinnati." The committee encouraged all neighborhood groups to hold meetings on the social unit organization, request literature on the organization from the MBSUO headquarters, and invite speakers on the social unit organization to any type of gathering. During August and September numerous requests for speakers on the unit plan came to the MBSUO headquarters. By the beginning of October, groups such as the Avondale Citizens' Group, the Mothers' Club of the Twelfth District School, the Clovernook Mothers' Club, the Mothers' Club of the Mary Dell School in Carthage, the Oyler School Mothers' Club, the Fairmount Mothers' Club, the Northside Mothers' Club, and the Phoenix Council of the Daughters of America all had invited social unit speakers to meet with them, review the history of the social unit organization, and discuss its activities in Mohawk-Brighton.[52]

Other activities pursued by the supporters of the social unit organization during the months immediately following the presentation of the CSA report revolved around the arrangements for a conference on the social unit organization to be held in Cincinnati from October 23 to 25, 1919. A joint committee, made up of the executives of the CSUO and the NSUO, invited a number of impartial evaluators to come to Cincinnati to study the social unit organization and prepare reports detailing their conclusions for presentation at the conference. All those invited to evaluate the unit organization came to Cincinnati during late September to study various aspects of the MBSUO.[53]

The conference, entitled "Wanted: A Program for Community Organization," opened on Thursday evening, October 23, 1919, at the Gibson Hotel in downtown Cincinnati. Frederick C. Butler, director of the Americanization program of the Department of the Interior, presided over the opening session attended by nearly eight hundred people from cities around the nation and from various Cincinnati neighborhoods and local organizations. W.A. Julian, president of the Council of Social Agencies and chairman of the CSUO's convention committee opened the conference. According to Julian, "the purpose of the conference was to ascertain what success had attended the efforts of the NSUO in its efforts to organize a model community in Mohawk-Brighton and what methods should be pursued for the perfection of the plan and its application to other communities across the nation." Butler returned to the podium following Julian's remarks and announced that the subject for discussion that evening would be "The Need of a More Definite Plan of Group and Citizenship Organization."[54]

John C. Collier, president of the National Community Center Association, opened the session. He stressed that in an increasingly large and complex society, community organization offered the most practical way of "bringing the citizen into an intelligent and potent relationship with business and with government." Collier contended that the social unit organization provided a "momentous service for the American Commonwealth" by demonstrating how to organize a neighborhood "to conserve true democratic government." He concluded his introductory remarks with an affirmation of support for the work of the social unit organization and then introduced the main speaker, John Lovejoy Elliott, headworker of the Hudson Guild in New York City.[55]

Elliott spoke on "Some Neighborhood Needs: Will the Social Unit Help Solve Them?" He believed that men and women in America felt estranged from the nation's political and social life. Elliott said that he found from his work with tenement dwellers in New York City that the ameliorative efforts of reformers failed to change this attitude. What was needed, Elliott argued, was a scheme to get the alienated involved in the social and political life of the country, which could illustrate the value of such participation. The social unit organization, Elliott contended, provided a way "to bring forth out of the common people the great redeeming powers latent in the city and in the nation because it instructs them, gives them directions, and sets them to work." In other words, Elliott concluded, the unit organization offered the "machinery to realize the promise of America."[56]

A discussion, led by Randall J. Condon, superintendent of the Cincinnati Public Schools, and Dr. Thomas Hart, editor of the *Catholic Telegraph*, followed Elliott's remarks. Condon agreed with Elliott that the social unit engendered a "genuine American democracy" by getting everyone to work together for the common good. Dr. Hart echoed these sentiments. He found that participation in the social unit organization aroused community spirit and "the determination to help one another to solve the problems that arose in everyday life." The unit organization, Dr. Hart said, helped to make "democracy effective, progressive and durable, bringing all groups into the American system." Discussion by the audience was brief and centered on the importance of organizing people to understand and identify their needs and on the necessity of developing machinery capable of meeting the needs identified.[57]

The second day of the conference focused on nursing under the social unit organization, neighborhood health organization, the relationship between social unit organization and various community interests, gathering community statistics, and an overview and analysis of the social unit experiment. Zoe LaForge of the National Organization for Public Health Nursing discussed the health programs undertaken by the MBSUO. LaForge stated that she found the number of persons served by the unit extraordinary and far above the usual number cared for in most of the nation's health centers. She stressed that despite the inconclusive nature of the results due to the brevity of the experiment, the frequent examinations resulted in improved health for the entire neighborhood. She recommended that the social unit health care programs be continued in Mohawk-Brighton, that plans be laid to extend similar programs to other areas of the city, and that all public health nursing organizations study closely the unit's method of generalized nursing. Haven Emerson, health officer of New York City, also spoke on the importance of organizing communities for the protection of health. After a brief review of the health programs of the MBSUO, he commended the MBSUO for raising the level of health care rendered and increasing the understanding of the need for preventive health organization. Discussion following LaForge's and Emerson's remarks supported the MBSUO's health program and called for its continuation.[58]

The session on the social unit and community interests, in which speakers discussed the organization's relationship to the church, housing, recreation, and Americanization[59], was followed by a talk by Robert E. Chaddock entitled "The Social Unit and Community

Statistics." Chaddock, secretary of the American Statistical Council, stressed the importance of collecting accurate information on social needs to plan social service programs wisely. He briefly sketched the various types of surveys conducted by the block workers in the MBSUO. These surveys, which included birth registration, preschool registration, and general family information, formed the core around which the organization could secure a picture of the local population. Chaddock stated that despite the fact that the unit's statistics were not complete in every instance, the social unit organization had facilitated the collection of statistics and increased public understanding of the importance of collecting social data. He concluded his talk by encouraging the collection of community statistics and commended the social unit organization for instituting a neighborhood census.[60]

Edward T. Devine, editor of *The Survey* magazine, gave a presentation on the social unit experiment as a whole. In "The Social Unit in Cincinnati: An Experiment in Organization," Devine spoke at some length abut the activities of the social unit organization and of its importance for the field of social work. He first briefly reviewed the origin of the social unit idea, the choice of Cincinnati as the demonstration city for the social unit experiment, and the selection of Mohawk-Brighton as the local unit laboratory.

Devine then proceeded to analyze different aspects of the experiment. First, he discussed the democratic features of the unit method of organization. He felt that the objective of the plan was democratic and that, during the life of the experiment, the members of the Citizens' Council, as "representatives of the people, consistently decided upon measures only after consultation with the residents of their respective blocks." For the most part, Devine believed, the executives, on any level, "did not arbitrarily impose their views and plans upon the district." In fact, Devine argued, the plan "penetrated to the very heart of the social order and raised the challenge as to whether the people were capable of deciding . . . what their needs were and how they were to be met." In addition, Devine pointed out that if this "democracy" were taken to its logical extreme, the philosophy of the unit organization "did look to an expansion of units across the city," which would alter the existing structures of government and those of the nation's social agencies. However, Devine concluded that the very nature of the organization, with its encouragement of local deliberation, meant that any major change would not come quickly, but would take, at the very least, a lifetime. Devine ended this section of his talk by stressing that, in his opinion, the tendency on the part of the unit organization for "slow and patient education and demonstration was not something to fear but to applaud" if it made America more democratic.

Devine then turned to a discussion of the accomplishments of the MBSUO experiment. From his talks with representatives of those agencies that cooperated with the MBSUO, such as the Better Housing League, the Anti-Tuberculosis League, and the Associated Charities, Devine discovered that the intensive block organization was helpful and that the cooperation between the block worker and the agency representatives resulted in "a higher quality of social services" and a reduction in unnecessary duplication of services. While all results were not conclusive, Devine believed that the "Social Unit added substantially to the physical and moral well-being of the residents of the district; that it led to more efficient and discriminating relief, to more thorough and constructive diagnosis of the needs of families in trouble; that it promoted neighborliness and sociability; that it made the ordinary family residing in the district more hospitable to visitors who came with a helpful purpose, and more discriminating as to the probable effect of sanitary and social measures brought forward for their benefit." These results were "sufficiently encouraging" and "warranted the expansion of the plan."

The final section of Devine's remarks focused on the controversy provoked by Mayor Galvin over the existence and continuation of the social unit organization in Cincinnati. Devine felt that the fact that the unit seemed to invite controversy indicated the importance of the unit in the development of plans to organize American communities. The social unit was different from other types of neighborhood work in that it embodied a distinct social philosophy. The social unit organization stressed the importance of community decisions rather than activities planned by a small number of "public spirited and altruistic individuals." It was this, Devine said, that unsettled many observers for "it was unheard of in current practice to consult the beneficiaries of any program and to train them to become active in their own behalf." The existence of the social unit forced people to think about what type of social service they wanted. Finally, he observed that the "most reasonable conclusion about the social unit organization was that it provoked thinking about social organization and that, this, if not for any other reason, meant that the social unit earned the right to a longer and more complete trial."[61]

The final day of the conference was Saturday, October 25. Collier addressed the gathering again and spoke on "Democracy and the Making of Budgets." After a review of the ways in which money was raised for community projects and then distributed, Collier stressed that the social unit organization provided an ideal way to administer community funds since "through the occupational council 'public servants' and through the citizens' council 'citizens' could participate in budgetary discussions, project determination, and program control."[62] Such administration of funds would be one way to break the stranglehold of large, annual giving campaigns that potentially predetermined what programs would be undertaken.

Mark Jones, secretary of the National Association of Employment Managers, and John Walker, ex-president of the Illinois Federation of Labor, addressed the assembly on "The Social Unit and the Worker and the Employer." Both Jones and Walker believed that the social unit organization had the potential to better relations between workers and businessmen.[63] In the final session of the conference, Phillips spoke on "The Social Unit in 1920." He stressed the importance of programs that emphasized "not the clashing of group against group" but rather the cooperation among groups. He argued that the hope of America lay in cooperative action and that more experiments were needed to devise the most efficient methods for fostering group interaction. Phillips said that, of course, the MBSUO was one such experiment, but even it needed more time "to perfect its democratic mechanism." Phillips stated that he hoped that Cincinnati would continue to support the MBSUO. He concluded by telling his audience that the NSUO planned "to survey the whole field of community effort" and then "begin to train people to organize their communities." Phillips then announced that he had submitted his resignation to the MBSUO's General Council and planned to return to New York City to work closely with the NSUO, studying the community organization movement and working to perfect the operation of the social unit organization. Following his talk, those present passed a resolution endorsing the social unit and urging its continuation.[64]

At the conclusion of the conference, the MBSUO turned its attention to the question of support for the organization after the experiment expired in January 1920. Although CSA investigators had recommended "limited and cautious" support for MBSUO activities in June, by November the CSA had decided not to follow the recommendations of the investigating committee. Many large contriibutors to the general fund-raising campaign, from which the CSA received its funds, refused to participate in the annual campaign if the social unit organization received support. Under pressure from the "conservative political and financial interests threatening to withdraw support from social welfare programs" described by Devine in his remarks at the NSUO conference,[65] the executive committee of the Council of Social Agencies declared that the MBSUO represented a menace to the established patterns of social work in the city and announced that it would not support the MBSUO in the future. In addition, the CSA threatened to cut off the support for any member organization. As a result, the MBSUO was forced to raise its own funds for any continuation of its programs.[66]

The CSA decision did not take the MBSUO completely by surprise. Shortly after the release of the CSA report in June, the MBSUO General Council decided not to count on continuing support from the Council of Social Agencies. In August the General Council had appointed a committee on the future of the social unit. This group spent the months of September and October talking with neighborhood residents and soliciting their opinions about support for MBSUO activities and about the programs the residents wished to see continued. After two months of discussion, the General Council, in response to the recommendation of the committee on the future of the social unit, called a general neighborhood meeting on November 21, 1919, to plan a financial campaign to raise enough money to carry on the work of the MBSUO in 1920. Those attending the meeting voted to raise funds in the neighborhood to show the district's dedication to the social unit organization.

The General Council appointed a campaign committee consisting of neighborhood residents, Dr. A. D. Brichard, Mrs. Charles Reinhardt, Caroline Severett, C.E. Neibaum, and Adolph Schreibman, to oversee the fund-raising campaign. The General Council also announced the proposed goal of the campaign—to raise thirty thousand dollars to finance fully all the MBSUO's activities.[67]

By December 5, 1919, the campaign committee had organized approximately 150 residents into thirty-two teams, one team for each block and one special team under the direction of Louis Destler to canvass all neighborhood business establishments. Block workers called block meetings to discuss the fund-raising campaign, and the *Social Unit Bulletin,* neighborhood churches, and local movie theaters all advertised the campaign. On December 5, 1919, the committee commenced a ten-day campaign to solicit money in the neighborhood to support the social unit work. On the first day of the campaign, over five hundred dollars was raised. Eventually over three thousand dollars was collected, representing "a contribution of about $1.00 from one out of every four residents," according to Phillips.[68]

The campaign committee, in cooperation with the MBSUO General Council, decided to launch a citywide drive for funds as well. Since the CSUO had voted to disband with the expiration of the experiment on January 1, 1920, the campaign committee, assisted by "friends of the Social Unit," organized teams to canvass the city. By the end of January 1920 approximately fourteen thousand dollars had been raised in Mohawk-Brighton and in the city at large. By the summer of 1920 almost twenty-five thousand dollars had been raised.[69]

Following the December fund-raising drive, the MBSUO made one final attempt to establish a formal relationship with the city of Cincinnati during 1920. Representatives of the MBSUO met several times with Mayor Galvin, asking him to alter his views on the social unit and support the neighborhood work. They requested that Galvin appoint a committee of thirty, consisting of representatives mainly from the city's social welfare agencies and related city departments, to act as an official advisory body for the social unit work in Cincinnati. Galvin, however, held fast to his 1919 stand on the social unit and refused to name an advisory committee.[70]

Throughout 1920 the MBSUO continued most of its activities at a somewhat reduced level. But the future looked bleak. The MBSUO was not sure it would be able to raise enough money to finance any programs in 1921. As a result, in October 1920 the MBSUO began to discuss the possibility of turning over all of its equipment to the Babies Milk Fund Association.[71] The MBSUO received permission from the NSUO to dispose of the property and equipment secured through the funds provided by the NSUO during the experimental years. In mid-November, when the Babies Milk Fund Association assumed possession of all the MBSUO property and equipment, the MBSUO had under its care 352 babies, 498 preschool children, 30 adult bedside classes, and 150 tuberculosis cases. The Babies Milk Fund Association absorbed the unit's child welfare work. Other agencies, such as the Visiting Nurse Association and the Anti-Tuberculosis League, took over the remaining social unit programs. On November 23, 1920, the MBSUO voted itself out of existence.[72]

The last two years of the Mohawk-Brighton social unit experiment had centered on the unit's fight for its life. Very few new or innovative activities were undertaken by the MBSUO staff. The mayor's attack diverted the unit's attention from its services and toward justification of its existence. As Courtenay Dinwiddie pointed out, the MBSUO "was forced to meet a new and difficult situation rather than perfect and extend itself."[73] By the end of 1920 the MBSUO, described by contemporaries as "an epoch-making experiment in democracy as applied to community problems,"[74] suffered a rather ignominious defeat.

Why did the mayor of Cincinnati attack an organization dedicated to democracy? According to most observers, contemporaries and more recent analysts alike, the social unit organization ultimately failed to survive in Cincinnati for two reasons—it was perceived as a threat to the city's dominant political organization and to the city's pattern of social work. Members of Cincinnati's political and social welfare establishments feared the rise of an organization that they did not control. The confluence of the fears exhibited by these groups resulted in a loss of funding that eventually forced the social unit organization out of existence.[75]

As Edward Devine had pointed out at the conference, the social unit theory of organization did possess political implications. From the very beginning, Phillips had stressed that it was "a plan to hasten the coming of a democracy, both genuine and efficient, by building upon a basis of geographic units an organization in which the people could get a clear idea of the common needs and could utilize the skilled groups in formulating and carrying out programs to meet those needs." Phillips believed that such a plan would provide the machinery for the interchange of information between citizens and experts in the development of sound rather than haphazard plans to meet neighborhood needs. As a result, it would correct any imbalance beween needs and solutions and make "democratic control more direct, effective and intelligent." Once functioning on the neighborhood level, the plan would spread across the city and, through intracity cooperation in a common organization, articulate city needs and strategies for action. Eventually, Phillips envisaged that this method of organization would be reproduced on the county, state, and federal levels. In short, he believed that citizen participation combined with expert analysis in the neighborhood setting would produce a working democracy—something lacking in the United States at that particular time.[76] Political life under such conditions would indeed differ from that under the prevailing system of representative democracy.

Although the social unit plan was the most developed scheme of its type, it was not unique. Rather, Phillips's plan represented a general inclination on the part of early twentieth century thinkers to view government as a "communion of citizens and experts." Mary P. Follett, for example, sketched a plan nearly as detailed as Phillips's in *The New State*. Like Phillips and others, Follett envisaged a governmental system in which the experts worked with a well-informed and active public; the "public would set the needs and the experts would devise the means." A civic leader in Boston who worked to establish community centers in public schools, Follett believed that "the most acute problem of modern life" was to make citizens feel that they were the government and directly responsible for everything that concerned it. She saw the neighborhood as an integral part of the city, state, and nation, and believed that an organized neighborhood in which citizens and experts cooperated provided "the opportunity for continuous political action directed towards supplying the needs of the citizenry." Eventually "neighborhood units across the city would unite and then multiply and form the people into a state, the New State."[77]

In the end, the feasibility of any or all of these plans to create a working democracy remains uncertain. Of these different schemes, only the social unit plan actually went into operation, and its demonstration never moved beyond the initial trial district. Also, since political institutions develop slowly, the three-year experimental period was too brief for a sufficient trial. And, finally, as political scientist Gale Lowrie found in his study of the social unit, the "unit form of government did not ensure that the Citizens' Council could avoid the evils of indirect representation, did not demonstrate how very many occupational councils would function, and did not indicate how to maintain a proper balance between the citizens and the experts." All in all, Lowrie concluded, the social unit plan offered "little that was tangible as a substitute for the American form of government."[78] The political implications inherent in any extension of the demonstration to other sections of the city proved to be unsettling to the local power structure. As contemporary community organization analyst Jesse Steiner pointed out in his study of the social unit organization, "beginning with a small phase of community life its expanding organization may . . . have absorbed new functions until it would finally take the place of existing political machinery."[79] Understandably, the vision of an ever-expanding organization capable of displacing the established political machinery, however improbable in reality, unnerved Galvin and his supporters and prompted them to launch an attack on the unit plan.

According to many observers, just such a vision led the local political organization in power, the Republican party, to conclude that the unit organization would supplant its political machine. In his study of politics and social welfare in Cincinnati during the first two decades of the twentieth century, Michael Bliss found that Cincinnati politicians disliked the unit "because it challenged the domination of the machine politicians at the machine's local geographical base."[80] Another observer noted that the block workers in particular appeared to threaten the position of the precinct captains by substituting "genuine leaders of the people." The politicans feared that the residents would look to their block workers before going to their precinct captains or ward bosses in times of need. Despite the fact that Phillips and the MBSUO staff made every effort to place the organization under popular control, Jesse Steiner concluded, the type of organization developed by the social unit could "lend itself to use as a political machine if its leaders were interested in using it for that purpose."[81] Not surprisingly, the local politicians mistrusted what they regarded as a challenge to the local power structure. As a result, when the MBSUO demonstrated that the people could participate directly in those affairs touching their interests, the politicians reacted harshly against an organization designed to foster "an intelligent citizenry that could not be so easily controlled," and which would "compromise the future of municipal administrations and local political machines which governed American cities."[82]

Philanthropic groups in Cincinnati mistrusted the social unit organization for similar reasons. Once the experiment got under way, a variety of health and social welfare organizations found that they did not favor the expansion of social-unit-style health and welfare activities. Like the politicians, these organizations feared a loss of control. As in the case of the MBSUO's decision to practice generalized nursing, organizations such as the Visiting Nurse Association and the Department of Health found they disapproved of changes that would affect the established methods of home nursing visitation. In essence, these groups fell into the very trap that Norton had warned them against in his report to the Trounstine Foundation. In his report Norton stressed that during an experiment it was important not to confuse a departure from "old time methods of organization and administration" with socialism.[83] When faced with change, these groups translated "change" into "radicalism." Rather than accept changes that might alter familiar organizational structures, a number of health and welfare groups reacted negatively—not seeing modification but rather fearing displacement.

In addition to this resistance to change, there was a clash between philosophies about the practice of social work. As Devine suggested in his remarks at the social unit conference, the idea of the social unit—"that of instituting a form of local philanthropic control"—ran against the "current of modern practice." It was unheard of, Devine said, "to consult the beneficiaries of any program and to train them to become active in their own behalf."[84] Cincinnati, like many other cities, favored the institution of financial federations, which centralized funding campaigns and, in many cases, program-making.[85] Leaders of those interested in financial federation were concerned,

not with cooperative democracy, but with the machinery and financing of social work. These proponents wanted "efficiency through
expert leadership rather than democractic self-determination
through the joint efforts of citizen and specialist."[86] As a result, the
thought of an ever-expanding social unit form of organization dis-
tressed the social welfare community just as it did the Republicans.

Hostility from either the political or the social welfare establishment would have hindered the development of any activity identified
as disruptive to established patterns of action. Together, these groups
represented a formidable force. Not only were the two establishments united in their hostility toward the unit, but they also shared
many of the same funding sources. Under such conditions, it was
extremely difficult for the MBSUO to continue its activities in Cincinnati.[87]

Ironically, given the ballyhoo raised by the political establishment
over the political implications of the social unit plan, the social welfare
leadership faced a more serious challenge from the social unit organization. To test his plan of organization, Phillips selected health programs rather than political programs. He believed that to plan
intelligently for change, the broader vision needed to be built on a
strong, tangible program. As a result, the social unit never was "the
workshop of the political scientist"; instead, it was that of the health
and social worker.[88] Health care activities were a good way to demonstrate a method of organization. Since health was regarded as a
fundamental of existence and health service was recognized as a
legitimate function of the community, health programs served as a
useful organizing tool. Phillips believed that preventive health programs allowed people to see how it was possible to work together.[89]

Of the various health services, child welfare programs represented
"an excellent cornerstone in the edifice of community organization."[90] Child welfare was necessary, it appealed to the sympathy and
the understanding of the general public, and it served as a means to
win the cooperation and the support necessary for social reconstruction. Phillips saw the child as the key to each family's appreciation of
programs to improve the conditions of life and to their involvement in
the execution of the programs.[91]

Phillips encouraged the NSUO and then the MBSUO to select an
infant health care service as the unit's pilot program. As it turned out,

tying health services to intensive geographic localization, administrative coordination, and the social organization of a neighborhood made the MBSUO one of the boldest early ventures in neighborhood health care. During the first two decades of the twentieth century, many health workers across the country attempted to relate health services to definite population units. Realizing that different areas of a city needed particular services, these health workers wanted to establish neighborhood health centers that served each particular area's need. They attempted to coordinate all health and welfare services that touched on the particular form of care offered by the health center. By mobilizing local sentiment in support of the health center, they hoped to instill in neighborhood residents an appreciation of preventive health care.[92] Of all efforts prior to 1920, the MBSUO represented the boldest and most celebrated of the health center experiments.[93]

The attraction of this form of health organization as a substitute for the more traditional types of programs became apparent after the mayor's attack on the MBSUO. Despite the enthusiastic support of the Mohawk-Brighton residents for the unit plan, Phillips recognized a fundamental difference of opinion between him and the neighborhood residents. Phillips's chief interest in the plan centered around the machinery through which he wished "to hasten the coming of democracy." The health center was to him merely a trial feature. But the members of the MBSUO felt differently. They viewed the experiment as a demonstration of democratic health and social work practices. To them, the health center was essential to the social unit plan, and the idea or theory behind the plan was incidental. As a result, when the controversy erupted, the MBSUO wanted Phillips to address only the practical side of the plan. They wanted the defense based on the efficiency of the programs offered at the MBSUO's health station. They asked Phillips to avoid any discussions of the theory for fear of endangering the practical services. After some spirited discussions, Phillips agreed to follow the MBSUO's wishes and defended the social unit organization primarily as a successful venture in health care. The defense, stripped of any theoretical underpinnings, further placed the experiment in the realm of health rather than political activity.[94] In this light, the continued existence of the unit organization, as the social welfare establishment quickly perceived, could shake the very foundation of Cincinnati's social and health care.

Harried out of existence by established elites who feared the larger implications of the social unit theory, the MBSUO failed to survive its three-year trial period. Nonetheless, while in operation, the social unit experiment provided the most comprehensive neighborhood health care service in the country. In the MBSUO health center, citizens identified local health needs and health specialists worked closely with the citizens to implement programs that met those needs. By bringing the health experts and the citizens together, the MBSUO demonstrated the feasibility of providing efficient health service under democratic citizen control. In addition, the MBSUO illustrated the principles that had guided Phillips from the very beginning in his work with the New York Milk Committee, for the health program in Mohawk-Brighton stressed not the part but the whole. Phillips's social unit demonstration showed for a short time that all aspects of the health environment could operate in a complementary manner for the well-being of the entire neighborhood. Although the MBSUO did not transform city, state, regional, or federal organizations as Phillips had hoped, it did represent the fullest implementation of the organic concept.

7

Metropolitan Community to Fragmented Metropolis, 1920-1940

When Phillips left Cincinnati, he did not abandon the social unit idea. The National Social Unit Organization remained intact, and Phillips began to work closely with the NSUO in New York City to promote the establishment of more social-unit-style community organizations. Accordingly, the NSUO entered into an agreement with the New York Community Councils (NYCC) in late 1919 and laid plans to establish another social unit laboratory. But within little more than a year both the NSUO and the NYCC disbanded. Although Phillips continued to champion the social unit theory of organization for another quarter century, he did so in a changed environment.

After 1920, a theory of organization that portrayed the urban environment as "a cluster of interlacing communities"[1] and stressed the organization of these communities to perfect their interaction with one another and with the city as a whole, no longer found a receptive public. A new image of the urban community, believed to be more appropriate to the post–World War I city, had emerged. As the studies of Chicago sociologists Robert Park, Harvey Zorbaugh, and Ernest Burgess and the activities organizer Saul Alinsky indicate, Americans thought of the city less as a whole composed of interdependent parts and more as a collection of fragments or disparate groups. In this context, community organization increasingly focused on strategies of advocacy and competition for scarce resources rather than a civic consciousness that identified with and yet transcended the local community and incorporated it into the whole American experience.

At the final session of the National Social Unit Conference in Cincinnati, Phillips announced his resignation from the Mohawk-Brighton Social Unit Organization and indicated that he planned to return to New York City to study the community organization movement and perfect the operation of the social unit theory of organization.[2] By mid-November, Phillips had reestablished himself in New York City and on December 8, 1919, Phillips and the NSUO announced that the NSUO had merged with the New York Community Councils "to bring about a unification of the scattered energies of the nation and to preserve the great national unity developed in America during the war." The NYCC was to be part of the NSUO demonstration in community organization following the tenets of the social unit theory of organization.[3]

The New York Community Councils were an outgrowth of the community council program set up during World War I by the Council of National Defense. Congress created the Council of National Defense, which included the secretaries of war, navy, interior, agriculture, commerce, labor, and seven civilians, after the outbreak of World War I to aid in the mobilization of the nation's resources. The council organized state, county, and city councils "so that the channels of communication between the government and the people would be more complete."[4] On the city level, the council, with the assistance of the U.S. Bureau of Education, fostered the creation of numerous community councils "to provide opportunities by which through continuous team work within the neighborhood people could gradually assume some responsibility for the prosecution of the war." The community councils, as envisaged by the Council of National Defense, were to assist the war-related financial programs, to rehabilitate returning soldiers, to provide neighborly home service to the families of the men on the front, and to encourage residents to participate in hospital volunteer work.[5]

By September 1918, barely six months after the formation of the Council of National Defense's Community Councils of National Defense (CCND), membership in the CCND stood at approximately 1.25 million. Most municipal governments in large American cities eagerly embraced the community council plan, and New York City was no exception. Shortly after the decision to create the CCND, the Mayor's Committee on Defense established an executive committee on community councils and coordination of war work under the co-chairmanship of George Gordon Battle, a New York City lawyer, and Albert Shiels, the former director of the Division of Reference and Research of the New York City Department of Education. Under their direction, community councils were formed throughout the city and were given official status by the Executive Committee on Community Councils and Coordination of War Work. After a number of these local councils were organized, the executive committee set up a city advisory committee to provide technical services to the various neighborhood councils and, when necessary, "to mediate between the local organization of people and government."[6]

According to the executive committee, the New York City CCND sought to "combine the good features of a federation of agencies and a community organization in which all citizens have membership."[7] Centered in neighborhood schools that carried the slogan, "Every Schoolhouse a Community Capital and Every Community a Little Democracy," the community councils in New York City were governed by neighborhood boards comprised of representatives from all the social and civic agencies active in the area and neighborhood citizens chosen by the residents "to express the will of the neighborhood to the social and civic 'experts.' "[8] These local community councils then were related to the city as a whole in a "city parliament" in which the representatives of the citizens and the social and civic agencies discussed important citywide issues.[9]

Following the armistice, the Mayor's Committee on Defense, after numerous consultations with the Executive Committee on Community Councils and Coordination of War Work and the CCND's City Parliament, recommended that the community council program continue and adjust its activities "to reflect peacetime issues."[10] The mayor's committee urged the CCND of New York City to establish permanent councils to advance both neighborhood and city welfare. Accordingly, in the winter of 1918, the CCND reorganized under the name of the New York Community Councils and attempted to adjust

its programs to promote the peacetime concerns of the citizens of
New York City.[11]

During the summer of 1919 the leadership of the NSUO, interested in expanding its social unit demonstration, contacted the executives of the New York Community Councils. The NSUO felt that
the work of the NYCC demonstrated the council's "ability to awaken
civic interest, to increase neighborliness, and to promote cooperative
endeavor." However, a limited budget hampered the NYCC in the
execution of its programs. With the MBSUO experiment drawing to a
close, the NSUO decided to invest in the work of the NYCC to help
"strengthen and intensify the work of the New York Community
Councils and to further its [the NSUO's] own research in the principles and practices of community organization."[12]

On December 2, 1919, the executives of the NSUO and the NYCC
announced that the two organizations had merged "to bring about a
unification of the scattered energies of the nation and to preserve the
great national unity which was developed in this country during the
war." With the merger, the leadership of both organizations,
according to George Gordon Battle of the NYCC and Mrs. Charles
Tiffany of the NSUO, hoped to centralize all "the major efforts in New
York City touching on community organization."[13] Under the terms
of the affiliation contract, signed by Albert Shiels of the NYCC and
Phillips, the two organizations pledged to foster "all efforts to
organize people democratically in local communities" throughout the
city of New York. The actual administration of the entire operation lay
in the hands of the NYCC, with the NSUO serving in an advisory
capacity. As an advisor, the NSUO agreed to conduct on behalf of the
NYCC, "a continuous program of education," during which the
NSUO would explain the aims, principles, and methods of community organization to the people of New York City and attempt to raise
enough money to support the programs of the local councils.[14]

On December 23, 1919, soon after the announcement of the
merger, members of the NSUO and the NYCC[15] met together at the
Cosmopolitan Club to set up their first major program. They decided
to focus first on a fund-raising campaign to finance the work of the
local community councils. Once the fund-raising campaign was under way, the NSUO planned to offer a lecture series on the fundamental principles of community councils and on the benefits to be gained
from banding together in neighborhood units.[16]

The community council organization that the NSUO allied with was similar to that of the social unit organization. Like the social unit organization, the peacetime councils sponsored by the NYCC wanted to foster a working relationship between citizens and specialists in the neighborhood and in the city. These councils—voluntary associations composed of neighborhood residents and representatives from agencies active in the neighborhood—were to meet frequently to discuss neighborhood problems. Once the members of the council had identified needs to be met, the councils were authorized to appoint special committees to seek solutions for neighborhood problems. A citywide organization of representatives from all the city's community councils and social welfare agencies maintained a staff of specialists to supplement the special committees set up by the various councils.[17] The major difference between the NYCC method of organization and that of the social unit plan was the absence of a definite organizational structure in the NYCC scheme. A council was considered organized if there was citizen participation on the neighborhood level. The social unit organization, on the other hand, had a "definite and detailed scheme of organization," one that was designed to effect the continuous interaction between citizen and specialist.[18] The NSUO hoped, by using the experience gained in Cincinnati, to provide "greater definiteness in organization" in the operation of the NYCC and to make the local councils "sound neighborhood organizations."[19]

The proposed budget reflected the division of activities between the NSUO and the NYCC. The budget divided the programs of the NSUO and the NYCC into two general areas—central administration and field service. Central administration included general administration, clerical help, a division of information and research, and a speaker's bureau. Field service covered all the organizers for the various councils and the organizers' secretaries. Most of the money for the projects, the headquarters, and the administrative staff came from the NSUO.[20]

But the plans of the NSUO and the NYCC never got off the ground. After a flurry of cooperative activity immediately following the merger, the two groups began to bicker. From late January 1920 to the eventual dissolution of the two organizations approximately one year later, the NSUO and the NYCC fought over the proposed budget, the repayment of an earlier loan given to the NYCC by the

NSUO, and the actual programs to be undertaken. No financial campaign was ever launched, and the NSUO did not begin its promised "educational campaign about community organization."[21]

The two organizations cooperated on only one project—Neighbors' Day on June 14, 1920. Neighbors' Day, "a national get together to promote community organization,"[22] was the outcome of a conference on community organization held in Washington, D.C., on March 20, 1920. At this meeting, called by Franklin K. Lane, former secretary of the interior and honorary president of the National Social Unit Organization, representatives from municipal governments, community organizations, labor and church groups, and social welfare agencies met to discuss the state of community organization in the United States. Those attending the conference repeatedly stressed the importance of community organization "in bringing people together to discuss needs and to begin to identify those needs to be met." At the conclusion of the conference, the participants voted to sponsor a Neighbors' Day on June 14, 1920, to promote the idea of community organization.[23]

In May the NSUO and the NYCC sponsored a follow-up conference in New York City to make final arrangements for the city's Neighbors' Day celebration. Representatives of a number of New York City civic, neighborhood, social, and political organizations discussed plans for programs to "highlight the need and the importance of preserving national unity through neighborhood organization."[24]

On June 14, 1920, New Yorkers celebrated Neighbors' Day. For two days before, the NSUO sponsored pageants, athletic events, tableaux, flag drills, baby parades, neighborhood dinners, community sings, and speeches in neighborhoods all across New York City. On Neighbors' Day itself the NSUO and the NYCC held a town meeting in Central Park on community organization in New York City. "All-in-all," according to a contemporary account, "Neighbors' Day was a success."[25]

After this show of cooperation and community spirit, the agreement between the NYCC amd the NSUO completely disintegrated. In late June the NYCC voted to go out of existence as soon as all outstanding bills and salaries were paid and "its financial relations with the NSUO were adjusted." On December 3, 1920, the executive committee of the NYCC formally voted to recognize a "state of indebtedness to the NSUO" that amounted to $30,521.93. The committee announced that it would try to pay off the NSUO, but the NYCC failed to secure the money. In March 1921 a brief note on the financial page of the *New York Times* reported that the NSUO had been placed in receivership to satisfy outstanding debts. An application for the appointment of a receiver for the NSUO was made in the New York Supreme Court by William C. Ewing on behalf of himself and other creditors. Ewing and the creditors contended that the operation of the NSUO had been suspended owing many thousands of dollars for salaries, wages, and supplies. The complainants alleged that the NSUO held no tangible assets, but that "solvent persons with the ability to pay" could provide the necessary $30,000 to satisfy the creditors. The office of the NSUO denied that it had suspended operation and declined to discuss the allegations of its inability to cover its debts. On this brief note the NSUO passed into history.[26]

With the dissolution of the NSUO, Phillips retired.[27] After his departure from Cincinnati and the Mohawk-Brighton Social Unit Organization, Phillips had begun to work on a manuscript which was to "put forth the underlying principles of the social unit idea."[28] Following the collapse of the NSUO, Phillips continued to work on his manuscript, which was eventually published in 1940 as *Adventuring for Democracy*. It was a discussion of the events leading up to the establishment of the MBSUO, the MBSUO experiment, and the social unit theory of organization. He followed this book with a series of unpublished manuscripts, all of which are variations on the material in *Adventuring for Democracy*.

Phillips did not spend all his remaining years writing, although he never again directed a demonstration. Supported for the most part by the generosity of friends and sympathizers, Phillips began to search for a way to make social units self-supporting. In the mid-1920s he came up with a vague plan based on profits to be derived from a cooperative milk production scheme to finance the operation of a social unit. He interested a number of people in his scheme, and with the help of Harvey W. Wiley, originator of the federal pure food laws, and Frederick M. Feiker, director of the American Engineering Council, formed the Consumers' and Producers' Association "to study the organization of milk cooperatives and the availability of useable profits." However, the first meeting of the Consumers' and Producers' Association was held a month after the stock market crash of 1929, and the onslaught of the Great Depression killed the fledgling organization.

Following the collapse of the Consumers' and Producers' Association, Phillips worked briefly for the Social Science Research Council. In the early 1930s Wesley C. Mitchell, the outgoing council president and a good friend of Phillips, invited Phillips to conduct a survey for the Social Science Research Council. In the ensuing report, entitled "A Criteria for Judging How the National Income Was Being Spent," Phillips emphasized the "role which organized Social Units, if combined with larger and larger units of population," could play in conveying information concerning the needs of American consumers. Although his study failed to interest the members of the Social Science Research Council, it inspired him to set up a new social unit organization.

Phillips decided that he wanted to establish a new organization that would "prove the ability of people in organized Social Units to support their own Health and Social activities through savings in distribution (which) they could achieve through concerted community-buying, and without affecting the profits of distributors and producers." He contacted a number of his old supporters who in turn interested new people in supporting the formation of an organization to "research social units and profits." In 1945 one hundred individuals joined Phillips in forming the Social Unit Institute, a nonprofit research and educational organization. The early programs of the institute centered on sporadic attempts "to investigate the causes of disunity among Americans and to develop a more detailed social unit program to promote unity in national life." The institute, like the NSUO, rested on the premise that every level of human organization, such as the neighborhood, the city, and the state, represented a unitary and integrated structure that operated in a complementary manner to form a larger whole.

Like the NSUO and the Consumers' and Producers' Association, the Social Unit Institute ceased to function. By the beginning of the 1950s, it was no more than a letterhead organization. While Phillips continued to write about the social unit theory of organization and its application for the next fifteen years or so, he did not organize another group. But he remained cheerful to the end and constant in his belief that social units could remake America into an organic democracy.[29]

The dissolution of the National Social Unit Organization and the New York Community Councils in 1921 represented more than just the end of an experiment; it marked the beginning of a major shift in urban definition and in the practice of community organization. The social unit organization illustrated, according to social-welfare historian Roy Lubove, "community organization in the years when its exponents believed literally in the possibility of a social harmony that transcended the fragmentation of American life."[30] Guided by their belief in the conception of interdependence, Phillips and his contemporaries possessed both a definition of urban form and a prescription for community action. Their city was the city of interdependence—an organic structure composed of an interdependent system of differentiated but complementary parts. As "a cluster of interlacing communities," each part or neighborhood simultaneously retained its "own vital ways of expression and action" and worked with all other sections of the city to create, as Robert A. Woods suggested, "the municipality which shall render the fullest service through the most spirited participation of its citizens."[31]

Community organization within the framework of the organic city rested on two basic premises: the wholeness of the environment and the importance of the neighborhood in nation-building. Organizational activities focused on strategies to facilitate communication between the different sections of the city to harmonize local community volition with the collective well-being of the city.[32] With the perfection of intracity cooperation, proponents of the organic city envisioned the duplication of such interaction on the state and national levels. At every juncture, community organizers stressed the totality of the world around them, and their activities were designed to further the interaction among all the parts of the whole.

Of all the plans to organize communities during the first two decades of the twentieth century, Phillips's social unit plan represents the most celebrated attempt to facilitate communication and cooperation between the interlacing communities comprising the city—despite the fact that the experimentation period proved too short to yield conclusive results. In very few communities were plans and policies so painstakingly submitted in advance to neighborhood residents. Decisions relating to MBSUO activities rested on neighborhood understanding and approval. The residents of Mohawk-Brighton studied some of their own problems, determined community needs, and conducted the proposed services themselves. The MBSUO stimulated local initiative so that as the life of the unit progressed the establishment of some services such as prenatal care and generalized nursing were not initiated by the founders of the plan.[33]

The key to the unit's success in stimulating local initiative and in widening participation in neighborhood decision-making were the block organizations. These organizations brought residents together, imbued them with a sense of common purpose, and included them in the decision-making process. The block workers developed the ability to diagnose local needs and to assist in the implementation of neighborhood programs.[34] Overall, because of the block representation system, residents became planners as well as recipients of neighborhood programs.

In addition to its concern with citizen participation, the social unit plan reflected the interest of early twentieth century social thinkers in cooperation between citizens and specialists. The MBSUO represented "a conscious effort on the part of the community to control its affairs democratically and to secure the highest service from its specialists, organizations, agencies, and institutions by means of recognized interrelatedness."[35] Within the confines of the neighborhood, interaction between citizens and specialists illustrated their joint responsibility in discerning local needs and then meeting those needs through consultation and cooperation.[36]

In operation, however, the social unit fell short of success. Various components of the organization failed to function properly. The block councils, for example, while supportive, did not cooperate with the block workers in a regular fashion. The councils rarely assumed responsibility for carrying out MBSUO policies. As a result, many block workers bypassed the councils and dealt directly with the residents of their blocks and with the larger MBSUO structure. Many councils, once they realized that the block workers would take care of everything, ceased to function altogether. On the occupational side, not all the groups in the MBSUO were as integrated into the organizational structure as the physicians, nurses, and social workers.

Periodically, the General Council lacked "unifying force in the formation of and execution of policies." In addition, since Phillips did not spend the entire three years in Cincinnati, the lack of an ever-present executive to coordinate and direct the local activities hindered the operation of the unit to some extent. Finally, the unit organization failed to sustain itself financially.[37]

Despite organizational malfunctions and controversies, the social unit organization demonstrated that a neighborhood could be organized to identify and resolve local needs. Residents discovered neighborhood problems and participated in the solution of those problems. The social unit organization stands as a bold effort to achieve neighborhood organization through the nurturing of the organic relationship believed to exist between citizen and specialist. And it attempted to foster a civic consciousness that identified with and yet transcended the neighborhood and worked directly into the fabric of American society.

During the first two decades of the twentieth century, the notion of the city as an organism captured the attention of urban analysts because of the apparent balance between the centripetal and centrifugal forces at work in the modern city. In this context it seemed possible to talk about an urban form "composed of differentiated parts which could work together to form a large viable whole."[38] This cohesion for civic progress ensured that localism did not separate and segregate the parts of the city from the greater civic structure of the urban community. By the mid-1920s, however, the balance between the unifying and decentralizing forces at work in the city collapsed as the forces of disunion and separatism overwhelmed the forces of union. As the centrifugal forces gained ascendancy, the tendency toward social and economic segregation, sparked by the demise of the walking city, intensified[39] and produced an urban form characterized by particularism rather than by interaction.

During the decade immediately following World War I, American communities appeared to move toward distinct ethnic, socioeconomic, and racial patterns of segregation far more pronounced than those existing before the war. Extensive highway development, the increasingly widespread use of the automobile, and the dispersion of industrial sites throughout the city both facilitated and encouraged the outward migration of residents and places of work that had begun with the introduction of mass transit in American cities during the nineteenth century.

The migration of significant numbers of blacks and southern whites to northern cities during the war years flooded inner-city areas and pushed the current residents out of central city neighborhoods into other residential areas. As these residents were displaced, they reacted negatively to those groups disrupting their world. Both racial and ethnic communities experienced turmoil, and in response, most urban groups attempted to segregate themselves from the disruptive elements of the urban environment. The combination of group antagonism and industrial and residential dispersion furthered by the automobile resulted in the "broad pattern of segregation and subcommunity formation"[40] that has characterized American urban areas up to the present.[41] Neighborhoods, in this context, were "natural areas"—communities defined in terms of the "common experiences of the group" that evoked an image of "territorial parochialism" rather than one of interconnected units within a larger whole.[42]

One of the earliest manifestations of the new view of the neighborhood and the city can be found in the work of Roderick D. McKenzie. In *The Neighborhood: A Study of Local Life in the City of Columbus, Ohio*,[43] McKenzie argued that neighborhoods were fragmented by "economic, racial, and cultural factors" and that these factors provided the only points of identification for neighborhood residents. When neighborhood groups organized, McKenzie found, they generally sought to protect the community from outside influences or groups. Nonetheless, neighborhood planning focused on the demarcation of an identifiable physical unit could allow the neighborhood to serve as the basis for delivery of various municipal services while enhancing local solidarity.[44] Despite his emphasis on neighborhood parochialism, McKenzie recognized neighborhoods as part of a large metropolitan structure. The city to McKenzie was an organism "essentially pluralistic in its composition, as much the product of competition as of cooperation."[45]

Fellow Chicago sociologist Harvey W. Zorbaugh agreed with McKenzie that neighborhoods were parochial, but unlike McKenzie, whose work represents a transitional piece, Zorbaugh portrayed neighborhoods as islands apart from the larger city. Little hope exists in his work, *The Gold Coast and the Slum,* for any positive neighborhood-city interaction. Zorbaugh based his conclusions on an examination of the experiences of one of Chicago's Community Councils of National Defense organized in an area composed of the Gold Coast and a vast slum district known as the Near North Side. After the war, caught up in a wave of enthusiasm over the "promises of community organization," this Chicago CCND reorganized into a peacetime venture under the name of the Lower North Community Council (LNCC). The aim of this council, according to Harvey Zorbaugh, was to coordinate the activities of all agencies in this area of the city, to ameliorate the condition of the Near North Side, "to cultivate a spirit of neighborliness," and to foster "the latent community of interest" believed to exist among the varied racial, ethnic, and socioeconomic groups living in the area served by the council.[46]

But once the work got under way and settled into a routine, interest in the council dropped, attendance dwindled, and groups went their own ways. The council became a shell of its former self. By 1921 it had all but disbanded, although a small group of organizers determinedly kept the council going. For a while the council drifted aimlessly and accomplished little. In 1922, however, Zorbaugh reported, the council became involved in two local controversies that marked a turning point in the history of the LNCC and fostered "a totally different conception of community organization."

The first controversy centered on the attempt to install a bathhouse on a residential street in the area, and the second revolved around the attempts of a group of property owners along Lake Shore Drive to change a provision in a zoning ordinance. In both cases, those living in the area served by the council found themselves pitted against each other. As a result of these experiences, the council concluded that it was impossible to champion the wishes of a whole area and reexamined its role in the community. Zorbaugh reported that council members rejected the notion of a whole area and "shed their idealistic view of community life." As a result of this reevaluation, council members began to describe the area as a conglomeration of groups—interested not in the well-being of the community at large but in the satisfaction of each group's particular interest. Each group attempted to manipulate the other to facilitate its own interests,[47] and community organizers emphasized advocacy and competition instead of cooperation.

Generalizing from his study of the Lower North Community Council, Zorbaugh stressed that traditional theories, which looked at the urban environment in terms of "hypothetical common interests and needs," failed to confront the realities of urban life. Neighborhood residents, Zorbaugh found, wished to protect their own interests rather than work for the interests of the community at large.[48] Although Zorbaugh continued to describe the city as an organism, he defined organism very differently than did his pre-1920 counterparts and his fellow sociologist McKenzie. Zorbaugh agreed with McKenzie that the city was pluralistic in its composition. Unlike McKenzie, however, he did not find evidence of cooperation. Instead, he argued that the urban community was composed of "mosaics of little cultural worlds" in which most areas ignored rather than cooperated with the larger society of which they were a part.[49]

The new definition of the city as a pluralistic structure reflected the attempt of those interested in the city to understand the dynamics of the urban environment of the two decades following World War I. This new definition of the city encouraged the formulation of a distinct philosophy of community organization and the development of a particular set of organizing techniques. Based on their acceptance of a pluralistic urban environment, organizers after 1920 were less interested in promoting cooperative action within a neighborhood and between neighborhoods. Instead, organizers such as Saul Alinsky and the activists involved in the New York Citywide Tenants' Council mobilized local residents around issue-oriented programs through which city residents could better confront the realities that shaped their lives.[50] In the context of the pluralistic metropolis, these organizers emphasized advocacy and competition for scarce resources. As a result, community organizing after 1920 increasingly fostered separatism rather than unity within a larger metropolitan community.

Urban definition and the principles and practices of community organization have continued to shift as the urban environment has changed in the years since 1940. As city form and structure have altered, contemporaries have developed new definitions to describe more accurately the urban community they saw about them. On the basis of these definitions, men and women active in urban affairs during these years devised programs to deal with the perceived realities of urban life. As during the first two decades of the twentieth century, the interaction between definition and action has provided both a basis for understanding urban environment and a prescription for activities to better that environment.

Notes

Introduction

1. Ernest C. Burgess, ed., *The Urban Community* (Chicago: Univ. of Chicago Press, 1926), viii.

2. Studies particularly helpful in thinking through this material include John Brewer, *Party Ideology and Popular Politics at the Accession of George III* (Cambridge: Cambridge Univ. Press, 1976); Thomas Bender, *Community and Social Change in America* (New Brunswick, N.J.: Rutgers Univ. Press, 1978); Zane L. Miller, *Suburb: Neighborhood and Community in Forest Park, Ohio, 1935-1976* (Knoxville: Univ. of Tennessee Press, 1981); Philip Abrams, "History, Sociology, Historical Sociology," *Past and Present* 87 (May 1980): 3-16.

3. Milton Kotler, "The Purpose of Neighborhood Power," *South Atlantic Urban Studies* 4 (1979): 29.

4. The terms *community organization* and *neighborhood organization*, from the very beginning of popular usage, have meant different things to different people. Because these terms have been used in so many different contexts, they have acquired decidedly ambiguous meanings. For the purposes of this study, the terms will be used interchangeably. They refer to organizing efforts designed to facilitate the development of local constituencies and formulation of strategies of action in specific geographic areas of cities. Although still diverse in the practices employed and in the beliefs held, organizational activities share three common elements. First, they all focus on the geographic community rather than on single-issue concerns. Second, they all hope to involve neighborhood residents in both the planning and implementation of local activities. And, third, they all share a commitment, however vaguely defined, not only to provide fuller services, but also to serve as agents of potential social change.

5. Robert Fisher, "Community Organization in Historical Perspective: A Typology," *The Houston Review* 4 (Summer 1982): 78-79.

6. Wilbur C. Phillips, *Adventuring for Democracy* (New York: Social Unit Press, 1940), 6-9; Wilbur C. Phillips, Birth Affidavit, March 22, 1966, Wilbur C. Phillips Papers, Social Welfare History Archives Center, Univ. of Minnesota, Minneapolis, Minn. (hereafter cited as Phillips Papers); Phillips Genealogy, Phillips Papers; Wilbur

C. Phillips to Raymond and Arthur, January 1, 1955, Phillips Papers; Harvard College, *Class of 1904*, Third Report, June 1914, 388.

7. Samuel Eliot Morrison, ed., *The Development of Harvard University Since the Inauguration of President Eliot 1869-1929* (Cambridge, Mass.: Harvard Univ. Press, 1930), xlv-xlvi; Laurence R. Vesey, *The Emergence of the Modern University* (Chicago: Univ. of Chicago Press, 1965), 272.

8. Phillips, *Adventuring*, 3-5, 9-15.

9. Miller, *Suburb*, xiii-xvi.

1. Neighborhood in the Organic City

Some of the material in this and subsequent chapters was originally published in Patricia Mooney Melvin, "A Cluster of Interlacing Communities: The Cincinnati Social Unit Plan and Neighborhood Organization, 1900-1920," in *Community Organization for Urban Social Change: A Historical Perspective*," ed. Robert Fisher and Peter Romanofsky (Westport, Conn.: Greenwood, 1981). Copyright 1981 by Robert Fisher and Peter Romanofsky. Used by permission of the publisher.

1. Arthur Mann, *The One and the Many: Reflections on the American Identity* (Chicago: Univ. of Chicago Press, 1979), 47, 55.

2. Ibid., 5-6, 98.

3. John Higham, *Strangers in the Land: Patterns of American Nativism, 1860-1925* (New York: Atheneum, 1971), 109.

4. Henry D. Shapiro, *Appalachia on Our Mind: The Southern Mountains and Mountaineers in the American Consciousness, 1870-1920* (Chapel Hill: Univ. of North Carolina Press, 1978), xi; Mann, *One and Many*, 95.

5. U.S. Bureau of the Census, *Historical Statistics of the United States, Colonial Times to 1970*, Bicentennial edition, vol. 1 (Washington, D.C.: Government Printing Office, 1975), 14.

6. Shapiro, *Appalachia*, xi; Higham, *Strangers*, 38-39; William Gaymon and John R. Garrett, "A Blueprint for a Pluralistic Society," *Journal of Ethnic Studies* 3 (1975): 59.

7. For a fuller discussion of the notion of a distended society, see Robert H. Wiebe, *The Search for Order, 1877-1920* (New York: Hill and Wang, 1967); David J. Russo, *Families and Communities: A New View of American History* (Nashville: Amer. Assn. for State and Local History, 1974), 292; David P. Thelen, *The New Citizenship: Origins of Progressivism in Wisconsin, 1885-1900* (Columbia: Univ. of Missouri Press, 1972), 56.

8. Shapiro, *Appalachia*, xi.

9. Within their description of reality, men and women define problems and think about, argue about, and act on those problems. As Henry Shapiro has argued, the need to understand the world "functions in a problem solving" manner. People, according to Shapiro, "acknowledge a dilemma explicitly, or more often implicitly, by attempting to deal with it." They attempt to restore any perceived lack of harmony between the way the world is and the way they believe the world should be. This harmonizing process has been called cognitive dissonance by Leon Festinger; Shapiro, in *Appalachia on Our Mind*, has analyzed Festinger's theory and illustrated its usefulness in understand-

ing what Thomas Bender has described as the "social framework of intellectual life."
    Those men and women who found that their notions about urban life failed to
correspond with the perceived actualities of urban life sought a means to harmonize the
situation. In so doing, these Americans "undertook to deal with the disparities they
recognized between their expectations and their experience by some form of thought."
Their ideas, poised between consciousness and reality, as representations of reality,
gave meaning to the world, through a process of both definition and action. Shapiro,
Appalachia, xvi-xviii; Leon Festinger, *A Theory of Cognitive Dissonance* (Stanford:
Stanford Univ. Press, 1957), 1-18; Rush Welter, "On Studying the National Mind," in
New Directions in Intellectual History, ed. John Higham and Paul K. Conkin (Bal-
timore: Johns Hopkins Univ. Press, 1979), 69; Gordon S. Wood, "Intellectual History
and the Social Sciences," in *New Directions*, ed. Higham and Conkin, 35.
    10. Jean B. Quandt, *From the Small Town to the Great Community: The Social
Thought of Progressive Intellectuals* (New Brunswick, N.J.: Rutgers Univ. Press, 1970),
passim; A.H. Lloyd, "The Organic Theory of Society," *American Journal of Sociology* 6
(March 1901): 577.
    11. Quandt, *Small Town*, 14, 27-28.
    12. Sidney Fine, *Laissez-Faire and the General Welfare State: A Study of Conflict
in American Thought, 1865-1901* (Ann Arbor: Univ. of Michigan Press, 1956), 41-43;
Robert C. Bannister, *Social Darwinism: Science and Myth in Anglo-American Social
Thought* (Philadelphia: Temple Univ. Press, 1979), 61-76.
    13. Quandt, *Small Town*, 86.
    14. Late nineteenth century men and women helped satisfy their desire for whole-
ness or oneness in a seemingly fragmented world by adopting metaphors or analogies.
In the process of redefining the environment to fashion a world view compatible with
their conception of the world, these men and women adopted a particular vocabulary to
talk about their ideas. Through the use of analogies and metaphors they attempted to
make clear the interrelationship between their theoretical formulations and their
descriptive interpretations of their conceptions. In other words, the symbols they
chose—the descriptive interpretations—provide the key to understanding their theoretical formulations. An examination of their symbolic structures for ordering the world
can reveal, according to Thomas Bender, "the ways in which specific ideas or ways of
thinking develop, gain hegemony or lose it, and are used in a particular setting." The
ideas are not divorced from reality, as if they were "detached causes or effects," but
rather the ideas simultaneously define that reality and create it by providing the
structure through which people order their world. Wood, "Intellectual," 31-35;
Thomas Bender, "The Culture of Intellectual Life: The City and the Professions," in
New Directions, ed. Higham and Conkin, 191; Shapiro, *Appalachia*, xvi-xvii; Clifford
Geertz, *The Interpretation of Cultures* (New York: Basic Books, 1973), 27-30; Thomas
Bender, *Towards an Urban Vision: Ideas and Institutions in Nineteenth Century
America* (Lexington: Univ. Press of Kentucky, 1975), ix-x; James Fernandez, "Persua-
sions and Performances: Of the Beast in Everybody . . . and the Metaphors of Every-
man," in *Myth, Symbol, and Culture*, ed. Clifford Geertz (New York: W.W. Norton and
Co., 1971), 41-42.
    15. Geertz, *Interpretation*, 27; Robert Bremner, *From the Depths: The Discovery
of Poverty in the United States* (New York: New York Univ. Press, 1956), 26; Robert A.

Woods, "The University Settlement Idea," in *Philanthropy and Social Problems*, ed. Henry C. Adams (New York: Thomas Y. Crowell and Co., 1893), 59. See also Stow Persons, *American Minds: A History of Ideas* (New York: Henry Holt and Co., 1958), 225-29; Merle Curti, *The Growth of American Thought* (New York: Harper and Row, 1964), 540-63; Stow Persons, ed., *Evolutionary Thought in America* (New Haven: Yale Univ. Press, 1950); Richard Hofstadter, *Social Darwinism in American Thought* (Boston: Beacon Press, 1955); Fine, *Laissez-Faire*; Bannister, *Social Darwinism*.

   16. Henry C. Adams, ed., *Philanthropy and Social Progress* (New York: Thomas Y. Crowell and Co., 1893), xi.

   17. Woods, "University Settlement," 58.

   18. Josiah Strong, *The Twentieth Century City* (New York: Baker and Taylor Co., 1898; reprint ed., New York: Arno Press, 1970), 117, 123-24, 173-74.

   19. M.P. Follett, *The New State: Group Organization, the Solution of Popular Government*, 2d ed. (New York: Longmans, Green and Co., 1923), 715.

   20. Edward T. Devine, "Some Elementary Definitions," *Charities*, June 4, 1904, 506; Wilbur C. Urban, "The Nature of Community, A Defense of Philosophical Orthodoxy," *Journal of Philosophy, Psychology and Scientific Methods* 16 (December 1919): 714-15; Herbert Croly, *The Promise of American Life* (New York: Macmillan Co., 1909; reprint ed., Cambridge, Mass.: Belknap Press, 1965), 176; Frederic Howe, *The City, The Hope of Democracy* (New York: C. Scribner's Sons, 1905), 294; Charles Horton Cooley, *Social Organization: A Study of the Larger Mind* (New York: C. Scribner's Sons, 1909), 9.

   21. Anselm L. Strauss, *Images of the American City* (New York: Free Press, 1961), 142; see also Kevin Lynch, *The Image of the City* (Cambridge, Mass.: Technology Press and Harvard Univ. Press, 1960), passim; Scott Greer, *The Emerging City: Myth and Reality* (New York: Free Press, 1962), 21; Blaine A. Brownell, *The Urban Ethos in the South 1920-1930* (Baton Rouge: Louisiana State Univ. Press, 1975), 39-45.

   22. Zane L. Miller, "Society, Abundance, and American Urban History," *Journal of Urban History* 4 (February 1978): 142.

   23. Robert A. Woods, "The City and Its Local Community," in *The Neighborhood in Nation-Building*, ed. Robert A. Woods (Boston: Houghton Mifflin, 1923; reprint ed., New York: Arno Press, 1970), 196.

   24. Jon C. Teaford, *City and Suburb: The Political Fragmentation of Metropolitan America, 1850-1970* (Baltimore: Johns Hopkins Univ. Press, 1979), 10-11; see also Mark Foster, *From Streetcar to Superhighway: American City Planners and Urban Transportation, 1900-1940* (Philadelphia: Temple Univ. Press, 1981), 11, 14-15; Joel A. Tarr, *Transportation and Changing Spatial Patterns in Pittsburgh, 1870-1934* (Chicago: Public Works Historical Society, 1978), 1-4; Sam Bass Warner, Jr., *Streetcar Suburbs: The Process of Growth in Boston, 1870-1900*, 2d ed. (Cambridge, Mass.: Harvard Univ. Press, 1978), 15, 46; Gideon J. Sjoberg, "The Pre-Industrial City, Past and Present," *American Journal of Sociology* 60 (January 1955): 438-45; Jon C. Teaford, *The Municipal Revolution in America: Origins of Modern City Government, 1650-1825* (Chicago: Univ of Chicago Press, 1975), passim; Clay McShane, *Technology and Reform: Street Railways and the Growth of Milwaukee, 1887-1900* (Madison: State Historical Society of Wisconsin, 1974), passim.

   25. Tarr, *Transportation*, 1, 4, 13; Joel A. Tarr, "From City to Suburb: The 'Moral'

Influence of Transportation Technology," in *American Urban History: An Interpretative Reader with Commentaries*, ed. Alexander B. Callow, 2d ed. (New York: Oxford Univ. Press, 1973), 203; Warner, *Streetcars*, passim; George Rogers Taylor, "The Beginnings of Mass Transportation in Urban America: Part I," *Smithsonian Journal of History* (Summer 1966): 35-50; George Rogers Clark, "The Beginnings of Mass Transportation in Urban America: Part II," *Smithsonian Journal of History* (Autumn 1966): 31-54.

26. Zane L. Miller, "The Role and Concept in Neighborhood in American Cities," typescript, August 11, 1978, 6; Mark Goldman, "Buffalo's Black Rock: A Neighborhood and the City," *Journal of Urban History* 5 (August 1979): 447-68; Tarr, "City," 203; George M. Smerk, "The Streetcar: Shaper of American Cities," *Traffic Quarterly* 21 (October 1967): 572-75.

27. Teaford, *City*, 39.

28. Ibid.

29. Ibid., 5-10; Tarr, *Transportation*, 1, 4, 13; Warner, *Streetcars*, passim; Tarr, "City," 203.

30. Zane L. Miller, "Neighborhood, Community and the Contemporary Metropolitan Crisis," in *Ohio in Century Three: Quality of Life*, ed. Ralph L. Pearson, Ohio American Revolution Bicentennial Conference Series, no. 6 (Columbus: Ohio Historical Society, 1977), 21; Goldman, "Buffalo," 467. The 1880 Census reports on cities reflect a similar view of society. In these reports society was defined as a unit composed of discrete groups and parts that contributed in some way to the larger social whole. See Zane L. Miller, "The Rise of the City," typescript, 1980.

31. Miller, "Neighborhood," 20-21; Miller, "Role," 3.

32. Arthur C. Holden, *The Settlement Idea: A Vision of Social Justice* (New York: Macmillan Co., 1922; reprint ed., New York: Arno Press, 1970), 43.

33. Robert A. Woods, "University Settlements as Laboratories in Social Science," in *The Neighborhood*, ed. Woods, 43.

34. Robert A. Woods, "The Neighborhood and the Nation," *Proceedings of the National Conference of Charities and Corrections*, vol. 36 (Buffalo, 1909), 102; Robert A. Woods, "The Recovery of the Parish," in *The Neighborhood*, ed. Woods, 135.

35. Robert A. Woods, "City and Community Life," p. 4, unpublished ms., in Robert A. Woods Papers, Houghton Library, Harvard Univ. (hereafter cited as Woods Papers).

36. Robert A. Woods, "The Neighborhood in Social Reconstruction," *American Journal of Sociology* 19 (March 1914): 579.

37. Woods, "Settlements as Laboratories," 43; Woods, "Recovery," 135.

38. Woods, "Neighborhood," 101-6; Woods, "Settlements as Laboratories," 43; Woods, "University Settlement," 87; Don S. Kirschner, "The Ambiguous Legacy: Social Justice and Social Control in the Progressive Era," *Historical Reflections* 2 (Summer 1975): 84-85; Robert A. Woods, "Success of the Settlement as a Means of Improving a Neighborhood," *Charities*, September 6, 1902, 225; South End House, *Annual Report*, 1908, 5, Woods Papers; South End House, *Annual Report*, 1909, 5, Woods Papers; Robert A. Woods, "Families and Neighborhoods," *The Survey*, June 26, 1909, 463.

39. Howe, *City*, 17, 22-23, 45.

40. Ibid., 21-22, 280; Woods, "Neighborhood," 106; Graham Taylor, "The Neighborhood and the Municipality," *Proceedings of the National Conference of Charities and Correction*, vol. 36 (Buffalo, 1909), 156-63.

41. Miller, "Scarcity," 142; Eric F. Goldman, *Rendezvous with Destiny: A History of Modern Reform* (New York: Vintage Books, 1956), 78; David W. Noble, "The New Republic and the Idea of Progress, 1914- 1920," *Mississippi Valley Historical Review* 36 (December 1951): 331.

42. Amos Griswold Warner, Stuart Alfred Queen, and Ernest Bouldin Harper, *American Charities and Social Work* (New York: Thomas Y. Crowell and Co., 1930), 456-57; Dwight Davis, "The Neighborhood Center—A Moral and Educational Factor," *Charities and the Commons*, February 1, 1908, 1504-6.

43. Jesse Steiner, *Community Organization* (New York: Century Press, 1925), 195.

44. Allen F. Davis, *Spearheads for Reform: The Social Settlements and the Progressive Movement 1890-1914* (New York: Oxford Univ. Press, 1967), 75.

45. Ibid., 3-18; Edward T. Devine and Lillian Brandt, *American Social Work in the Twentieth Century* (New York: Pioneer Press, 1921), 13-27; Ernest S. Griffith, *A History of American Government: The Progressive Years and Their Aftermath* (New York: Praeger Publishers, 1974), 15; Jane Addams, "The Subjective Necessity for Social Settlements," in *Philanthropy and Social Progress*, ed. Henry C. Adams (New York: Thomas Y. Crowell and Co., 1893), 22-23.

46. For examples of the belief in the importance of the neighborhood see Addams, "Subjective," 22-23; John Elliott, "The Function of the Settlement," *Ethical Record* 1 (April 1900): 80-81; Robert A. Woods and Albert Kennedy, *The Settlement Horizon: A National Estimate* (New York: Russell Sage, 1922), 59; Delos F. Wilcox, *The American City, A Problem in Democracy* (New York: Macmillan Co., 1904), 230; Davis, *Spearheads*, passim; Walter I. Trattner, *From Poor Law to Welfare State: A History of Social Welfare in America* (New York: Free Press, 1974), 141.

47. Davis, *Spearheads*, 75.

48. Addams, "Subjective," 22-23.

49. Holden, *Settlement Idea*, 84-91; Graham Taylor, "Survival and Revival of Neighborhoodship," *The Survey*, May 4, 1912, 231.

50. Davis, *Spearheads*, 75-76; South End House, *Annual Report*, 1908, 4; South End House, *Annual Report*, 1910, 5, Woods Papers; Eleanor Woods, *Robert A. Woods: Champion of Democracy* (Boston: Houghton Mifflin, 1929), 241; (Woods), "Suggestions for Work to be Undertaken," unpublished ms., Woods Papers; Woods, "Neighborhood in Reconstruction," 579.

51. In 1891 the Neighborhood Guild was reorganized and renamed the University Settlement.

52. Davis, *Spearheads*, 8-9; Woods and Kennedy, *Settlement*, 64, 227; Charles B. Stover, "The Neighborhood Guild in New York," *Johns Hopkins Univ. Studies in Historical and Political Science* 7 (1889): 65-68; Stanton Coit, *Neighborhood Guilds: An Instrument of Social Reform* (London: Swan Sonneschein and Co., 1891), passim; Edward King, review of *Neighborhood Guilds: An Instrument of Social Reform*, by Stanton Coit, *Charities Review* 1 (December 1891): 77; Albert J. Kennedy, review of *The Neighborhood in Nation-Building*, by Robert A. Woods, *American Review* 1 (November-December 1923): 727; Albert J. Kennedy, "Community Organization," 38,

127, unpublished ms., in Albert J. Kennedy Papers, Social Welfare History Archives Center, Univ. of Minnesota (hereafter cited as Kennedy Papers).

53. Woods and Kennedy, *Settlement*, 212, 215; "Hudson Guild's Success and Its New Quarters," *Charities and The Commons*, October 10, 1907, 925; Freda Davidson, "Fifty Years of the Hudson Guild," *Ethical Outlook* 31 (April 1945): 181; Sidney Dillick, *Community Organization for Neighborhood Development—Past and Present* (New York: William Morrow, 1953), 56-57; *The Hudson Guild, 1895-1927* (New York, 1927), passim.

54. Robert A. Woods, ed., *The City Wilderness: A Settlement Study* (Boston: Riverside Press, 1891; reprint ed., New York: Arno Press, 1970), 274.

55. Davis, *Spearheads*, 23; Steiner, *Community*, 116; Harvey Zorbaugh, *The Gold Coast and the Slum* (Chicago: Univ. of Chicago Press, 1929), 263.

56. Joseph K. Hart, *Community Organization* (New York: Macmillan Co., 1920), 6, 98-99; Holden, *Settlement*, 193-94; Ida C. Clarke, *The Little Democracy: A Text-Book on Community Organization* (New York: D. Appleton and Co., 1918), 4-5; Eduard C. Lindeman, *The Community* (New York: Association Press, 1921), 58.

57. Davis, *Spearheads*, 76.

58. Ibid.; Steiner, *Community*, 57; Hart, *Community*, 218.

59. Dillick, *Community*, 47; Davis, *Spearheads*, 76; Steiner, *Community*, 57; Clarence Perry, *Ten Years With the Community Center Movement* (New York: Russell Sage, 1921), passim; Robert Fisher, "Community Organization Practice in the Early Twentieth Century: The Community Center Movement," typescript, 1977, 3-9.

60. Dillick, *Community*, 47, 76-79; Lindeman, *Community*, 68-69; Warner, Queen, and Harper, *American Charities*, 462-63; Jesse Steiner, "Community Organization: A Study of Its Rise and Recent Tendencies," *Social Forces* 1 (November 1922): 13; Jesse Steiner, "An Appraisal of the Community Movement," *Social Forces* 7 (March 1929): 341; Davis, *Spearheads*, 76-81; "The Playground and the Social Center," *Common Ground* (June 1910): 57-59; Fisher, "Community Organization," 3-9.

61. Clarke, *Democracy*, 14.

62. Miller, "Neighborhood," 21; see also Griffith, *American*, 115; Woods, "Families," 463; Woodrow Wilson, "The Need of Citizenship Organization," *American City*, November 1911, 265-68; Joseph Arnold, "The Neighborhood and City Hall: The Origin of Neighborhood Associations in Baltimore, 1880-1911," *Journal of Urban History* 7 (November 1979): 5.

63. Griffith, *American*, 117.

64. Miller, "Role," 7-9; Patricia Mooney Melvin, " 'With Interests Common to All': Cincinnati's Neighborhood Improvement Associations 1880-1920," Organization of American Historians, April 19, 1975.

65. Arnold, "Neighborhood," 6-23.

66. Wilbur C. Phillips and Elsie C. Phillips, "Social Unity: A Philosophy for Democracy," 66, unpublished ms., Phillips Papers.

67. Quandt, *Small Town*, 1, 48; Woods, "Neighborhood," 106; Taylor, "Neighborhood," 156-63; Cooley, *Social Organization*, 26.

2. Infant Health and Neighborhood Organization

Some of the material in this chapter first appeared in Patricia Mooney Melvin, "Milk to Motherhood: The New York Milk Committee and the Beginning of Well Child Programs," *Mid-America* 65 (October 1983): 111-34. Material about the Milwaukee Child Welfare Commission first appeared in Patricia Mooney Melvin, "Make Milwaukee Safe for Babies: The Child Welfare Commission and the Development of Urban Health Centers," 1911-1912, *Journal of the West* 17 (April 1978): 83-93.

1. For a good discussion of the notion of the human as organism, see Dom Cavallo, "Social Reform and the Movement to Organize Children's Play During the Progressive Era," *History of Childhood Quarterly* 3 (Spring 1976): 509-22.

2. Roy Lubove, "The New York Association for Improving the Condition of the Poor: The Formative Years," *New York Historical Society Quarterly* 43 (1959): 308; Roy Lubove, *The Professional Altruist: The Emergence of Social Work as a Career 1880-1930* (New York: Atheneum Press, 1971), 3; Robert Bremner, *American Philanthropy* (Chicago: Univ. of Chicago Press, 1960), 61; Charles E. Rosenberg, *No Other Gods: On Science and American Social Thought* (Baltimore: Johns Hopkins Univ. Press, 1976), 116-22; Edward K. Spann, *The New Metropolis: New York City, 1840-1857* (New York: Columbia Univ. Press, 1981), 83-90.

3. Distillery or brewer's slop came from diffusing grain refuse through water once the alcohol had been removed. Robert M. Hartley, *An Historical, Scientific and Practical Essay on Milk as an Article Human Substance* (New York: Leavitt, 1842; reprint ed., New York: Arno Press, 1977), 109; James Flexner, "The Battle for Pure Milk in New York City," in *Is Loose Milk a Health Hazard?*, ed. Edward Brown and Leland Spencer (New York: Milk Commission, 1931), 164.

4. William H. Allen, *Civics and Health* (Boston: Ginn and Co., 1909), 257; Norman Shaftel, "A History of the Purification of Milk in New York, or 'How Now, Brown Cow,' " in *Sickness and Health in America: Readings in the History of Medicine and Public Health*, ed. Judith W. Leavitt and Ronald L. Numbers (Madison: Univ. of Wisconsin Press, 1978), 277-78; John Spargo, *The Common Sense of the Milk Problem* (New York: Macmillan Co., 1908), 14; John Duffy, *A History of Public Health in New York City 1625-1866* (New York: Russell Sage, 1968), 427-29; Hartley, *Essay*, 139.

5. Shaftel, "Purification," 276-77; Chester Linwood Roadhouse and James Lloyd Henderson, *The Milk Market Industry* (New York: McGraw Hill, 1941), 3-4. For a fuller discussion of urban growth and the rising interest in public health, see Michael H. Frisch, *Town into City: Springfield, Massachusetts, and the Meaning of Community, 1840-1880* (Cambridge, Mass.: Harvard Univ. Press, 1972), 236-37; Charles Glaab and Theodore Brown, *A History of Urban America*, 2d ed. (New York: Macmillan Co., 1976), 66-84; Kenneth T. Jackson and Stanley K. Schultz, eds. *Cities in American History* (New York: Alfred A. Knopf, 1972), 249-57; George Rosen, *A History of Public Health* (New York: MD Publications, 1958), 183, 238-60, 339, 344; Jon A. Peterson, "The Impact of Sanitary Reform Upon American Urban Planning 1840-1890," *Journal of Social History* 13 (Fall 1979): 83-84; Charles E. Rosenberg, *The Cholera Years: The United States in 1832, 1849, and 1866* (Chicago: Univ. of Chicago Press, 1962), 5-6, 98, 133-50.

6. *Cholera infantum*, also called infantile diarrhea, "summer complaint," "bowel

complaint," and dysentery, represented the most serious of all gastrointestinal diseases. It was spread through bowel excreta under conditions of inadequate sanitary facilities or through water or milk contamination. Judith W. Leavitt, "Public Health in Milwaukee 1867-1910" (Ph.D. diss., Univ. of Chicago, 1975), 28.

7. Duffy, *Public Health 1625-1866*, 427-34; Shaftel, "Purification," 278-80; John Mullaly, *The Milk Trade in New York City and Vicinity* (New York: Fowles and Welles, 1853), passim; *Frank Leslie's Illustrated Newspaper*, June 5, 1858; *Frank Leslie's Illustrated Newspaper*, August 2, 1858.

8. Duffy, *Public Health 1625-1866*, 436-37; Shaftel, "Purification," 281.

9. W.T. Sedgewick, Massachusetts Association of Boards of Health *Journal* 2 (1892): 30, quoted in Manfred J. Waserman, "Henry Coit and the Certified Milk Movement in the Development of Modern Pediatrics," *Bulletin of the History of Medicine* 46 (July-August 1972): 359.

10. Spargo, *Common Sense*, 25; R.L. Duffus and L. Emmett Holt, Jr., *L. Emmett Holt: Pioneer of a Children's Century* (New York: D. Appleton and Co., 1940), 166; Rosen, *History*, 332-33.

11. Dr. Henry L. Coit organized a medical milk commission to oversee the milk industry in the Newark area. Created in 1893, this body entered into contractual agreements with individual dairymen to supervise the production of high-grade milk. Dairy owners participating in the program were required to hire bacteriologists and chemists to inspect their dairying operations. In return, the commission allowed dairymen to label their milk "certified," signifying that it had met pure milk standards. Stuart Galishoff, *Safeguarding the Public Health: Newark, 1895-1918* (Westport, Conn.: Greenwood Press, 1975), 85-86; Duffus and Holt, *L. Emmett Holt*, 169; Charles E. North, "Milk and Its Relation to Public Health," in *A Half Century of Public Health*, ed. Mazÿck P. Ravenel (New York: American Public Health Assn., 1921), 267.

12. Dr. George Goler organized in 1897 the first municipally regulated milk protection system in the United States. Under his direction, inspectors appointed by Rochester's Health Department made certain that dairymen sterilized their utensils, gave their cows periodic tuberculin tests, and checked for diseased employees. In addition, Dr. Goler required the pasteurization of all milk to kill off any stray germs that might have escaped normal sanitary procedures. Duffus and Holt, *L. Emmett Holt*, 169; North, "Milk," 267; George B. Mangold, *Child Problems* (New York: Macmillan Co., 1910), 74, 78-79.

13. Certified milk, or milk inspected by a medical commission, sold for roughly 20 to 24 cents. This was double the price for commercial milk, much of which was of dubious quality.

14. At his station, Dr. Koplik modified raw milk for all infants under his care. Rosen, *History*, 354; Henry Koplik, "The History of the First Milk Depot of *Gouttes de Lait* with Consultations in America," *Journal of the American Medical Association* 63 (October 1912): 1574.

15. Straus opened his first of twenty-six stations on July 1, 1893, on the pier at the foot of Thirty-second Street. All milk at his stations was pasteurized to remove all harmful bacteria, and then dispensed in nursing bottles that were given free or at cost to needy tenement mothers. North, "Milk," 277-78; Lina Gutherz Straus, *Disease in Milk, The Remedy Pasteurization: The Life Work of Nathan Straus*, 2d ed. (New York:

E. P. Dutton and Co., 1917), 51-52; Rosen, *History* 355; Duffus and Holt, *L. Emmett Holt*, 169-70.

16. North, "Milk," 278; Phillip Van Ingen, "The History of Child Welfare Work in the United States," in *A Half Century of Public Health*, ed. Mazÿck P. Ravenel (New York: American Public Health Assn., 1921), 306; S. Josephine Baker, *Child Hygiene* (New York: Harper and Bros., 1925), 215; U.S. Department of the Treasury, Public Health and Marine Hospital, *Milk and Its Relation to Public Health*, Bulletin 41 (Washington, D.C.: Government Printing Office, 1908), 582-84. The cities with infant depots in 1908 were New York, Yonkers, Rochester, Newark, Pittsburgh, Cleveland, Chicago, Philadelphia, Baltimore, St. Louis, Detroit, Columbus, Cambridge, Providence, Cincinnati, Toledo, Jersey City, New Bedford, Boston, Kansas City, Mo., and Kansas City, Kans.

17. Demographically, infants are defined as an exact age group—all children who have not yet reached year one. The infant mortality rate is intended to be a measure of the risk of death during the first year of life rather than an age specific death rate. The rate is computed according to the following formula:

$$m_i = \frac{d\text{-}_{lk}.}{B}$$

m_i is the infant mortality rate. $d\text{-}_l$ represents the deaths of infants under one year of age, exclusive of stillbirths during a specific time period. k equals 1,000. B equals the total number of births occurring during the same time period.

It is important to remember, particularly when studying the early twentieth century, that all vital statistics for the first year of life are somewhat vague. Many babies who died soon after birth may never have been registered as either births or deaths. Nonetheless, the infant death rate is usually adequate to reveal the level of infant mortality in a population and to permit preliminary conclusions about trends and patterns within the population. U.S. Department of Commerce, Bureau of the Census, *Sixteenth Census of the United States, 1940: Vital Statistic Rates in the United States*, 43; George W. Barclay, *Techniques of Population Analysis* (New York: John Wiley and Sons, 1958), 47-48, 135-38, 143.

18. Van Ingen, "Child Welfare," 291-92; Joyce Antler and Daniel M. Fox, "The Movement Toward a Safe Maternity: Physician Accountability in New York City, 1915-1940," in *Sickness and Health in America: Readings in the History of Public Health*, ed. Judith W. Leavitt and Ronald L. Numbers (Madison: Univ. of Wisconsin Press, 1978), 376; James H. Cassedy, *Charles V. Chapin and the Public Health Movement* (Cambridge, Mass.: Harvard Univ. Press, 1962), 146.

19. U.S. Department of Commerce and Labor, Bureau of the Census, *Mortality Statistics 1900 to 1904*, cc, ccii; S. Josephine Baker, *Fighting For Life* (New York: Macmillan Co., 1959), 83; Barclay, *Techniques*, 123; Joseph S. Neff, "Recent Public Health Work in the United States Especially in Relation to Infant Mortality," *American Journal of Public Health* 5 (October 1915): 966-67.

20. S. Josephine Baker, "Reduction of Infant Mortality in New York City," *American Journal of Diseases of Children* 5 (1913): 150-55, 159.

21. Ibid.

22. Duffus and Holt, *L. Emmett Holt*, 166; Rosen, *History*, 351, 358-59; J.D. Burks, "Clean Milk and Public Health," *Annals of the American Academy of Political and Social Science* 37 (March 1911): 199-200; Charles R. Henderson, "Infant Welfare: Methods of Organization and Administration in Italy," *American Journal of Sociology* 17 (November 1911): 290; New York Association for Improving the Condition of the Poor, *Annual Report*, vol. 62 (September 30, 1905), 18 (hereafter cited as AICP); New York Milk Conference, *Clean Milk for New York City*, Report of the New York Milk Conference (November 20, 1906), 3.

23. Neff, "Recent Work," 966-67; U.S. Department of Commerce and Labor, Bureau of the Census, *Mortality Statistics 1906*, 266, 430.

24. Lillian Brandt, *Growth and Development of AICP and COS*, Report to the Committee in the Institute of Welfare and Research (New York: Community Service Society of New York, 1942), 186; New York Milk Conference, *Clean Milk*, 3-4.

25. The participants included Dr. Walter Bensel, the assistant sanitary superintendent of the New York City Department of Health; Dr. Herman M. Briggs, medical officer of the City of New York; Dr. John S. Fulton, the secretary of the Maryland State Board of Health; Dr. George Goler, health officer of Rochester; Dr. Charles Harrington, secretary of the Massachusetts State Board of Health; Dr. Walter Greene, commissioner of health in Buffalo; Dr. A. Clark Hunt, assistant secretary of the New Jersey State Board of Health; Dr. William Park, the director of research laboratories of the New York Department of Health; Dr. Louis Ager, pathologist at the Long Island College Hospital and attending physician at the Sheltering Arms Nursery; Dr. S.T. Armstrong, the superintendent of Bellevue Hospital; Dr. John Winters Brannan, president of the Board of Trustees of the Bellevue and Allied hospitals; Dr. Henry V. Chapin, Professor of Diseases of Children at the New York Post-Graduate Medical School and Hospital; Professor H.W. Conn, professor of bacteriology at Wesleyan University; Dr. E.K. Dunham, the professor of pathology at the University and Bellevue Hospital Medical College; Dr. John T. Fitzgerald, a superintendent of Kings County Hospital; George L. Flanders, assistant commissioner of agriculture for the State of New York; Dr. Simon Flexner, the director of the Rockefeller Institute for Medical Research; Dr. E. Elliot Harris, visiting physician at the City Children's Hospital; Dr. L. Emmett Holt, professor of children's diseases at Columbia University; Dr. A. Jacobi, the consulting physician at Mt. Sinai Hospital; Dr. Alexander Lambert, consulting physician at the New York Infirmary for Women and Children; Clarence B. Lane, assistant chief of the Dairying Division, Bureau of Animal Husbandry, U.S. Department of Agriculture; Dr. William Perry Northup, visiting physician at the Presbyterian and Foundling hospitals; Dr. Horst Oertel, pathologist at City Hospital; Professor Leonard Pearson, dean of the Department of Veterinary Medicine at the University of Pennsylvania; Professor R.A. Pearson of the Dairying Department at Cornell University; Dr. G.H. Swift, a visiting physician at St. Mary's Free Hospital for Children; Dr. Linsly R. Williams, the chief of clinic of the Department of Medicine of Vanderbilt Clinic; Dr. Joseph E. Winters, Professor of Children's Diseases at the Medical Department of Cornell University; President Nicholas Murray Butler of Columbia University; Dr. H.L. Coit, Newark; Commissioner Robert W. Hebberd of the Department of Charities; Dr. Ernst Lederle, former New York City health commissioner; Mr. Nathan Straus, founder of the Straus Milk Depots in New York City; Professor H.T. Vulte of Teachers College; Commissioner C.A. Wieting; Dr. Henry

Mitchell of the New Jersey Board of Health. New York Milk Conference, *Clean Milk*, 10.

26. Ibid.

27. North, "Milk," 240-41; Allen, *Civics*, 258-59; Phillip Van Ingen and Paul Emmons Taylor, *Infant Mortality and Milk Stations* (New York: New York Milk Committee, 1912), 24 (hereafter cited as NYMC); Phillips, *Adventuring*, 3-5, 24; Brandt, *Growth*, 186; Wilbur C. Phillips and Elsie Phillips, "A Plan for Social Organization or the Unit Method of Gradually Building Up a Complete System for Studying and Meeting Social Needs," 79, unpublished ms., Phillips Papers. Phillips served as active director of the NYMC's affairs from 1907 until April 1911.

28. Baker, *Child Hygiene*, 217; George B. Mangold, *Problems of Child Hygiene* (New York: Macmillan Co., 1914), 93-94, Rosen, *History*, 344; Neff, "Recent Work," 973.

29. Rosen, *History*, 351.

30. Mangold, *Problems*, 93-94; Phillips, *Adventuring*, 23; John B. Blake, *Origins of Maternal and Child Welfare Programs* (New Haven: Yale Univ. Press, 1953), 8.

31. Rosen, *History*, 353.

32. R.W. Bruère, "A Plan for the Reduction of Infant Mortality," *Bulletin of the American Academy of Medicine* 11 (1910): 251-52; NYMC, *Infant Milk Depots and Their Relation to Infant Mortality* (New York: NYMC, 1908), 11; John Duffy, *A History of Public Health in New York City, 1866-1966* (New York: Russell Sage, 1974), 464.

33. Phillips, *Adventuring*, 24; NYMC, *Milk Depots*, 10-12; Edward T. Devine, "The Waste of Infant Life," *The Survey*, December 4, 1909, 320; Allen, *Civics*, 251.

34. NYMC, *Milk Depots*, 24.

35. Ibid., 26; Wilbur C. Phillips, "The New York Milk Committee: What It Is and What It Hopes To Do," Phillips Papers.

36. NYMC, *Milk Depots*, 26-27; Wilbur C. Phillips, "Infants' Milk Depots and Infant Mortality," *American Association for the Study and Prevention of Infant Mortality* 1 (1910): 78.

37. AICP, *Annual Report*, vol. 65 (September 30, 1908), 71.

38. NYMC, *Milk Depots*, 26-27; Phillips, "Milk Depots," 81; Wilbur C. Phillips, "The Mother and The Baby," *The Survey*, August 7, 1909, 626.

39. AICP, *Annual Report* 65: 70; NYMC, *Milk Depots*, 28; Phillips, "Mother and Baby," 626.

40. NYMC, *Milk Depots*, 28; Phillips, "Mother and Baby," 626.

41. AICP, *Annual Report* 65: 71.

42. Ibid., 71-72; NYMC, *Milk Depots*, 64-65, 80.

43. AICP, *Annual Report* 65: 72; NYMC, *Milk Depots*, 65-66; Wilbur C. Phillips, "Infant Mortality," *Dietetic and Hygienic Gazette* (1911-1912): 93.

44. NYMC, *Milk Depots*, 28, 66-67; Phillips, *Adventuring*, 25.

45. NYMC, *Milk Depots*, 64; Galishoff, *Safeguarding*, 87-93. See also M.J. Rosenau, *The Milk Question* (Boston: Houghton Mifflin, 1912), for a good discussion of the pasteurization controversy.

46. Galishoff, *Safeguarding*, 87-93; AICP, *Annual Report* 65: 15.

47. *New York Times*, January 19, 1909; *New York Times*, January 24, 1909.

48. *New York Times*, January 20, 1909; *New York Times*, January 22, 1909; *New York Times*, January 30, 1909.

49. Duffy, *Public Health 1866-1966*, 480; Trattner, *Poor Law*, 111; Baker, *Fighting*, 129.

50. For a fuller discussion of Phillips's efforts to illustrate the possibility of securing a pure milk supply and to establish milk standards see Patricia Mooney Melvin, "Neighborhood in the Organic City: The Social Unit Plan and the First Community Organization Movement 1900-1920," (Ph.D. diss., Univ. of Cincinnati, 1978), 68-79.

51. Phillips and Phillips, "Plan," 188; Phillips, *Adventuring*, 46-48; Wilbur C. Phillips, "The Achievements and Future Possibilities of the New York Milk Committee," *Proceedings of the Child Conference for Research and Development*, vol. 1 (Worcester, Mass., 1909), 191-92.

52. Sally M. Miller, *Victor Berger and the Promise of Constructive Socialism 1910-1920* (Westport, Conn.: Greenwood Press, 1973), 36; Frederick I. Olson, "Milwaukee's First Socialist Administration 1910-1912: A Political Examination," *Mid-America* 43 (July 1961): 197-205; Sally M. Miller, "Milwaukee: Of Ethnicity and Labor," in *Socialism and the Cities*, ed. Bruce Stave (Port Washington: Kennikat Press, 1975), 45-50; Bayrd Still, *Milwaukee: The Story of a City* (Madison: State Historical Society of Wisconsin, 1948), 515-17; Roderick Nash, "Victor Berger: Making Marx Respectable," *Wisconsin Magazine of History* 47 (Summer 1947): 301-2; Samuel Haber, *Efficiency and Uplift: Scientific Management in the Progressive Era 1890-1920* (Chicago: Univ. of Chicago Press, 1964), 147; "Municipal Reform in Milwaukee," *Outlook*, June 10, 1911, 275; Zane L. Miller, *Boss Cox's Cincinnati: Urban Politics in the Progressive Era* (New York: Oxford Univ. Press, 1968), 113-28.

53. Phillips, *Adventuring*, 60-63; Olson, "First Socialist Administration," 200-204; Miller, "Milwaukee," 51.

54. Phillips and Phillips, "Plan," 52-54; Louis Frederick Frank, *The Medical History of Milwaukee 1834-1914* (Milwaukee: Germania Publishing Co., 1915), 167-68; Leavitt, "Public Health," 251-323.

55. *Milwaukee Journal*, May 3, 1911; *Milwaukee Sentinel*, May 2, 1911; *Milwaukee Free Press*, April 29, 1911; *Milwaukee Free Press*, April 30, 1911.

56. *Milwaukee Journal*, May 3, 1911; *Milwaukee Sentinel*, May 3, 1911; *Milwaukee Journal*, May 5, 1911.

57. *Milwaukee Free Press*, May 19, 1911; Milwaukee, Wisconsin, *Proceedings of the Common Council of the City of Milwaukee for the Year Ending April 11, 1912*, File #272 (May 8, 1911), 77-78; Phillips, *Adventuring*, 66; National Social Unit Organization, *A Statement of the Practical Experience on Which the Unit Plan is Based*, Bulletin 2-A (Cincinnati: NSUO, 1918), 4-5 (hereafter cited as NSUO); Sherman C. Kingsley, "Children," *The Survey*, July 6, 1912, 527.

58. *Milwaukee Sentinel*, May 14, 1911.

59. "Statement of Infant Mortality Rate in the Fourteenth Ward Showing Why the Child Welfare Commission had Selected this District for the Establishment of Baby Welfare Centers," (1911), 1, Phillips Papers; Leavitt, "Public Health," 10; Roger David Simon, "The Expansion of an Industrial City: Milwaukee 1880-1910," (Ph.D. diss., Univ. of Wisconsin, 1971), 216, 220; U.S. Department of Commerce, Bureau of the Census, *Thirteenth Census of the United States, 1910: Population*, vol. 3, 1101.

60. "Statement of Infant Mortality," 1; Leavitt, "Public Health," 10.

61. Phillips, *Adventuring*, 67; NSUO, *Statement*, 4; Thaddeus Borum, comp., *We,*

the Milwaukee Poles: The History of Milwaukeeans of Polish Descent and a Record of Their Contributions to the Greatness of Milwaukee (Milwaukee: Nowing Publishing Co., 1946), 18.

62. "List of Physicians in the Baby District," Phillips Papers; NSUO, *Statement*, 16-18; Phillips and Phillips, "Plan," 94-99.

63. *Milwaukee Journal*, July 21, 1911; *Milwaukee Sentinel*, July 24, 1911; *Milwaukee Free Press*, July 25, 1911.

64. Phillips, *Adventuring*, 72-73; *Milwaukee Sentinel*, July 24, 1911; *Milwaukee Free Press*, July 19, 1911; "Baby Station," (1911), Phillips Papers.

65. Phillips, *Adventuring*, 72-73; NSUO, *Statement*, 5-7; Phillips and Phillips, "Plan," 99.

66. Phillips, *Adventuring*, 73; NSUO, *Statement*, 7-14.

67. NSUO, *Statement*, 22, 28-29; Phillips, *Adventuring*, 74, 83.

68. *Milwaukee Leader*, May 20, 1912; *Thirty-fifth Annual Report of the Commissioner of Health for the Year 1911*, 180-82; *Milwaukee Sentinel*, July 8, 1911; *Milwaukee Journal*, December 26, 1911; "Community Planning for Infant Welfare Work," Phillips Papers; *Milwaukee Journal*, October 10, 1911; *Milwaukee Journal*, September 28, 1911.

69. "Educating a Nation About Its Children," *Outlook*, November 11, 1914, 569.

70. *Milwaukee Sentinel*, July 24, 1911; *Milwaukee Leader*, May 20, 1912; Milwaukee, Wisconsin, *Proceedings of the City of Milwaukee for the Year Ending April 11, 1912*, File #1743 (January 29, 1913), 1181; NSUO, *Statement*, 22-29.

71. Olson, "First Socialist Administration," 197-98; Miller, "Milwaukee," 48-50; Still, *History*, 519; Leavitt, "Public Health," 355; Wilbur C. Phillips, "The Trend of Medico-Social Effort in Child Welfare Work," *American Journal of Public Health* 2 (November 1912): 876-82.

72. Duffy, *Public Health 1866-1966*, 634; Leavitt, "Public Health," 355; Phillips, "Trend," 880.

73. *Milwaukee Free Press*, April 14, 1912.

74. *Milwaukee Free Press*, June 5, 1912; *Milwaukee Free Press*, June 9, 1912.

75. *Milwaukee Sentinel*, June 8, 1912.

76. *Milwaukee Sentinel*, June 25, 1912; Milwaukee, Wisconsin, *Proceedings of the Common Council for the City of Milwaukee for the Year Ending April 14, 1913*, File #2262 (June 17, 1912), 270; *Thirty-sixth Annual Report to the Commissioner of Health of Milwaukee for the Year 1912*, 11, 13, 87, 89. For a fuller discussion of the demise of the Child Welfare Commission see Melvin, "Neighborhood," 135-53.

77. Wilbur C. Phillips, "The Need of Community Planning in Child Welfare Work," *Transactions of the Fifteenth International Congress on Hygiene and Demography* (Washington, D.C., 1912), 291-93.

78. George Rosen, "The First Neighborhood Health Center Movement: Its Rise and Its Fall," in *From Medical Police to Social Medicine: Essays on the History of Health Care*, ed. George Rosen (New York: Science Publications, 1974), 304-27; Duffy, *Public Health 1866-1966*, 268-69; Michael M. Davis and Andrew R. Warner, *Dispensaries: Their Management and Development* (New York: Macmillan Co., 1918), 321-23; Michael M. Davis, "The Health Center Idea: A New Development in Public Health Work," *Public Health Nurse Quarterly* 8 (January 1916): 27-30.

79. Phillips, "Need," 290-94.

80. Wilbur C. Phillips, "A New Design for Democracy or the Social Unit Theory and Plan for Evolving a Functional Consumers' and Producers' Democracy," unpublished ms., Phillips Papers.

81. Phillips, *Adventuring*, 165.

82. Ibid.; Phillips, "Need," 291.

83. Woods, "City and Community," 196.

3. The Social Unit Theory of Organization

1. Charles C. Forcey, *The Crossroads of Liberalism: Croly, Weyl, Lippman, and the Progressive Era* (New York: Oxford Univ. Press, 1961), 41; Quandt, *Small Town*, passim.

2. Robert A. Woods, "Social Work: A New Profession," in *The Neighborhood in Nation-Builing*, ed. Robert A. Woods (New York: Houghton Mifflin, 1923; reprint ed., New York: Arno Press, 1970), 91.

3. Follett, *New State*, 174.

4. Ibid., 51, 11, 174; Quandt, *Small Town*, 38-41; Gabriel Kolko, *The Triumph of Conservatism: A Reinterpretation of American History, 1900-1916* (Glencoe, Ill.: Free Press, 1963), 305.

5. Haber, *Efficiency*, 110.

6. "The Expert and American Society," *New Republic*, May 4, 1918, 6-8.

7. Sidney Kaplan, "Social Engineers as Saviors: Effects of World War I on Some American Liberals," *Journal of the History of Ideas* 17 (June 1956): 347-49.

8. Quandt, *Small Town*, 139-45; Cooley, *Social Organization*, 147; Walter Lippman, *Public Opinion* (New York, 1922), 362-96.

9. Herbert Croly, *Progressive Democracy* (New York: MacMillan Co., 1915), 283.

10. Ibid., 301; Forcey, *Crossroads*, 27, 157, 165; Wiebe, *Search for Order*, 161-62; David W. Noble, "Herbert Croly and American Progressive Thought," *Western Political Quarterly* 7 (December 1954): 547-50.

11. NSUO, *The Unit Experiment from the Standpoint of Popular Control, Theoretical Soundness, Practical Efficiency, Educational Value and Cost*, Bulletin 6 (Cincinnati: NSUO, 1919), 19.

12. Phillips, *Adventuring*, 166-67.

13. Phillips and Phillips, "Plan," 271; Phillips and Phillips, "Social Unity," 4.

14. Phillips used *consumer* and *citizen* interchangeably. The citizen was the consumer of goods and sources.

15. Phillips, *Adventuring*, 84-85; Phillips and Phillips, "Plan," 431-56.

16. Phillips and Phillips, "Plan," 451-56.

17. Ibid., 271; Phillips, "Need," 293-94.

18. Phillips, *Adventuring*, 162-65.

19. Woods, "Recovery," 135.

20. Phillips, *Adventuring*, 93.

21. Ibid., xii-xiv; James Weinstein, *The Corporate Ideal in the Liberal State: 1900-1918* (Boston: Beacon Press, 1968), xiv.

22. Phillips, *Adventuring*, 94-104.

23. Ibid., 64-104; Phillips and Phillips, "Plan," 277-318.

24. Courtenay Dinwiddie, *Community Responsibility: A Review of the Cincinnati Social Unit Experiment* (New York: New York School of Social Work, 1921), 2.

25. Phillips, *Adventuring*, 167-69; "NSUO," 7-8, Phillips Papers; Phillips and Phillips, "Plan," 306.

26. NSUO, *Description of the Unit Plan*, Bulletin 4 (Cincinnati: NSUO, 1919), 6-7.

27. Phillips, *Adventuring*, 169-70.

28. Ibid., 103-4, 170-71.

29. Ibid., 150-51; Phillips and Phillips, "Plan," 177; NSUO, *Description of Plan*, 7.

30. Phillips and Phillips, "Plan," 355; Phillips, *Adventuring*, 153, 160, 163.

31. One of Richard Cabot's most important contributions to medical science was the inauguration of medical social service programs. The commencement of such service at Massachusetts General Hospital in 1905 ended his search for means to create awareness of the importance of physical and social factors in the treatment of disease. Cabot believed that disease could not be understood or treated without reference to the total environment of the individual.

32. NSUO, *History of the Unit Plan*, Bulletin 1 (Cincinnati: NSUO, 1917), 3; Phillips, *Adventuring*, 143; Wilbur C. Phillips to Ethel Pew, March 9, 1964, Phillips Papers.

33. Committee on Unit Organization, "A Plan for Making the City of Washington a National Social Unit Laboratory By Developing a Model Program for Community Organization, Beginning with Work for Children," 13, Phillips Papers.

34. Phillips, *Adventuring*, 144-45; Phillips to Pew, March 9, 1964.

35. NSUO, *History of Plan*, 3; Phillips, *Adventuring*, 145.

36. Phillips, *Adventuring*, 145.

37. U.S. Department of Commerce and Labor, Children's Bureau, *The Children's Bureau*, 1912.

38. Dorothy E. Bradbury and Martha M. Eliot, *Four Decades of Action for Children: A Short History of the Children's Bureau*, Bulletin 358 (Washington, D.C., 1956), 5-6; Phillips, *Adventuring*, 145; *The Children's Bureau*, 2, 5; Trattner, *Poor Law*, 183; Grace Abbott, *Ten Years Work for Children* (Washington, D.C., 1923), 1-3.

39. Phillips, *Adventuring*, 143.

40. Ibid., 145-46; NSUO, *History of Plan*, 3-4.

41. NSUO, *History of Plan*, 3-4.

42. Ibid., 4.

43. Ibid., 3-4; Phillips, *Adventuring*, 148.

44. Phillips, *Adventuring*, 147-48.

45. NSUO, *History of Plan*, 4.

46. Ibid.; Minutes of the National Temporary Committee on the Unit Program, February 9, 1916, Phillips Papers.

47. Those interested in supporting the social unit plan included the Honorable Oliver P. Newman, Norman Hapgood, Justice Frederick L. Siddons, and John Joy Edson of Washington, D.C.; William F. Cochran and Dr. James Mason-Knox from Baltimore; John Collier, Dr. Charles E. North, Mrs. Charles Tiffany, Mrs. William Baldwin, George W. Perkins, Dr. S.S. Goldwater, Julia Lathrop, William Loeb, Jr., Mrs. Mowbray Clark, and Harry B. Monasmith of New York City; Dr. John Beffel of

Milwaukee; Michael M. Davis and Mrs. William Lowell Putnam of Boston; Roy Smith Wallace of Philadelphia; and Mrs. H.O. Wittpenn of Hoboken. Minutes of the National Temporary Organizing Committee, February 15, 1916, Phillips Papers.

48. NSUO, "Draft," Gifford Pinchot Papers, Library of Congress (hereafter cited as Pinchot Papers).

49. Minutes of the National Temporary Organizing Committee, March 9, 1916, Phillips Papers,

50. Phillips, *Adventuring*, 148-49.

51. "Health Centers as an Aid to Democracy," *The Survey*, April 22, 1916, 93.

52. NSUO, *History of Plan*, 5; Minutes of the NSUO, April 11, 1916, Phillips Papers.

53. NSUO, *History of Plan*, 5; *New York Times*, April 12, 1916.

54. NSUO, *History of Plan*, 5.

55. Ibid., 5-6.

56. *New York Times*, April 12, 1916.

57. "Health Centers," 93.

58. Ibid.

59. Ibid.; *New York Times*, April 12, 1916; Wilbur C. Phillips, "Health and Commonwealth," *Proceedings of the National Conference of Social Work*, vol. 44 (Pittsburgh, 1917), 252.

60. NSUO, *History of Plan*, 7.

61. Martin Duberman, *The Uncompleted Past* (New York: Random House, 1964), 8.

62. Phillips, "Need," 290.

63. Ibid., 290-94; Wiebe, *Search for Order*, 169; "Health Center," 93; Wilbur C. Phillips to Mrs. Gifford Pinchot, April 5, 1916, Pinchot Papers.

64. Haber, *Efficiency*, 87-88; "Expert," 6-7; Forcey, *Crossroads*, 27, 257, 264; Anatole Shaffer, "The Cincinnati Social Unit Experiment: 1917-1919," *Social Service Review* 45 (June 1971): 163.

65. Appeal Letter, (April 1916), Pinchot Papers; William J. Norton, *The Cooperative Movement in Social Work* (New York: Macmillan Co., 1927), 1; Warner, Queen, and Harper, *American Charities*, 456-57.

66. Phillips to Pinchot, April 8, 1916; Phillips, "Need," 192; Wilbur C. Phillips, "The Trend of Medico-Social Effort in Child Welfare Work, *American Journal of Public Health* 2 (November 1912): 875; Athel C. Burnham, *The Community Health Problem* (New York: Macmillan Co., 1920), passim; Davis, "Health Center Idea," 22-39; *New York Times*, April 12, 1916; "Health Center," 93.

67. Phillips, *Adventuring*, 175.

68. Ibid.; *New York Times*, November 20, 1916; NSUO, *History of Plan*, 7; "Mr. and Mrs. Phillips' Big Idea," *Everybody's Magazine*, June 1916, 785.

69. "Release for Use in Monday Morning's Paper, November 20th," November 1916, Pinchot Papers; NSUO, *History of Plan*, 7; "Health Center," 93; Committee on Unit Organization, "Plan for Washington."

70. Organized in 1907, the Anti-Tuberculosis League worked to "stimulate and arouse the public conscience . . . to assume its real responsibility" in the prevention of tuberculosis. It campaigned for better tenement house regulations and inspection,

sought to collect statistics on the causes and spread of tuberculosis in Cincinnati, and in conjunction with the Health Department operated a tuberculosis dispensary. See Samuel E. Allen, "A Brief History of Anti-Tuberculosis Work in Cincinnati," *Lancet-Clinic* (Cincinnati) 113 (May 1915): 512; Phillip P. Jacobs, "The Cincinnati Municipal Tuberculosis Program," *Lancet-Clinic* (Cincinnati) 113 (May 1915): 516.

71. The Municipal Tuberculosis Committee consisted of all public and private agencies engaged in fighting tuberculosis in the Cincinnati area. Courtenay Dinwiddie, "The Tuberculosis Problem of Cincinnati Today," *Lancet-Clinic* (Cincinnati) 113 (May 1915): 515.

72. J.H. Landis, "The Co-Ordination of Public and Private Effort in the Anti-Tuberculosis Fight," *Lancet-Clinic* (Cincinnati) 113 (May 1915): 517; Courtenay Dinwiddie, "An Outline of the Proposed Plan for a Health Center," *Lancet-Clinic* (Cincinnati) 113 (May 1915): 518.

73. Cincinnati *Commercial Tribune*, June 22, 1916.

74. NSUO, *History of Plan*, 8; Wilbur C. Phillips to Gifford Pinchot, August 29, 1916, Pinchot Papers; Phillips, *Adventuring*, 174-75; Phillips, "Health and Commonwealth," 253; N.A. Nelson, "Neighborhood Organization vs. Tuberculosis," *Modern Medicine* 1 (October 1919): 516; Dillick, *Community Organization*, 81.

75. Wilbur C. Phillips to Gifford Pinchot, October 6, 1916, Pinchot Papers.

76. Cincinnati *Commercial Tribune*, October 22, 1916.

77. Phillips, *Adventuring*, 175-77; NSUO, *History of Plan*, 8; Meeting of the NSUO, November 9, 1916, Phillips Papers.

78. "Release for Use"; NSUO, *History of Plan*, 7; *New York Times*, November 20, 1916.

79. Steiner, *Community*, 241; *New York Times*, November 20, 1916; "The Social Unit District Chooses Itself," *The Survey*, July 21, 1917, 355; NSUO, *History of Plan*, 7-10; NSUO, "Report of the Executive Committee," November 9, 1916, Phillips Papers.

80. Cincinnati *Commercial Tribune*, November 20, 1916; Wilbur C. Phillips to Gifford Pinchot, January 1, 1917, Pinchot Papers; Phillips, *Adventuring*, 177.

4. The Social Unit Comes to Cincinnati

1. Phillips, *Adventuring*, 117; NSUO, *Experiment*, 2.

2. NSUO, *Creation and Purpose of the Social Unit Organization*, Bulletin 3 (Cincinnati: NSUO, 1918), 5-7.

3. Wilbur C. Phillips and Elsie Phillips to Gifford Pinchot, March 5, 1917, Pinchot Papers.

4. Organizations represented in the meeting of the Temporary Organizing Committee included the Academy of Medicine, Central Labor Council, Chamber of Commerce, Federation of Mothers' Clubs, Visiting Nurse Association, Federated Improvement Association, Anti-Tuberculosis League, Bureau of Catholic Charities, Woman's City Club, Council of Social Agencies, Allied Printing Trades Council, Santa Maria Institute, National Conference of Jewish Charities, Young Men's Christian Association, Cincinnati Woman's Club, Cincinnati Schoolmasters' Club, Municipal Tuberculosis Committee, Associated Charities, Housewives' League, Optimists' Club,

Board of Health, Board of Education, University of Cincinnati, General Hospital, Board of Park Commissioners, Cincinnati Woman's Teachers' Association, Rotary Club, United Jewish Charities, Court of Domestic Relations, Ohio-Miami Medical College, Council of Jewish Women, American Red Cross, Graduate Nurses' Association, Probate Court, Woman's Missionary Federation, Better Housing League, Harriet Beecher Stowe School, Children's Clinic, Cincinnati Dental Society, Commissioner of Buildings, Schmidlapp Foundation, Consumers' League, Physicians' Society, and Department of Public Welfare. NSUO, *Description of Plan*, 13-15.

5. Ibid.; NSUO, *Creation*, 7-8; Dinwiddie, *Community Responsibility*, 111.

6. NSUO, *Creation*, 8; Phillips, "Health and Community," 153; Cincinnati *Commercial Tribune*, March 2, 1917.

7. NSUO, *Creation*, 9; Cincinnati *Commercial Tribune*, March 23, 1917; Courtenay Dinwiddie, "The Work Accomplished by the Social Unit Organization," *Proceedings of the National Conference of Social Work*, Vol. 45 (Kansas City, 1918), 496.

8. Dinwiddie, *Community Responsibility*, 104; NSUO, *Creation*, 9-10; Dinwiddie, "Work Accomplished," 496.

9. Cincinnati Social Unit Organization (hereafter cited as CSUO), "Constitution," in Randall J. Condon Papers, Univ. of Maine (hereafter cited as Condon Papers).

10. NSUO, *Outline of the Unit Plan*, Bulletin 2 (Cincinnati: NSUO, 1917), 5.

11. CSUO, "Constitution."

12. Ibid., "Social Unit District Chooses Itself," 355.

13. Dinwiddie, *Community Responsibility*, 104; Cincinnati *Commercial Tribune*, April 17, 1917.

14. Dinwiddie, *Community Responsibility*, 104-12.

15. This committee consisted of Drs. Charles T. Souther, president in 1916; John W. Murphy, president in 1915; A.B. Thrasher, president in 1912; and W.D. Haines, president in 1911. "Relation of the Unit Plan to the Cincinnati Academy of Medicine," p. 1, Phillips Papers.

16. Cincinnati *Commercial Tribune*, April 24, 1917; Dinwiddie, *Community Responsibility*, 108.

17. "Relation of Unit Plan," 7.

18. Ibid.

19. Dinwiddie, *Community Responsibility*, 104-12; Phillips, *Adventuring*, 231-32.

20. Phillips, *Adventuring*, 179; Cincinnati *Commercial Tribune*, May 6, 1917; Dinwiddie, "Work Accomplished," 497.

21. *Cincinnati Enquirer*, May 14 through May 21, 1917; Cincinnati *Commercial Tribune*, May 14 through May 21, 1917.

22. "Will You Vote Yes or No?" Phillips Papers.

23. NSUO, *Creation*, 10; Dinwiddie, "Work Accomplished," 497; Phillips, *Adventuring*, 180; Cincinnati *Commercial Tribune*, June 8, 1917; Cincinnati *Commercial Tribune*, June 3, 1917; "Social Unit District Chooses Itself," 355; "Report of the Secretaries to the Members of he Executive Council of the NSUO, April 16 to April 23, (1917)," Pinchot Papers.

24. Cincinnati *Commercial Tribune*, June 3, 1917; Cincinnati *Commercial Tribune*, June 8, 1917; Phillips, "Health and Commonwealth," 255.

25. The organizations promising aid were the Congregation of the Lincoln Park Baptist Church; the Official Board of the Lincoln Park Baptist Church; the Ladies Aid Society of the York Street Methodist Episcopal Church; the Sunday School of the York Street Methodist Episcopal Church; the Young People's Society, the Sunday School Teachers, the Baracca Class, and the Church Committee of the First German Presbyterian Church; the Sands School Social Center Woman's Club of District School 28; the Poplar Street Presbyterian Church; the Mothers' Club of District School 28; the Board of Elders of the Second German Presbyterian Church; Bloom Civics Club; the West End Medical Society; the Teachers of Bloom School; the Cincinnati Woman's Teacher Association; the Sands Center Social Club; the Brotherhood of the Second German Presbyterian Church; the Ladies Aid Society of the Poplar Street Presbyterian Church; the Men's Bible Club of the Poplar Street Presbyterian Church; the Kindergarten Mother's Club of Sands School; the Mothers' Club of District 27, Cincinnati Lodge #1 of the Order of Hercules; the Hubert Playground Association; and St. Luke's Church. Cincinnati *Commercial Tribune*, June 8, 1917.

26. Ibid.; Cincinnati *Commercial Tribune*, June 1, 1917; NSUO, *Creation*, 11; Phillips, "Health and Commonwealth," 254; Dinwiddie, "Work Accomplished," 497.

27. Phillips, *Adventuring*, 182.

28. For an extended discussion of the notion of the Zone of Emergence and its use as a descriptive term for city structure see Robert A. Woods and Albert J. Kennedy, *The Zone of Emergence*, ed. Sam Bass Warner, Jr. (Cambridge, Mass.: M.I.T. Press, 1962).

29. Cincinnati Bureau of Governmental Research, *A Survey Defining the Boundaries of the Cincinnati Region*, Report No. 43 (Cincinnati, 1933), 6-8.

30. Tarr, "City," 205.

31. See Zane L. Miller, "Boss Cox and the Municipal Reformers: Cincinnati Progressivism, 1880-1914," (Ph.D. diss. Univ. of Chicago, 1966) for a fuller discussion of the Circle, Zone, and Hilltop breakdown in Cincinnati for this period.

32. Miller, *Boss Cox's Cincinnati*, 9-24.

33. Ibid., 25-40.

34. Miller, "Boss Cox," 58-96; *Historic Brighton* (Cincinnati, 1902), 91; William C. Smith, *Queen City Yesterdays: Sketches of Cincinnati in the Eighties* (Crawfordsville, Ind.: R.E. Banta, 1959), 3; Woods and Kennedy, *Zone*, 64.

35. Woods and Kennedy, *Zone*, 64; Miller, *Boss Cox's Cincinnati*, 25-34; Warner, *Streetcar Suburbs*, 65-66.

36. Miller, "Boss Cox," 72-78. According to the Fourteenth Census of the United States, the population of the three wards comprising Mohawk-Brighton stood at 39,835. Of this number, the native white population totaled 33,355 and the foreign-born population accounted for 5,918 people. Of the foreign-born population, the Census registered 967 Hungarians, 283 Rumanians, and 2,929 Germans. United States, Bureau of the Census, *Fourteenth Census of the United States, 1920: Population*.

37. Gertrude Mathews Shelby, "Extending Democracy: What the Cincinnati Social Unit Plan Has Accomplished," *Harpers Magazine*, April 1920, 690; Woods and Kennedy, *Zone*, 21; Miller, *Boss Cox's Cincinnati*, 27-28.

38. *Cincinnati Post*, June 11, 1913. See also Miller, *Boss Cox's Cincinnati*, and Woods and Kennedy, *Zone*.

39. "Report of the Secretaries."

40. Miller, *Boss Cox's Cincinnati*, 25-40.

41. Ralph E. Diffendorfer, *The Church and the Community* (New York: Council of Women for Home Missions and Interchurch Movement of North America, 1920), 18.

42. Ibid., 18-19.

43. Dinwiddie, "Work Accomplished," 497-98.

44. See Patricia Mooney Melvin, "With 'Interests Common to All': Cincinnati's Neighborhood Improvement Associations 1880-1920" (paper delivered at the annual meeting of the Organization of American Historians, April 19, 1985); Lyle Koehler, *Westwood in Cincinnati: Community, Continuity, and Change* (Cincinnati: no publisher, 1981); Arnold, "Neighborhood."

45. For a complete listing of the members of the committee responsible for the creation of the Mohawk-Brighton Social Unit Organization see NSUO, *Description of Plan*, 12-15. Members of the committee, in general, were active in the Mohawk-Brighton Social Unit Organization either as members of the neighborhood Occupational Council or as block workers.

46. Dinwiddie, "Work Accomplished," 498; Cincinnati *Commercial Tribune*, June 16, 1917.

47. NSUO, *The Beginning of Work in the Social Unit*, Bulletin 5 (Cincinnati: NSUO, 1918), 3.

48. Ibid.; Cornelius J. Petzhold, "The Social Unit," in Social Unit Organization Papers, Cincinnati Historical Society (hereafter cited as Social Unit Papers).

49. Petzhold, "Social Unit;" NSUO, *Beginning of Work*, 5; NSUO, *Experiment*, 7; Phillips, *Adventuring*, 184; Cincinnati *Commercial Tribune*, August 2, 1917.

50. Petzhold, "Social Unit;" NSUO, *Beginning of Work*, 5.

51. Mary L. Hicks and Roe S. Eastman, "Blockworkers," *The Survey*, September 1, 1920, 672.

52. Democracy on the Social Unit Pattern," *The Survey*, February 6, 1918, 551.

53. NSUO, *Beginning of Work*, 6; Phillips, *Adventuring*, 186.

54. Dinwiddie, *Community Responsibility*, 6.

55. Ibid., 6, 15-16; NSUO, *The Social Unit: A National Experiment on Democracy*, n.d., 7-8.

56. Dinwiddie, *Community Responsibility*, 40; NSUO, *Experiment*, 10; Phillips, *Adventuring*, 187.

57. Dinwiddie, *Community Responsibility*, 40-41.

58. Phillips, *Adventuring*, 188.

59. Ibid.

60. Ibid., 197-98; NSUO, *Beginning of Work*, 6; NSUO, *Experiment*, 11.

61. "Medical Organization in the Social Unit and Work During the First Six Months of 1918," July 1, 1918, p. 4, Phillips Papers.

62. Dinwiddie, *Community Responsibility*, 51; NSUO, *Experiment*, 12; NSUO, *Beginning of Work*, 7.

63. NSUO, *Experiment*, 10-12.

64. Ibid., 10; Dinwiddie, *Community Responsibility*, 72-73; Petzhold, "Social Unit."

65. Dinwiddie, *Community Responsibility*, 66-67; NSUO, *Beginning of Work*, 7.

66. Dinwiddie, *Community Responsibility*, 89; NSUO, *Beginning of Work*, 7.

67. Phillips, *Adventuring*, 192; NSUO, *Beginning of Work*, 7.

68. Ibid.

69. Dinwiddie, "Work Accomplished," 499; NSUO, *Beginning of Work*, 10.

70. NSUO, *Experiment*, 15.

71. Ibid.; NSUO, *Beginning of Work*, 10; Phillips, *Adventuring*, 196-99.

72. NSUO, *Beginning of Work*, 10.

73. Ibid.; *Social Unit Bulletin*, November 24, 1917.

74. "Blockworkers," Phillips Papers. The women who served as block workers were Mrs. John Oberdahn, Mrs. G.W. Baldock, Mrs. E.T. Gillick, Miss Anna Felix, Mrs. Frank Moellers, Mrs. B. Clift, Mrs. Emma Garner, Mrs. A. Eberle, Miss Nellie Bekner, Mrs. T. Schone, Mrs. Frank Woodall, Mrs. J. Doerman, Mrs. H. Harmuth, Mrs. Louis Hudepohl, Mrs. Mary Edmondson, Mrs. Henry Palmer, Mrs. William Pahner, Mrs. Otto Wurtz, Mrs. Staudacher, Mrs. S. Stewart, Mrs. Charles Reinhardt, Mrs. R. Pfeister, Mrs. Benjamin Hall, Mrs. August Kruse, Mrs. Fred Giese, and Mrs. M.J. Durkin.

75. NSUO, *Beginning of Work*, 4. Members of the MBSUO Occupational Council included William A. Evans (executive), Dr. T. Warrington Gosling, Miss Ruth A. Gottlieb, Dr. John Grothaus, William T. Jack, Alexander Landesco, Miss Kathryn Nordman, Rev. Albert E. Wirth, and Miss Ellen McCarthy.

76. "Financial Report of the NSUO from February 9, 1916, to January 1, 1918," 2-6, Phillips Papers; Phillips, *Adventuring*, 193-98. For the period February 9, 1916 to December 31, 1917 receipts totaled $33,733.72. Of these, 46 percent went for salaries, 14 percent for office equipment and supplies, 7 percent for travel expenses, 5 percent for printing expenses, and 9 percent for miscellaneous expenses. The remaining 19 percent was carried over into the 1918 budget.

77. *Social Unit Bulletin*, November 24, 1917; Phillips, *Adventuring*, 199-200.

78. NSUO, *Experiment*, 16; Phillips, *Adventuring*, 193-208; "Financial Report of the National Social Unit Organization From February 9, 1916 to January 1, 1918," 11-13, Phillips Papers. The proposed budget of 1918 divided up a total of $50,483.92 between the NSUO (12 percent), the CSUO (18 percent), and the MBSUO (70 percent).

79. Dinwiddie, *Community Responsibility*, 8; Edward T. Devine, "Social Unit in Cincinnati: An Experiment in Organization," *The Survey*, November 1919, 117.

5. An Experiment in Neighborhood Health Care

Some of the material in this chapter first appeared in Patricia Mooney Melvin, "Mohawk-Brighton: A Pioneer in Neighborhood Health Care," *Bulletin of the Cincinnati Historical Society*, now entitled *Queen City Heritage*, 36 (Spring 1978): 57-72.

1. Rosen, *History*, 472.

2. *Social Unit Bulletin*, December 22, 1917.

3. Dinwiddie, *Community Responsibility*, 41; Burnham, *Community Health*, 111; A.G. Kreidler and Wilbur C. Phillips, "Medical Organization in the Social Unit and Work During the First Six Months of 1918," July 1, 1918, 2-3, Phillips Papers.

4. Dinwiddie, *Community Responsibility*, 53-54; Abbie Roberts, "Report of the

Nurses' Council for the Year 1918," 6, Phillips Papers; Zoe LaFarge, "The Social Unit and Public Health Nursing," *National Social Unit Conference* (Cincinnati, 1919; proceedings in Boston Public Library), 13-14; Mohawk-Brighton Social Unit Organization, "Blanks and Forms," Public Library of Cincinnati and Hamilton County, Cincinnati, Ohio (hereafter cited as MBSUO).

5. Phillips, "Health and Commonwealth," 254-55.

6. Roberts, "Nurses' Report," 7; Elsie Phillips, "A Plan for Community Organization," *Vassar Quarterly* 2 (February 1917): 77-78; NSUO, *Experiment*, 23-25.

7. NSUO, *Experiment*, 23-25; Wilbur C. Phillips, "A New Design for Democracy or the Social Unit Theory and Plan for Evolving a Functional Consumers' and Producers' Democracy," 5, Phillips Papers.

8. Phillips, *Adventuring*, 212.

9. Ibid.; Roberts, "Nurses' Report," 7; Dinwiddie, "Work Accomplished," 499. It is impossible to date precisely the chain of events that led to the opening of the baby station. I believe that the sequence of events presented above is essentially correct. However, I feel that much of the preparatory work—for instance the education of the block workers—preceded the official decision to launch the infant health campaign. While I have no conclusive evidence of this, I find it very hard to believe that the mobilization and instruction of the block workers and the registration of the babies could have occurred only during the first two and one-half weeks of December.

10. Roberts, "Nurses' Report," 7, 11; Kreidler and Phillips, "Medical Organization," 2.

11. Phillips, *Adventuring*, 218; Cincinnati *Commercial Tribune*, March 22, 1918; Courtenay Dinwiddie and A.G. Kreidler, "A Community Self-Organized for Preventive Health Work," *Modern Medicine* 1 (May 1919): 27.

12. Roberts, "Nurses' Report," 7.

13. Nelson, "Neighborhood," 519.

14. Dinwiddie, *Community Responsibility*, 147-48, 168; Petzhold, "Social Unit."

15. Dinwiddie and Kreidler, "Community," 28; Kreidler and Phillips, "Medical Organization," 2; Roberts, "Nurses' Report," 8.

16. Dinwiddie and Kreidler, "Community," 28; Dinwiddie, *Community Responsibility*, 147; Roberts, "Nurses' Report," 8.

17. Phillips, *Adventuring*, 222-23.

18. Abbott, *Ten Years*, 2.

19. U.S. Department of Labor, Children's Bureau, *Children's Year: A Brief Summary of Work Done and Suggestions for Follow-Up Work* (Washington, D.C., 1920), 5.

20. Ibid.; Abbott, *Ten Years*, 9; Anna E. Rude, "Children's Year Campaign," *American Journal of Public Health* 9 (May 1919): 348; James A. Tobey, *The Children's Bureau* (Baltimore: Johns Hopkins Univ. Press, 1925), 7-10.

21. Phillips, *Adventuring*, 222-23.

22. U.S. Department of Labor, Children's Bureau, *Save 100,000 Babies: Get a Square Deal for Children* (Washington, D.C., 1918), 4-5; Phillips, *Adventuring*, 224.

23. Dinwiddie and Kreidler, "Community," 27.

24. Ibid.; Phillips, *Adventuring*, 224.

25. Mary Hicks to Julia Lathrop, April 4, 1918, in U.S. Children's Bureau Records, National Archives (hereafter cited as Children's Bureau Records).

26. Julia Lathrop to Mary Hicks, April 1918, Children's Bureau Records.

27. Mary Hicks to Julia Lathrop, April 20, 1918, Children's Bureau Records; Dinwiddie, *Community Responsibility*, 146.

28. Cincinnati *Commercial Tribune*, April 23, 1918; Dinwiddie, *Community Responsibility*, 78-79; Phillips, *Adventuring*, 26; *Social Unit Bulletin*, n.d.; NSUO, *Experiment*, 26-27.

29. *Social Unit Bulletin*, June 22, 1918; *Social Unit Bulletin*, July 20, 1918; Roberts, "Nurses' Report," 9; U.S. Department of Labor, Children's Bureau, *April and May Weighing and Measuring Test*, pt. 1 (Washington, D.C., 1918), 4; U.S. Department of Labor, Children's Bureau, *April and May Measuring Test*, pt. 2 (Washington, D.C., 1918), 3. It is unclear how Cincinnati as a whole reponded to the drive. What little information exists in the newspapers about Children's Year concerns the MBSUO. Nationwide, the Children's Bureau felt that the drive was successful. All but two states participated in the Children's Year program. Over 16,500 cities, towns, villages, and rural communities conducted the tests. Seven and one-half million weight and measurement tests were sent in to the bureau. As a direct result of the publicity generated by the campaign, nineteen states established state child hygiene divisions, bringing the nationwide total of such organizations to thirty-two. Abbot, *Ten Years*, 9; Children's Bureau, *Childen's Year*, 8-9; Tobey, *Children's Bureau*, 7-10.

30. Elsie Phillips, "Cincinnati's Social Unit," *Vassar Quarterly* (1919): 273.

31. Phillips, *Adventuring*, 255; Dinwiddie, *Community Responsibility*, 10-11.

32. Roberts, "Nurses' Report," 3, 13; Dinwiddie, *Community Responsibility*, 50-51; LaForge, "Social Unit and Nursing," 13.

33. Dinwiddie, *Community Responsibility*, 55-59; LaForge, "Social Unit and Nursing," 10; Roberts, "Nurses' Report," 11.

34. Cincinnati *Commercial Tribune*, September 8, 1918.

35. LaForge, "Social Unit and Nursing," 10, 14; Roberts, "Nurses' Report," 11-12.

36. Dinwiddie, *Community Responsibility*, 147; N.A. Nelson, "Neighborhood Organization vs. Tuberculosis," (1919), 2, Social Unit Papers; Phillips, "Cincinnati's Social Unit," 274.

37. Roberts, "Nurses' Report," 10; Petzhold, "Social Unit"; Burham, *Community Health*, 111.

38. Edward T. Devine, "An Appraisal of the Cincinnati Experiment," *National Social Unit Conference*, 9.

39. Nelson, "Organization," 518; Dinwiddie, *Community Responsibility*, 147.

40. Nelson, "Organization vs. Tuberculosis," 9.

41. Alfred W. Crosby, Jr., *Epidemic and Peace 1918* (Westport, Conn.: Greenwood Press, 1976), 53, 203; Louis I. Dublin, *Twenty-five Years of Health Progress* (New York: Metropolitan Life Insurance Co., 1957), 128; Robert S. Katz, "Influenza 1918-1919: A Study in Mortality," *Bulletin of the History of Medicine* 48 (Fall 1974): 418. For a discussion of the epidemiology of influenza, see Martin M. Kaplan and Robert G. Webster, "The Epidemiology of Influenza," *Scientific American*, December 1977, 88-106.

42. "Flu," Phillips Papers; NSUO, *Experiment*, 32; Phillips, *Adventuring*, 244; "The Social Unit Plan in the Epidemic," *The Survey*, January 11, 1919, 503.

43. Dinwiddie, *Community Responsibility*, 12; Roberts, "Nurses' Report," 10-11; Petzhold, "Social Unit"; NSUO, *Experiment*, 34.

44. Roberts, "Nurses' Report," 11.

45. No figures for the influenza epidemic are complete so actual totals cannot be ascertained. Many cases of influenza were listed as pneumonia, especially during the early months of the epidemic. U.S. Department of Commerce, Bureau of the Census, *Mortality Statistics, 1919*, 28-29; Roberts, "Nurses' Report," 11; Dublin, *Twenty-five Years*, 127-28.

46. "Flu;" Roberts, "Nurses' Report," 11; NSUO, *Experiment*, 34; "The Social Unit Plan," *Outlook*, July 23, 1919, 460.

47. Dinwiddie, *Community Responsibility*, 148-49; Dinwiddie and Kriedler, "Community," 29.

48. *Social Unit Bulletin*, March 3, 1919.

49. Phillips, *Adventuring*, 231-32; NSUO, *Experiment*, 28-29.

50. Phillips, *Adventuring*, 232-33; Dinwiddie, *Community Responsibility*, 11.

51. Phillips, *Adventuring*, 232-33; Dinwiddie, *Community Responsibility*, 12.

52. Courtenay Dinwiddie, "Report to the National and City Statistical Councils of the Social Unit Organization," January 1, 1919, 1, Phillips Papers.

53. Ibid., 2; NSUO, *Experiment*, 29-30; Phillips, *Adventuring*, 233-38; Dinwiddie, *Community Responsibility*, 12; Robert E. Chaddock, "Municipal Statistics and the Social Unit Organization," *Quarterly Publication of the American Statistical Association* 16 (December 1919): 549.

54. Dinwiddie, "Report to Statistical Councils," 3.

55. Petzhold, "Social Unit"; NSUO, *Experiment*, 37; Devine, "Social Unit in Cincinnati," 121.

56. Dinwiddie, *Community Responsibility*, 151.

57. Ibid., Minutes of the Board of Directors of the Better Housing League, January 14, 1919, Better Housing League Papers, Urban Studies Collection, Univ. of Cincinnati.

58. "Statement of the Work of the Better Housing Leauge in the Social Unit District," August 11, 1919, 3, Social Unit Papers.

59. Ibid.; Dinwiddie, *Community Responsibility*, 151.

60. "Statement of Better Housing League," 3.

61. Dinwiddie, *Community Responsibility*, 151; Devine, "Appraisal," 8.

62. Dinwiddie, *Community Responsibility*, 61-65; Phillips, "Cincinnati's Social Unit," 275.

63. Devine, "Appraisal," 8.

64. Ibid., 8-10; Dinwiddie, "Work Accomplished," 504; *Social Unit Bulletin*, August 8, 1919; Dinwiddie, *Community Responsibility*, 62-66.

65. Dinwiddie, *Community Responsibility*, 63-66.

66. Ibid., 68-60, 89; Petzhold, "Social Unit."

67. Dinwiddie, *Community Responsibility*, 80-81; Cincinnati *Commercial Tribune*, January 9, 1919.

68. Cincinnati *Commercial Tribune*, February 16, 1919.

69. Cincinnati *Commercial Tribune*, February 22, 1919.

70. Ibid.; Dinwiddie, *Community Responsibility*, 81; NSUO, *Experiment*, 41.

71. Dinwiddie, "Work Accomplished," 504.

72. Cincinnati *Commercial Tribune*, June 1, 1918; *Social Unit Bulletin*, April 13, 1918; Dinwiddie, *Community Responsibility*, 83; NSUO, *Experiment*, 41; Phyllis Duganne, "Country Neighborliness in City Blocks," *World Outlook*, July 1919, 13.

73. Dinwiddie, *Community Responsibility*, 85.

74. Ibid., 152; Rosen, "Neighborhood Health Center," 304-27; C.E.-A. Winslow, "The Health Center Movement," *Modern Medicine* 1 (August 1919): 328.

75. Dinwiddie and Kreidler, "Community," Dinwiddie, 27; *Community Responsibility*, 47.

76. Haven Emerson, "The Social Unit and Medical Organization," *National Social Unit Conference* (Cincinnati, 1919), 4.

77. Dinwiddie, *Community Responsibility*, 15, 69-70, 79; Dinwiddie and Kreidler, "Community," 31.

6. Politics and the Social Unit, 1919-1920

1. Little information exists about the selection or composition of this committee.

2. Minutes of the National Social Unit Organization, September 17, 1918, Phillips Papers.

3. Dinwiddie, *Community Responsibility*, 28; "Financial Statements for the Expenditures Estimated for the Calendar Year 1919," Phillips Papers. Total monies approved for 1919 came to $60,441.11 and was divided between the NSUO and the MBSUO. Of this $60,441.11, 69 percent was to go to the MBSUO and the remaining 31 percent to the NSUO.

4. Ibid., 25; Cincinnati *Commercial Tribune*, March 5, 1919.

5. Anyone over eighteen years of age was eligible to vote. Phillips provided no rationale for this decision. Also, it is not clear why the MBSUO focused on families rather than on eligible voters. The fact that the percentage of voter turnout appeared higher for families than for individuals may have influenced the organization's decision to report the results in this way.

6. Dinwiddie, *Community Responsibility*, 25-26; NSUO, *Experiment*, 9.

7. Shaffer, "Social Unit Experiment," 168.

8. NSUO, *Experiment*, 9; Dinwiddie, *Community Responsibility*, 26; Phillips, *Adventuring*, 277; Cincinnati *Commercial Tribune*, March 5, 1919.

9. Michael Bliss, "Politics and Social Welfare in Cincinnati: 1900-1920," (M.A. thesis, Univ. of Cincinnati, 1970), 61; Cincinnati *Commercial Tribune*, June 23, 1918; Dinwiddie, *Community Responsibility*, 122-23.

10. Cincinnati *Commercial Tribune*, June 23, 1918.

11. Dinwiddie, *Community Responsibility*, 122; William J. Norton, *The Social Unit Organization in Cincinnati*, Report of the Helen S. Trounstine Foundation (Cincinnati, 1919), frontispiece.

12. An organization designed to centralize fund-raising efforts for charitable work.

13. Norton, *Social Unit*, 183.

14. Ibid., 183-85.

15. Untitled ms., n.d., Condon Papers; Dinwiddie, *Community Responsibility*, 122.

16. A religious forum in Boston, founded under the auspices of the Boston Social Union in 1908.

17. Wilbur C. Phillips to Gifford Pinchot, August 4, 1917, Pinchot Papers; "Statement of Wilbur C. Phillips and Elsie Phillips," September 19, 1917, Pinchot Papers.

18. Mail vote, January 1919, Phillips Papers; Cincinnati *Commercial Tribune,* March 10, 1919; *New York Times,* March 11, 1919.

19. *New York Times,* March 11, 1919; Cincinnati *Commercial Tribune,* March 11, 1919; *Cincinnati Enquirer,* March 11, 1919.

20. Cincinnati *Commercial Tribune,* March 11, 1919.

21. Ibid.; Cincinnati *Commercial Tribune,* March 13, 1919; Dr. John Landis to Wilbur C. Phillips, June 24, 1918, Phillips Papers; Note on the letter from Dr. Landis to Wilbur C. Phillips, Phillips Papers; Cincinnati *Commercial Tribune,* June 23, 1919.

22. Members of this advisory council included Drs. E.H. Bradford, dean of the Harvard Medical School; Christian R. Holmes, dean of the Medical School of the University of Cincinnati; Walter P. James, president of the New York Academy of Medicine; John H. Mason-Knox, ex-president of the American Association for the Study and Prevention of Infant Mortality; Charles Mayo, president of the American Medical Association; William Mayo, president of the American Surgical Association; Victor Vaughan, ex-president of the American Medical Association; and William H. Welch, director of the School of Hygiene and Public Health at Johns Hopkins University.

23. *Cincinnati Enquirer,* June 6, 1918; Cincinnati *Commercial Tribune,* September 25, 1918; Wilbur C. Phillips to Ethel Pew, February 14, 1957, Phillips Papers; Phillips to Pew, March 9, 1964; Dinwiddie, *Community Responsibility,* 108-10, 125-31; Phillips, *Adventuring,* 296-97; "Health and Welfare Work under the Social Unit Plan," *Ohio State Medical Journal* 15 (December 1919): 831.

24. Cincinnati *Commercial Tribune,* September 25, 1918; Phillips, *Adventuring,* 296. Congress created the Council of National Defense shortly after the outbreak of World War I to help facilitate the mobilization of the nation's resources. See Chapter 7.

25. *New York Times,* March 11, 1919; *Cincinnati Times-Star,* March 10, 1919; Cincinnati *Commercial Tribune,* March 11, 1919.

26. *Cincinnati Enquirer,* March 11, 1919; Cincinnati *Commercial Tribune,* March 12, 1919; Phillips, *Adventuring,* 301-7.

27. *Cincinnati Enquirer,* March 12, 1919.

28. *Cincinnati Enquirer,* March 13, 1919; *Cincinnati Enquirer,* April 7, 1919; Cincinnati *Commercial Tribune,* April 7, 1919; *Cincinnati Times-Star,* April 7, 1919.

29. Cincinnati *Commercial Tribune,* March 12, 1919; *Cincinnati Enquirer,* March 13, 1919.

30. Mr. and Mrs. Guggenheim to Wilbur C. Phillips, March 18, 1919, Phillips Papers; Cincinnati *Commercial Tribune,* March 11, 1919; Cincinnati *Commercial Tribune,* March 25, 1919.

31. Cincinnati *Commercial Tribune,* March 12, 1919; Cincinnati *Commercial Tribune,* April 3, 1919; *Cincinnati Times-Star,* April 3, 1919; Dinwiddie, *Community Responsibility,* 132-36.

32. Cincinnati *Commercial Tribune,* March 12, 1919; Cincinnati *Commercial Tribune,* March 13, 1919; *Cincinnati Enquirer,* March 12, 1919; *Social Unit Bulletin,* March 28, 1919.

33. *Social Unit Bulletin,* March 28, 1919; Cincinnati *Commercial Tribune,* March 14, 1919.

34. Dinwiddie, *Community Responsibility,* 19; Phillips, *Adventuring,* 309-10; *Cincinnati Times-Star,* March 19, 1919; Cincinnati *Commercial Tribune,* March 17, 1919;

Cincinnati *Commercial Tribune,* March 19, 1919; *Social Unit Bulletin,* March 26, 1919; Nelson, "Organization," 519; Petzhold, "Social Unit."

35. *Social Unit Bulletin,* March 26, 1919; *Social Unit Bulletin,* March 28, 1919; Cincinnati *Commercial Tribune,* 22, 1919; Cincinnati *Commercial Tribune,* March 26, 1919; *Cincinnati Times-Star,* March 25, 1919; Petzhold, "Social Unit"; Dinwiddie, *Community Responsibility,* 75.

36. *Social Unit Bulletin,* March 26, 1919, to April 8, 1919; Cincinnati *Commercial Tribune,* April 19, 1919; *Cincinnati Times-Star,* April 5, 1919; Phillips, *Adventuring,* 310-11; Cincinnati *Commercial Tribune,* April 9, 1919.

37. Phillips, *Adventuring,* 312-14; *Social Unit Bulletin,* April 16, 1919; Cincinnati *Commercial Tribune,* April 11, 1919; *Cincinnati Times-Star,* April 11, 1919; Petzhold, "Social Unit"; Charles A. Reed, "The 'Social Unit' in Cincinnati," *American Review of Reviews,* May 1919, 524.

38. *Cincinnati Times-Star,* April 11, 1919; *Cincinnati Times-Star,* April 26, 1919; *Cincinnati Enquirer,* April 26, 1919; Cincinnati *Commercial Tribune,* May 5, 1919; *Social Unit Bulletin,* May 10, 1919. The members of the Executive Committee of Nine included Dr. William B. Wherry, Mrs. L.C. Fillmore, Professor Guy A. Tawney, Mrs. Paul Wooley, Dr. Thomas Hart, the Reverend F.L. Flinchbaugh, Kathryn Nordman, Mrs. A.L. Whitaker, and Martin Love.

39. The Council of Social Agencies (CSA) was founded in 1913. Its planned functions included explaining to the public the types of charitable work undertaken in the city, a drive to reduce duplication of services, an attempt to safeguard the public against fraudulent solicitation, and a variety of schemes to educate the public on its obligation to finance the social needs of the community. Cincinnati *Commercial Tribune,* May 9, 1919.

40. Bliss, "Politics and Welfare," 65-66; *Cincinnati Times-Star,* May 6, 1919; *Cincinnati Enquirer,* May 6, 1919.

41. *Cincinnati Times-Star,* May 16, 1919; *Cincinnati Enquirer,* May 6, 1919.

42. Cincinnati *Commercial Tribune,* May 8, 1919; Cincinnati *Commercial Tribune,* May 9, 1919; Cincinnati *Commercial Tribune,* March 21, 1919.

43. Committee's underlining.

44. Wilbur C. Phillips to the committee appointed by the Council of Social Agencies to Investigate the Social Unit, May 27, 1919, Phillips Papers; Council of Social Agencies, *Investigation of the Charges Against the Social Unit Organization* (Cincinnati, 1919), 5-7; Cincinnati *Commercial Tribune,* July 2, 1919.

45. CSA, *Investigation,* 7-10.

46. CSA, *Investigation,* 11-17; "Summary of Committee from the Council of Social Agencies on the Social Unit Organization," 1919, 3, Phillips Papers.

47. CSA, *Investigation,* 18-20; "Summary," 3-4.

48. CSA, *Investigation,* 21-33; "Summary," 4; Cincinnati *Commercial Tribune,* July 2, 1919.

49. CSA, *Investigation,* 35; Cincinnati *Commercial Tribune,* July 2, 1919; *Cincinnati Enquirer,* July 2, 1919.

50. Courtenay Dinwiddie, "Comment on the Report of the Council of Social Agencies," n.p., n.d., Public Library of Cincinnati and Hamilton County, Cincinnati, Ohio.

51. Concinnati *Commercial Tribune,* July 12, 1919; Executive Committee of the

Committee of Citizens on the Social Unit, "Comment Upon the Published Report of the Council of Social Agencies on the Social Unit Organization," July 12, 1919, 1-5, Phillips Papers.

52. Cincinnati *Commercial Tribune,* July 22, 1919; Cincinnati *Commercial Tribune,* September 10, 1919; Cincinnati *Commercial Tribune,* September 17, 1919; Cincinnati *Commercial Tribune,* October 7, 1919; Duganne, "Country Neighborliness," 13.

53. Dinwiddie, *Community Responsibility,* 136-37; Phillips, *Adventuring,* 346; Cincinnati *Commercial Tribune,* September 12, 1919 to September 30, 1919; *Social Unit Bulletin,* October 25, 1919.

54. Dinwiddie, *Community Responsibility,* 137; Phillips, *Adventuring,* 358; Cincinnati *Commercial Tribune,* October 23, 1919.

55. John Collier, "Why Community Organization?" *National Social Unit Conference,* 2-3.

56. John Lovejoy Elliott, "Some Neighborhood Needs: Will the Social Unit Help Solve Them?" in *National Social Unit Conference,* 4-5.

57. Ibid., 5-8.

58. LaForge, "Social Unit and Public Health," 10-19; *Cincinnati Times-Star,* October 24, 1919; Emerson, "Social Unit and Medical Organization," 3-9.

59. *Cincinnati Times-Star,* October 24, 1919; Charles Stelzle, "The Social Unit and the Church," *National Social Unit Conference,* 2-4. The other three speeches were not published.

60. Robert E. Chaddock, "The Social Unit and Community Statistics," *National Social Unit Conference,* 2-4.

61. Edward T. Devine, "The Social Unit in Cincinnati: An Experiment in Organization," *National Social Unit Conference,* 3-15. Devine's talk was reprinted in the November 15, 1919, issue of *The Survey* and summarized in the January 1920 issue of the *Journal of Delinquency* under the title of "The Social Unit as a Means of Democratizing Social Work."

62. John Collier, "Democracy and the Making of Budgets," *National Social Unit Conference,* 3-6.

63. Mark M. Jones, "The Social Unit from the Point of View of Business," *National Social Unit Conference,* 3-4; John Walker, "The Social Unit from the Point of View of Labor," Ibid., 5-8. Walker's talk was reprinted under the title "The Social Unit Plan" in the *Illinois State Federation of Labor Weekly Newsletter,* January 10, 1920.

64. Cincinnati *Commercial Tribune,* October 25, 1919; Wilbur C. Phillips, "The Social Unit in 1920," *National Social Unit Conference,* 3-6.

65. Devine, "Social Unit in Cincinnati," 119.

66. Phillips, *Adventuring,* 355; Shaffer, "Social Unit Experiment," 168-69; Bliss, "Politics and Welfare," 76-77.

67. *Social Unit Bulletin,* August 3, 1918; Dinwiddie, *Community Responsibility,* 137-38; Cincinnati *Commercial Tribune,* November 19, 1919; *Social Unit Bulletin,* November 22, 1919.

68. Phillips, *Adventuring,* 363, Cincinnati *Commercial Tribune,* December 4, 1919; Cincinnati *Commercial Tribune,* December 5, 1919; *Social Unit Bulletin,* December 16, 1919; *Social Unit Bulletin,* December 10, 1919; *Social Unit Bulletin,* March 13, 1920.

69. *Social Unit Bulletin,* December 20, 1919; Dinwiddie, *Community Responsibility,* 139; Cincinnati *Commercial Tribune,* January 13, 1920; "Social Unit Survey," *The Survey,* August 2, 1920, 589.

70. Cincinnati *Commercial Tribune,* January 27, 1920; *Social Unit Bulletin,* January 31, 1920.

71. Organized in 1909 under the direction of Dr. Benjamin K. Rachford, the Babies Milk Fund Association established infant milk clinics throughout the city of Cincinnati to help combat milk-related infant deaths. In 1919 the Babies Milk Fund Association became part of the newly formed Community Chest.

72. *Social Unit Bulletin,* July 3, 1920; Chaddock, Elliott, Stelzle, Straight, and Phillips to Mary Hicks, n.d., Phillips Papers; Mary Hicks to Wilbur C. Phillips, November 4, 1920, Phillips Papers; Mary Hicks to Wilbur C. Phillips and Elsie C. Phillips, November 6, 1920, Phillips Papers; Conference Relative to Future Work in the Mohawk-Brighton District, Phillips Papers; Warwick Black, "The Social Unit Ended in Cincinnati," *National Municipal Review.* February, 1921, 73; Dr. B.K. Rachford to Mary Hicks, November 11, 1920, Babies Milk Fund Association and Maternity Service, Cincinnati, Ohio.

73. Dinwiddie, *Community Responsibility,* 132.

74. Robert C. Dexter, *Social Adjustment* (New York: Alfred A. Knopf, 1927), 392.

75. Shaffer, "Social Unit Experiment," 169; Bliss, "Politics and Welfare," 78; Minutes of the National Social Unit Organization, December 6, 1920, Phillips Papers; Dinwiddie, *Community Responsibility,* 128; "Who Makes Bolshevism in Cincinnati?" *New Republic,* April 19, 1919, 367.

76. Phillips, *Adventuring,* 153-63; Petzhold, "Social Unit"; Phillips and Phillips, "Plan," 271, 284, 355; Delos F. Wilcox, *The American City, A Problem in Democracy* (New York: Macmillan Co., 1904), 265; Kenneth Fox, *Better City Government: Innovation in American Urban Politics 1850-1937* (Philadelphia: Temple Univ. Press, 1977), 82; Devine, "Social Unit," 7-8.

77. Follett, *New State,* passim; see also Quandt, *Small Town,* 16, 41, 139-45; Haber, *Efficiency,* 127.

78. S. Gale Lowrie, "Social Unit: An Experiment in Politics," *National Municipal Review,* September 1920, 561-66.

79. Steiner, *Community,* 248.

80. Bliss, "Politics and Welfare," 78.

81. Petzhold, "Social Unit"; Steiner, *Community,* 246; see also "Statement of Better Housing League," 3.

82. *Minutes,* December 6, 1920; "Who Wants Bolshevism," 367; see also Follett, *New State,* 217; Hart, *Community,* 189; Phillips, "New Design," 65; Griffith, *American,* 132; Steiner, *Community,* 246.

83. Norton, *Social Unit Organization,* 183.

84. Devine, "Social Unit," 7-8.

85. Financial federations, ventures in the joint financing of social welfare agencies, first began in America in Denver during 1888. The Denver Associated Charities sought to relieve the "generous and well-to-do" givers to philanthropic organizations from continual solicitation. A number of cities followed Denver's lead. The drive for joint financing received a boost during World War I with the establishment of War Chests designed to centralize fund raising for war-related charitable organizations.

In Cincinnati, the first venture in joint financing—the Federation of Jewish Charities—occurred soon after the Denver experiment. But for most Cincinnati organizations, centralized fund raising did not become the practice until the Cincinnati Council of Social Agencies "created a financial federation within itself." The CSA set up a special department, composed of representatives of all those participating in the joint campaign. Each cooperating agency prepared in advance a detailed budget. Once accepted by the special CSA budget committee, the participating agency could alter its budget only with the permission of the CSA. Once the various budgets were accepted by the CSA, the CSA sponsored a campaign in which a large number of solicitors would canvass the city for approximately ten days to raise all the money necessary to meet the cooperating agencies' budgets. Warner, Queen, and Harper, *American Charities*, 540-44.

86. Lubove, *Professional Altruist*, 181-83.

87. Bliss, "Politics and Welfare," 75-78; "The Social Unit Plan," *Outlook*, July 23, 1919, 640; Steiner, *Community*, 175-80.

88. Black, "Social Unit," 72.

89. Steiner, *Community*, 248; Dexter, *Social Adjustment*, 391; Burnham, *Community Health*, 54; Phillips, "Need," 290-94.

90. Woods and Kennedy, *Settlement*, 251.

91. Phillips, "Need," 291-94.

92. Patricia Mooney Melvin, "Mohawk-Brighton: A Pioneer in Neighborhood Health Care," Cincinnati Historical Society *Bulletin* 38 (Spring 1978): 57-72; "The Historical Development," *American Journal of Public Health* 11 (March 1919): 212; Winslow, "Health Center," 327; *The Reminiscences of Dr. Haven Emerson*, 33, Oral History Project, Columbia University, New York; "What is a Health Center," *American Journal of Public Health* 10 (August 1920): 677; Michael M. Davis, *Clinics, Hospitals and Health* (New York: Harper and Bros., 1927), 357; Davis and Warner, *Dispensaries*, 318-19; Melvin, "Make Milwaukee Safe," 83-93.

93. Winslow, "Health Center," 327; Warner and Davis, *Dispensaries*, 321-23; Burnham, *Community Health*, 55-56; Rosen, "Neighborhood Health Center," 304-27.

94. Phillips, *Adventuring*, 326-30; Lowrie, "Social Unit," 560-61.

7. Metropolitan Community to Fragmented Metropolis, 1920-1940

1. Woods, "City and Local Community," 196.

2. Phillips, "Social Unit in 1920," 6; Cincinnati *Commercial Tribune*, October 25, 1919.

3. *New York Times*, December 8, 1919.

4. Steiner, "Community Organization," 15.

5. Dillick, *Community*, 72.

6. Ibid., 71-72; John Collier, "Community Councils—Democracy Everyday: III," *The Survey*, September 28, 1918, 710.

7. Steiner, "Community Organization," 15.

8. Ibid.

9. Dillick, *Community*, 72-73; Lindeman, *Community*, 168-69.

10. Lindeman, *Community*, 70.

11. Holden, *Settlement Idea*, 57.

12. Program and Budget for 1920 of the Community Councils of Greater New York and the National Social Unit Organization, (1920), 2, Phillips Papers; Agreement between the Executives of the National Social Unit Organization and the Community Councils of New York Contingent to Ratification by the Boards of the Two Organizations, n.d., Phillips Papers.

13. *New York Times*, December 8, 1919; Cincinnati *Commercial Tribune*, December 8, 1919; Wilbur C. Phillips to the General Council of the NSUO, December 2, 1919, Phillips Papers.

14. "Plan of Cooperation between the Community Councils of New York, Community Service, Inc., and the National Social Unit Organization," (1919), 1, Phillips Papers. At the time of the merger, Community Service, Inc., planned to join forces with the NYCC and NSUO. Community Service, Inc., focused its efforts on the leisure-time activities of neighborhood residents. However, soon after the plans for the merger were drawn up, Community Service, Inc., decided to sever its relationship with the NYCC and the NSUO. Draft of a Statement of Work Being Carried on by the New York Community Councils, Community Service, Inc., and the National Social Unit Organization, (1920), Phillips Papers.

15. Participants in this meeting included, for the NYCC, George G. Battle, Harriet B. Lowenstein, Lawson Purdy, A.W. Richardson, Thomas Rock, Mrs. C.C. Rumsey, Eugene Gibney, Ruth Morgan, Albert Shiels, Irwin Mills, Mayo Tolman, G.S. Fouger, Mildred Taylor, and Ben Howe; for the NSUO, Mrs. Charles Tiffany, Felix M. Warburg, Mrs. Daniel Guggenheim, Mrs. Willard Straight, Virginia Potter, Helen Hartley Jenkins, Mrs. Henry Ollesheimer, Edward Lyman, Phillips, and Dorothy Thompson. Minutes of the Meeting of the Executive Committee of the New York Community Councils and the National Social Unit Organization, December 23, 1919, Phillips Papers.

16. Ibid.

17. Lindeman, *Community*, 69-70; Dillick, *Community*, 71-72.

18. Leebron Harvey, "The Democratic Community," *The Survey*, June 19, 1920, 409.

19. Program and Budget for 1920, 2.

20. Ibid.

21. Minutes of the Joint Campaign Committee of the New York Community Councils and the National Social Unit Organization, April 16, April 20, May 4, 1920, Phillips Papers; Minutes of the National Social Unit Organization, June 7, September 30, December 6, 1920, Phillips Papers.

22. "An American Folk-Day," *The Survey*, June 26, 1920, 427-28.

23. *New York Times*, March 21, 1920; "A Day for Neighbors," *The Survey*, March 27, 1920, 798.

24. Minutes of the National Social Unit Organization, February 16, March 13, 1920, Phillips Papers.

25. *New York Times*, June 13, 1920; "Day for Neighbors," 798; "American Folk-Day," 427.

26. Minutes of the National Social Unit Organization, September 30, December 6,

1920; *New York Times,* March 30, 1921, 18; Shaffer, "Social Unit Experiment," 170.

27. Joan Phillips Reed to the author, September 27, 1977.

28. "To Members of the General Council of the National Social Unit Organization from the Executive Council," n.d., Phillips Papers.

29. Wilbur C. Phillips, "Brief Summary of His Past Activities Which Led Him Step By Step to His Present Conclusions," n.d., 1-3, Phillips Papers.

30. Lubove, *Altruist,* 177.

31. Woods, "City and Local Community," 196.

32. Clarence E. Rainwater, "Community Organization," *Studies in Sociology* 4 (February 1920): 5.

33. Dinwiddie, *Community Responsibility,* 33-36.

34. Ibid., 23-24, 33-36; Seba Eldridge, "Community Organization and Citizenship," *Social Forces* 7 (September 1928): 139; Lubove, *Altruist,* 177.

35. Lindeman, *Community,* 173.

36. Ibid.; Lubove, *Altruist,* 177-78.

37. Dinwiddie, *Community Responsibility,* 23-24, 37-38, 97; Lubove, *Altruist,* 177.

38. Miller, "Neighborhood," 21; Goldman, "Buffalo," 467.

39. Teaford, *City,* 84.

40. Gerald D. Suttles, "Community Design: The Search for Participation in a Metropolitan Society," in *Metropolitan America in Contemporary Perspective,* ed. Amos Hawley and Vincent P. Rock (New York: John Wiley and Sons, 1975), 243.

41. Kenneth T. Jackson, *The Ku Klux Klan in the City 1915-1930* (New York: Oxford Univ. Press, 1967), 244-49; Zorbaugh, *Gold Coast,* 221; Zane L. Miller, "Turning Inward: The Concept and Role of Neighborhood in American Cities," typescript, October 14, 1977, delivered at Neighborhood Preservation: The Case of Lubbock's Overton South, Texas Tech Univ., October 14-15, 1977, 15.

42. Robert E. Park, "The Urban Community as a Spatial Pattern and a Moral Order," in *The Urban Community,* ed. Ernest Burgess (Chicago: Univ. of Chicago Press, 1926), 3-11.

43. Roderick D. McKenzie, *The Neighborhood: A Study of Local Life in the City of Columbus, Ohio,* (Chicago: Univ. of Chicago Press, 1923; reprint ed. New York: Arno Press, 1970).

44. Christopher Silver, "Neighborhood Planning in Historical Perspective, *Journal of the American Planning Association* 51 (Spring 1985): 161-74.

45. Zane L. Miller, "The Role and Concept of Neighborhood in American Cities," in *Community Organization for Urban Social Change: A Historical Perspective,* ed. Robert Fisher and Peter Romanofsky (Westport, Conn.: Greenwood Press, 1981), 12-13.

46. Zorbaugh, *Gold Coast,* 204-11.

47. Ibid., 214-16.

48. Ibid., 204-43.

49. Ibid., 221-48.

50. Ibid., 16-17; Charles F. Grosser, *New Directions in Community Organization: From Enabling to Advocacy* (New York: Praeger Publishers, 1976), 23, 171-72; Roy Bailey and Mike Brake, "Introduction: Social Work in the Welfare State," in *Radical*

Social Work, ed. Roy Bailey and Mike Brake (New York: Pantheon Books, 1975), 11; Robert Bailey, Jr., *Radicals in Urban Politics: The Alinsky Approach* (Chicago: Univ. of Chicago Press, 1974), 45; Saul D. Alinsky, *Reveille for Radicals* (New York: Random House, 1946; Vintage Book ed., 1969), 53-190; Joseph A. Spencer, "Tenant Organization and Housing Reform in New York City: The Citywide Tenants Council, 1936-1943," in *Community Organization,* ed. Fisher and Romanofsky, 127-56.

Bibliographic Essay

This study of the interrelationship between urban definition and community organization during the first two decades of the twentieth century draws on a wide variety of sources. Of these sources, manuscripts, newspapers, periodicals, published reports, conference proceedings, and government documents provided most of the material necessary for the reconstruction of the development of the social unit theory of organization and of the operation of the social unit organization in its various manifestations. Printed materials, published between 1880 and 1930, helped document contemporary attitudes about the city, child welfare, health centers, and community organization. Certain secondary sources proved useful in working out an approach to and understanding of urban definition and the dynamics of community organization. Other secondary sources offered important background information for an understanding of the dynamics of late nineteenth century urban growth and the turn-of-the-century crusade for child welfare. And, finally, this study drew on a variety of secondary sources for specific information about the development of the social unit theory of organization and the operation of the social unit demonstration.

Manuscripts

The Wilbur C. Phillips Papers at the Social Welfare History Archives Center of the University of Minnesota offer the richest source of material on the social unit theory and on the organizational activities of the National Social Unit Organization and the Mohawk-Brighton Social Unit Organization. Material in the Phillips Papers can be grouped into five different categories: the campaign for child welfare, the social unit theory of organization, the National Social Unit Organization, the Mohawk-Brighton Social Unit Organization, and social-unit-style activities after 1921. Included in each category are correspondence, published and unpublished reports, minutes of meetings, financial records, and public relations information. Three unpublished manuscripts—Wilbur C. Phillips and Elsie C. Phillips, "Social Unity: A Philosophy for Democracy," n.d.; Wilbur C. Phillips and Elsie C. Phillips, "A Plan for Social Organization or the Unit Method of Gradually Building Up a Complete System for Studying and Meeting Social Needs," n.d.; and Wilbur C. Phillips, "A New Design for Democracy or the Social Unit Theory and Plan for Evolving a Functional Consumers' and Producers' Democracy," n.d.—provide detailed accounts of Phillips's activities in New York City, Milwaukee, and Cincinnati. These studies also supplement nicely material covered in Phillips's autobiography, *Adventuring for Democracy* (New York: Social Unit Press, 1940).

Material related to social unit activities also appears in a variety of other manuscript collections. The Gifford Pinchot Papers at the Library of Congress include important correspondence relating to the organization of the National Social Unit Organization and the decision to select Cincinnati for the unit demonstration. The Randall J. Condon Papers at the University of Maine contain information on the organization of the Cincinnati Social Unit Organization and on the selection of Mohawk-Brighton as the demonstration district. Other collections that include material pertaining to the Mohawk-Brighton Social Unit Organization and its activities are the Better Housing League Papers in the Special Collections Department of the University of Cincinnati Library; the Social Unit Papers and the Southwestern Lung Association Papers at the Cincinnati Historical Society; the Mohawk-Brighton Social Unit Organization Collection at the Public Library of Cincinnati and Hamilton County; the United States Children's Bureau Records at the National Archives, and the Dorothy Thompson Papers at the George Arents Research Library at Syracuse University. Collections with minimal correspondence relating to Phillips's activities are the Frank A. Vanderlip Papers, the Nicholas Murray Butler Papers, and the Wesley C. Mitchell Papers located in the Butler Library at Columbia University.

Other manuscript collections and oral history documents provided information on urban health care activities and on turn-of-the-century beliefs about the importance of community organization. Material on contemporary views about community organization and its relationship to city organization can be found in the Robert A. Woods Papers in the Houghton Library at Harvard University, the Albert J. Kennedy Papers in the Social Welfare History Archives Center of the University of Minnesota, the Eduard C. Lindeman Papers in the Butler Library at Columbia University, and *The Reminiscences of William J. Norton*, Oral History Project, Columbia University. Information on urban health activities during the early twentieth century is contained in the Henry L. Coit Papers at the National Library of Medicine and in *The Reminiscences of Dr. Haven Emerson*, Oral History Project, Columbia University.

Newspapers

Newspapers yielded invaluable information on the history of the Milwaukee Child Welfare Commission and on the Cincinnati social unit demonstration. The three major Milwaukee daily newspapers—the *Milwaukee Free Press*, the *Milwaukee Journal*, and the *Milwaukee Sentinel*—and the Socialist daily—the *Milwaukee Leader*—provided extensive coverage of the operation of the Child Welfare Commission and the controversy surrounding its dissolution.

Of the three major Cincinnati newspapers during these years, the *Cincinnati Commercial Tribune* represented the single most important source on the creation of the Mohawk-Brighton Social Unit Organization, its operation, and its fight for survival. The *Cincinnati Enquirer* furnished relatively detailed coverage of the mayor's attack on the social unit and on the various investigations undertaken to ascertain the soundness of the beliefs held by those involved in the creation and direction of social unit activities in Cincinnati. Articles in the *Cincinnati Times-Star*—a newspaper owned by a friend and political supporter of the mayor—captured the flavor of the attack on the social unit and serve as excellent documents of the antiradical hysteria that swept the U.S. after World War I. The *New York Times* not only provided material on social unit activities in Cincinnati but also furnished regular coverage of the activities of the National Social Unit Organization. Articles in the *New York Times* on the national organization also helped place the Cincinnati demonstration in context and served as barometers of public opinion about the value of neighborhood work. All of these newspapers are available on microfilm. Articles in the *Social Unit Bulletin,* the official newspaper of the Mohawk-Brighton Social Unit Organization, provided important information about the daily activities of the unit demonstration and on the neighborhood's response to the mayor's attack. Copies of the *Bulletin* can be found in the Cincinnati Historical Society and in the Wilbur C. Phillips Papers.

Periodicals

Selected periodicals proved especially important in documenting the early twentieth century crusade to improve child health, in detailing contemporary views about the social unit organization, and in recording assumptions about urban organization held during the first two decades of the century. These periodicals include the *American City*, the *American Journal of Public Health, Charities and The Commons*, the *New Republic, Outlook*, and *The Survey*.

Published Reports

Several published reports aided in documenting different aspects of neighborhood work undertaken prior to 1920 and Phillips's baby health activities in New York City and Milwaukee. The South End House, *Annual Reports* (1908-1910) provided information about one particular settlement house—the South End House in Boston—and the relationship between its activities and the general welfare of Boston as a whole. Lillian Brandt's report to the Committee in the Institute of Welfare and Research of the Community Service Society, *Growth and Development of AICP and COS* (New York: Community Service Society, 1942), contains helpful material on the activities of the New York Association for Improving the Condition of the Poor. The association's *Annual Reports* (1907-1912) likewise provided useful information. The report published by the New York Milk Committee in 1916—*Ten Years of Work 1907-1916*—places the early work of the committee in perspective and assesses the impact of the programs designed by Phillips for the committee from 1906 to 1911 on the New York City child health crusade. The *Annual Reports of the Commissioner of Health for Milwaukee* for 1911 and 1912 help detail the work undertaken by the Milwaukee Child Welfare Commission and assess the impact of the work on the Fourteenth Ward.

Other reports helped document the operation of the social unit demonstration and the controversy surrounding the social unit experiment in Cincinnati. The reports issued by the Council of Social Agencies, *Investigation of the Charges Against the Social Unit Organization* (Cincinnati, 1919), and by William J. Norton, *The Social Unit Organization*, (Cincinnati: Helen S. Trounstine Foundation, 1919), help in the reconstruction of events surrounding the mayor of Cincinnati's attack on the social unit organization and the city's eventual decision to abandon its commitment to the social unit demonstration. The Harvard College, Class of 1904, *Reports*, for the years 1904 through 1954, located in the Weidner Library at Harvard University, help trace the different stages of Phillips's career. Sketches in these yearly reports include information about the graduates' employment, residence, and future plans. And, finally, the Cincinnati Bureau of Governmental Research's *A Survey Defining the Boundaries of the Cincinnati Region*, Report No. 43 (Cincinnati, 1933) provided information necessary for understanding Cincinnati's pattern of urban development prior to 1933.

Conference Proceedings

Those active in the early twentieth century child health crusade and in the turn-of-the-century community organization programs participated in numerous conferences. In their presentations, these health and urban activists outlined their own activities and speculated on the importance of their efforts. As a result, their papers represent a rich mine of information for anyone interested in social welfare activities during the first two decades of the twentieth century. The most important of these conferences include the Child Conference for Research and Welfare (1909); the International Congress on Hygiene and Demography (1912); the annual sessions of the National Conference of Charities and Correction, later renamed the National Conference of Social Work (1909-1920); the National Social Unit Organization Conference (1919); the special conference called by the New York Association for Improving the Condition of the Poor, "Clean Milk for New York City," (1906); and the special conference sponsored by the New York Milk Committee, "Conference on Milk Problems" (1910).

Government Documents

Reports issued by the federal government provided information on child health activities between 1900 and 1920 and on characteristics of various groups in the population. Reports detailing child health programs include Dorothy E. Bradbury and Martha M. Eliot's *Four Decades of Action for Children: A Short History of the Children's Bureau*, U.S. Department of Health, Education and Welfare, Bulletin No. 358 (Washington, D.C.: Government Printing Office, 1956); U.S. Department of Commerce and Labor, Children's Bureau, *The Children's Bureau* (Washington, D.C.: Government Printing Office, 1912); U.S. Department of Labor, Children's Bureau, *April and May Weighing and Measuring Tests*, Parts 1, 2, 3 (Washington, D.C.: Government Printing Office, 1918); U.S. Department of Labor, Children's Bureau, *Children's Year: A Brief Summary of Work Done and Suggestions for Follow-Up Work* (Washington, D.C.: Government Printing Office, 1920); U.S. Department of Labor, Children's Bureau, *Save 100,000 Babies: Get a Square Deal for Children* (Washington, D.C.: Government Printing Office, 1918); and U.S. Department of the Treasury, Public Health and Marine Hospital Service of the United States, Hygienic Laboratory, *Milk and Its Relation to Public Health*, Bulletin No. 41 (Washington, D.C.: Government Printing Office, 1908).

Government documents that provide the necessary demographic information inlcude U.S. Department of Commerce, Bureau of the Census, *Mortality Statistics*, 1919; U.S. Department of Commerce, Bureau of the

Census, *Sixteenth Census of the United States, 1940: Vital Statistics Rates in the United States 1900-1940;* U.S. Department of Commerce and Labor, Bureau of the Census, *Mortality Statistics 1900-1904;* U.S. Department of Commerce and Labor, *Mortality Statistics, 1906;* U.S. Department of Commerce and Labor, Bureau of the Census, *Fourteenth Census of the United States, 1920: Population,* Vol. 1; U.S. Department of Commerce and Labor, *Thirteenth Census of the United States, 1910: Population,* Vol. 3; U.S. Department of Commerce and Labor, Bureau of the Census, *Twelfth Census of the United States, 1900: Population,* Vol. 1; and U.S. Bureau of the Census, *Historical Statistics of the United States, Colonial Times to 1970,* Vol. 1 (1975).

The most important local government documents were the *Proceedings of the Common Council of the City of Milwaukee for the Year Ending April 11, 1912,* and the *Proceedings of the Common Council of the City of Milwaukee for the Year Ending April 14, 1913.* These documents provided information on the formation, operation, and demise of the Milwaukee Child Welfare Commission.

Monographs and Articles

This examination of the history of the social unit organization and its relationship to prevailing beliefs about urban definition draws on the accounts of individuals active during the period under study and on the work of other scholars. Many materials are primary sources in that they date from the years under scrutiny. The secondary sources focus on periods of which their authors were not a part. The books and articles included in this essay represent all those sources most useful in this study.

Several studies have proved critical in my understanding of and my approach to the history of neighborhood and the city between 1880 and 1930. Most helpful in structuring my overall approach have been Thomas Bender, *Community and Social Change in America* (New Brunswick, N.J.: Rutgers Univ. Press, 1978); Thomas Bender, *Toward an Urban Vision: Ideas and Institutions in Nineteenth-Century America* (Lexington: Univ. Press of Kentucky, 1975); Blaine A. Brownell, *The Urban Ethos in the South 1920-1930* (Baton Rouge: Louisiana State Univ. Press, 1975); Zane L. Miller, "Defining the City—and Urban History," *Reviews in American History* 4 (September 1976): 436-41; and Henry D. Shapiro, *Appalachia on Our Mind: The Southern Mountains and Mountaineers in the American Consciousness, 1870-1920* (Chapel Hill: Univ. of North Carolina Press, 1978).

Other studies proved useful specifically in thinking through the relationship between ideas and action. The collection of essays edited by John

Higham and Paul K. Conkin, *New Directions in American Intellectual History* (Baltimore: Johns Hopkins Univ. Press, 1979) not only provoked new ways of looking at my material, but also served as a constant reminder of the problems associated with any investigation of the interaction between definition and action. Other important works include Robert C. Bannister, *Social Darwinism: Science and Myth in Anglo-American Social Thought* (Philadelphia: Temple Univ. Press, 1979); John Brewer, *Party Ideology and Popular Politics at the Accession of George III* (Cambridge: Cambridge Univ. Press, 1976); Leon Festinger, *A Theory of Cognitive Dissonance* (Stanford: Stanford Univ. Press, 1957); Sidney Fine, *Laissez-faire and the General Welfare State: A Study of Conflict in American History 1865-1901* (Ann Arbor: Univ. of Michigan Press, 1956); Jean B. Quandt, *From the Small Town to the Great Community: The Social Thought of Progressive Intellectuals* (New Brunswick, N.J.: Rutgers Univ. Press, 1970); Robert H. Wiebe, *The Search for Order 1877-1920* (New York: Hill and Wang, 1967); and Robert H. Wiebe, *The Segmented Society: An Introduction to the Meaning of America* (New York: Oxford Univ. Press, 1975).

Several sources have proved useful in my analysis of early twentieth century beliefs about the organization of society. Among contemporary sources, the most helpful include Herbert Croly, *Progressive Democracy* (New York: Macmillan and Co., 1915); Herbert Croly, *The Promise of American Life* (New York: Macmillan Co., 1909; reprint ed., Cambridge, Mass.: Belknap Press, 1965); A.H. Lloyd, "The Organic Theory of Society," *American Journal of Sociology* 6 (March 1901): 577-601; M.P. Follett, "Community as a Process," *Journal of Philosophy, Psychology and Scientific Methods* 16 (December 1919): 715-17; M.P. Follett, *The New State: Group Organization, the Solution of Popular Government*, 2d ed. (New York: Longmans, Green and Co., 1923); and Walter E. Weyl, *The New Democracy: An Essay on Certain Political and Economic Tendencies in the United States* (New York: Macmillan Co., 1913). Charles Forcey, *The Crossroads of Liberalism: Croly, Weyl, Lippman and the Progressive Era 1900-1925* (New York: Oxford Univ. Press, 1961); Samuel Haber, *Efficiency and Uplift: Scientific Management in the Progressive Era 1890-1920* (Chicago: Univ. of Chicago Press, 1964); Samuel P. Hayes, *Conservation and the Gospel of Efficiency: The Progressive Conservation Movement 1890-1920* (Cambridge, Mass: Harvard Univ. Press, 1959); Samuel P. Hays, *The Response to Industrialism 1885-1914* (Chicago: Univ. of Chicago Press, 1957); Sidney Kaplan, "Social Engineers as Saviors: Effects of World War I on Some American Liberals," *Journal of the History of Ideas* 17 (June 1956): 347-69; Don S. Kirschner, "The Ambiguous Legacy: Social Justice and Social Control in the Progressive Era," *Historical Reflections* 2 (Summer 1975): 69-88; Gabriel Kolko, *The Triumph of Conservatism:*

A *Reinterpretation of American History 1900-1916* (Glencoe, Ill.: Free Press, 1963); David W. Noble, "Herbert Croly and American Progressive Thought," *Western Political Quarterly* 7 (December 1954): 537-53; David W. Noble, "The New Republic and the Idea of Progress," *Mississippi Valley Historical Review* 38 (December 1951): 387-402; David W. Noble, *The Paradox of Progressive Thought* (Minneapolis: Univ. of Minnesota Press, 1958); and David E. Price, "Community and Control: Critical Democratic Theory in the Progressive Period," *American Political Science Review* 68 (December 1974): 1663-78, help provide the necessary context for an understanding of the environment in which the social unit organization developed.

Sam Bass Warner, Jr.'s *Streetcar Suburbs: The Process of Growth in Boston, 1870-1900*, 2d ed. (Cambridge, Mass: Harvard Univ. Press, 1978), remains the best starting point for an understanding of the development of the late nineteenth century city. Other important studies that focus on the dynamics of urban growth include Mark S. Foster, *From Streetcar to Superhighway: American City Planners and Urban Transportation, 1900-1940* (Philadelphia: Temple Univ. Press, 1981); Clay McShane, *Technology and Reform: Street Railways and the Growth of Milwaukee, 1887-1900* (Madison: State Historical Society of Wisconsin, 1974); Gideon J. Sjoberg, "The Pre-Industrial City, Past and Present," *American Journal of Sociology* 60 (January 1955): 438-45; George M. Smerk, "The Streetcar: Shaper of American Cities," *Traffic Quarterly* 21 (October 1967): 569-84; Joel A. Tarr, "From City to Suburb: The 'Moral' Influence of Transportation Technology," in *American Urban History: an Interpretative Reader with Commentaries*, 2d ed., edited by A.B. Callow (New York: Oxford Univ. Press, 1973), 202-12; Joel A. Tarr, *Transportation and Changing Spatial Patterns in Pittsburgh, 1850-1934* (Chicago: Public Works Historical Society, 1978); and George Rogers Taylor, "The Beginnings of Mass Transportation in Urban America: Part 1," *Smithsonian Journal of History* (Autumn 1966): 31-54.

Works that explore the interaction that develops between the city as a whole and its component parts as a result of late nineteenth urban growth are Joseph L. Arnold, "The Neighborhood and City Hall: The Origin of Neighborhood Associations in Baltimore, 1880-1911," *Journal of Urban History* 6 (November 1979): 3-30; Zane L. Miller, "The Rise of the City," typescript, 1980; Zane L. Miller, "Role and Concept of Neighborhood in American Cities," typescript, August 11, 1978; Zane L. Miller, "Scarcity, Abundance, and American Urban History," *Journal of Urban History* 4 (February 1978): 131-56; Zane L. Miller, *Suburb: Neighborhood and Community in Forest Park, Ohio, 1935-1976* (Knoxville: Univ. of Tennessee Press, 1981); Zane L. Miller, "Turning Inward: The Concept and Role of Neighborhood in American Cities," typescript, October 14, 1977, delivered at Neighborhood Preservation: The Case of Lubbock's Overton South, Texas Tech Univ., October 14-15, 1977; and Jon C. Teaford, *City and Suburb: The Political Fragmentation of Metropolitan America, 1850-1970* (Baltimore: Johns Hopkins Univ. Press, 1979).

Contemporary sources that detail concerns about the city, contain descriptions of urban life, and include discussions of urban organization are plentiful. Ernest W. Burgess, ed., *The Urban Community* (Chicago: Univ. of Chicago Press, 1926); John Daniels, *America Via the Neighborhood* (New York: Harper and Row, 1920); Frederic C. Howe, *The City, The Hope of Democracy* (New York: C. Scribner's Sons, 1905); R.D. McKenzie, *The Neighborhood* (Chicago: Univ. of Chicago Press, 1923: reprint ed., New York: Arno Press, 1970); Robert E. Park, "The City: Some Suggestions for the Investigation of Human Behavior in the Urban Environment," *American Journal of Sociology* 20 (1916): 577-612; L.S. Rowe, "The City in History," *American Journal of Sociology* 5 (May 1900): 721-45; T.V. Smith and L.D. White, eds., *Chicago: An Experiment in Social Research* (Chicago: Univ. of Chicago Press, 1929); Josiah Strong, *The Challenge of the City* (New York: Young People's Missionary Movement, 1907); Josiah Strong, *The Twentieth Century City* (New York: Baker and Taylor Co., 1898; reprint ed., New York: Arno Press, 1970); Delos F. Wilcox, *The American City, A Problem in Democracy* (New York: Macmillan Co., 1904); Robert A. Woods, *The Neighborhood in Nation-Building* (Boston: Houghton Mifflin, 1923; reprint ed., New York: Arno Press, 1970); Robert A. Woods, "The Neighborhood in Social Reconstruction," *American Journal of Sociology* 19 (March 1914): 577-91; Robert A. Woods and Albert J. Kennedy, *The Zone of Emergence*, edited by Sam Bass Warner, Jr., (Cambridge, Mass.: M.I.T. Press, 1962), and Harvey W. Zorbaugh, *The Gold Coast and the Slum: A Sociological Study of Chicago's Near North Side* (Chicago: Univ. of Chicago Press, 1929), rank among the most useful of these works.

Contemporaries involved in the efforts to organize urban areas or in the analysis of these attempts document the rise of the early twentieth century drive to organize the nation's neighborhoods. The most important of these sources include Ida C. Clarke, *The Little Democracy* (New York: D. Appleton and Co., 1918); Joseph K. Hart, *Community Organization* (New York: Macmillan Co., 1920); Eduard C. Lindeman, *The Community* (New York: Association Press, 1921); B.A. McClenahan, *Organizing the Community: A Review of Practical Principles* (New York: Century Co., 1922); Clarence Perry, *Ten Years with the Community Center Movement* (New York: Russell Sage, 1921); Clarence E. Rainwater, "Community Organization," *Studies in Sociology* 4 (February 1920); Jesse F. Steiner, *The American Community in Action* (New York: Henry Holt and Co., 1928); Jesse F. Steiner, "An Appraisal of the Community Movement," *Social Forces* 7 (March 1929): 333-42; Jesse F. Steiner, *Community Organization* (New York: Century Co., 1925); Jesse F. Steiner, "Community Organization: A Study of Its Rise and Recent Tendencies," *Social Forces* 1 (November 1922): 11-18; and Jesse F. Steiner, "Community Organization in Relation to Social Change," *Social Forces* 1 (November 1922): 102-8.

Individuals active in the settlement house movement were instrumental in furthering our understanding of urban definition and strategies of neighborhood organization. General works that provide pertinent discussions of the settlements and their role in the city include Robert H. Bremmer, *American Philanthropy* (Chicago: Univ. of Chicago Press, 1960); Robert H. Bremmer, *From the Depths: The Discovery of Poverty in the United States* (New York: New York Univ. Press, 1956); Clarke Chambers, *Seedtime of Reform: American Social Service and Social Action 1918-1933* (Minneapolis: Univ. of Minnesota Press, 1963); Allen F. Davis, *Spearheads of Reform: The Social Settlements and the Progressive Movement 1890-1914* (New York: Oxford Univ. Press, 1967); Edward T. Devine, *When Social Work Was Young* (New York: Macmillan Co., 1939); John Elliott, "The Function of the Settlement," *Ethical Record* 1 (April 1900): 80-81; Susan E. Foote, "The Settlement as a Social Laboratory," *Ethical Record* 4 (February-March 1903): 83-86; Arthur C. Holden, *The Settlement Idea: A Vision of Social Justice* (New York: Macmillan Co., 1922; reprint ed., New York: Arno Press, 1970); Roy Lubove, *The Professional Altruist: The Emergence of Social Work as a Career 1880-1930* (New York: Atheneum Press, 1971); William J. Norton, *The Cooperative Movement in Social Work* (New York: Macmillan Co., 1927); Amos Griswold Warner, Stuart Alfred Queen, and Ernest Bouldin Harper, *American Charities and Social Work* (New York: Thomas Y. Crowell and Co., 1930); Robert A. Woods and Albert J. Kennedy, eds., *Handbook of Settlements* (New York: Charities Publication Committee, 1911; reprint ed., New York: Arno Press, 1970); and Robert A. Woods and Albert J. Kennedy, *The Settlement Horizon: A National Estimate* (New York: Russell Sage, 1922).

Studies of specific settlements that illuminate the issues of urban definition and community organization include Stanton Coit, *Neighborhood Guilds: An Instrument of Social Reform* (London: Swan Sonnenschein and Co., 1891); Freda Davidson, "Fifty Years of the Hudson Guild," *Ethical Outlook* 31 (April 1945): 180-81; *The Hudson Guild* (New York, 1927); Mary K. Simkhovitch, *Neighborhood: My Story of Greenwich House* (New York: W.W. Norton and Co., 1938); and Charles B. Stover, "The Neighborhood Guild in New York," *Johns Hopkins Univ. Studies in Historical and Political Science* 7 (1889): 60-65.

Although much secondary literature on community organization lacks historical perspective, there are a number of useful discussions on the importance of community organization in American cities and on the popular organizational strategies employed by community organizers. In addition, these studies help document the shifting aims of community organizers over time. The most important of these sources include Saul Alinsky, *Reveille for Radicals* (New York: Random House, 1946; Vintage Book edition, 1969); Michael J. Austin and Neil Betten, "Intellectual Origins of Community Organizing, 1920-1939," *Social Service Review* 51 (March 1977): 155-70; Robert Bailey, Jr., *Radicals in Urban Politics: The Alinsky Approach* (Chicago: Univ. of Chicago Press, 1974); Roy Bailey and Mike Brake, eds., *Radical Social Work* (New York: Pantheon Books, 1975); Sidney Dillick, *Community Organization for Neighborhood Development—Past and Present* (New York: William Morrow, 1953); Robert Fisher, "Community Organization Practice in the Early Twentieth Century: The Community Center Movement," typescript, 1977; Robert Fisher, *Let the People Decide: Neighborhood Organizing in America* (Boston: Twayne, 1984); Robert Fisher and Peter Romanofsky, eds., *Community Organization for Urban Social Change: A Historical Perspective* (Westport, Conn.: Greenwood Press, 1981); Charles F. Grosser, *New Directions in Community Organization: From Enabling to Advocacy* (New York: Praeger Publishers, 1976); and Christopher Silver, "Neighborhood Planning in Historical Perspective," *Journal of the American Planning Association* 51 (Spring 1985): 161-74.

The literature on the public health movement at the turn of the century is abundant. Studies such as those by Ida M. Cannon, *On the Social Frontier of Medicine: Pioneering in Medical Social Service* (Cambridge, Mass.: Harvard Univ. Press, 1952); James H. Cassedy, *Charles V. Chapin and the Public Health Movement* (Cambridge, Mass.: Harvard Univ. Press, 1962); John Duffy, *A History of Public Health in New York City 1625-1866* (New York: Russell Sage, 1968); John Duffy, *A History of Public Health in New York City 1866-1966* (New York: Russell Sage, 1974); Stuart Galishoff, *Safeguarding the Public Health: Newark 1895-1918* (Westport, Conn.: Greenwood Press, 1975); George Rosen, *From Medical Police to Social Medicine: Essays on the History of Health Care* (New York: Science History Publications, 1974); George Rosen, *A History of Public Health* (New York: MD Publications, Inc., 1958); George Rosen, *Preventive Medicine in the United States 1900-1975: Trends and Interpretations* (New York: Science History Publications, 1975); Charles E. Rosenberg, *The Cholera Years: The United States in 1839, 1849, and 1866* (Chicago: Univ. of Chicago Press, 1962); Wilson G. Smillie, *Preventive Medicine and Public Health* (New York: Macmillan Co., 1952); Wilson G. Smillie, *Public Health Administration in the United States*, 3d ed. (New York: Macmillan Co., 1947); and Wilson G. Smillie, *Public Health: Its Promise for the Future* (New York: Macmillan Co., 1955), help provide the necessary context for an understanding of public health activities in the United States between 1880 and 1920. Reformers evinced considerable interest in child health during the nineteenth and early twentieth centuries. Most helpful in understanding the problems facing children during this period have been S. Josephine Baker, *Child Hygiene* (New York: Harper and Bros., 1925); S. Josephine Baker, *Fighting for Life* (New York: Macmillan Co., 1939); S. Josephine Baker, *Healthy Babies* (Boston: Little, Brown and Co., 1923); Henry Koplik, "The History of the First Milk Depot or *Gouttes de Lait* with Consultations in America," *Journal of the American Medical Association* 63 (October 1914): 1574-75; George B. Mangold, *Child Problems* (New York: Macmillan Co., 1910); George B. Mangold, *Problems of Child Welfare* (New York: Macmillan Co., 1914); and Ravenel Mazÿck, ed., *A Half Century of Public Health* (New York: American Public Health Association, 1921).

An important aspect of the campaign for child health was the drive to clean up the milk supply. Edward Brown and Leland Spencer, eds., *Is Loose Milk a Health Hazard?* (New York: Milk Commission, 1931); J.D. Burks, "Clean Milk and Public Health," *Annals of the American Academy of Political and Social Science* 37 (March 1911): 199-200; Robert M. Hartley, *An Historical Scientific and Practical Essay on Milk as an Article of Human Substance* (New York: Leavitt, 1842; reprint ed., New York: Arno Press, 1977); John Mullaby, *The Milk Trade in New York and Vicinity* (New York: Fowles and Welles, 1853); Chester Linwood Roadhouse and James Lloyd Henderson, *The Milk Market Industry* (New York: McGraw-Hill, 1941); M.J. Rosenau, *The Milk Question* (Boston: Houghton Mifflin, 1912); Judith W. Leavitt and Ronald L. Numbers, eds., *Sickness and Health in America: Readings in the History of Medicine and Public Health* (Madison: Univ. of Wisconsin, 1974); John Spargo, *The Common Sense of the Milk Question* (New York: Macmillan Co., 1908); and Lena Gutherz Straus, *Disease in Milk, the Remedy Pasteurization: The Life Work of Nathan Straus*, 2d ed. (New York: E.P. Dutton and Co., 1917), all provide basic information on the history of the efforts to purify the milk supply between 1800 and 1920.

Other studies focus not only on the campaign for clean milk but look more directly at its impact on the state of child health. Contemporary sources that focus on the issue of clean milk and its relationship to child health in New York City from 1880 to 1920 include S. Josephine Baker, "Reduction of Infant Mortality in New York City," *American Journal of Diseases of Children* 5 (1913): 151-61; Ernst C. Meyer, *Infant Mortality in New York City: A Study of the Results Accomplished by Infant Saving Agencies, 1885-1920* (New York: Rockefeller Foundation, 1921); New York Milk Committee, *Infant Milk*

Depots and Their Relation to Infant Mortality (New York: New York Milk Committee, 1908); Wilbur C. Phillips, "Infant Mortality in New York City," *Medical Record*, January 28, 1911, 146-47; and Phillip Van Ingen and Paul Emmons Taylor, *Infant Mortality and Milk Stations* (New York: New York Milk Committee, 1912).

Among the best studies of the early twentieth century child health crusade in Milwaukee are Gerald Burgardt, "History of the Child Welfare Clinic in Milwaukee," typescript, February 3, 1941; George A. Dundon, "Health Chronology of Milwaukee," typescript, 1946; Louis Frederick Frank, *The Medical History of Milwaukee 1834-1914* (Milwaukee: Germania Publishing Co., 1915); and Judith W. Leavitt, "Public Health in Milwaukee 1867-1910," (Ph.D. diss., Univ. of Chicago, 1975). Secondary studies that provide more specific information about the crusade for child health include John B. Blake, *Origins of Maternal and Child Health Programs* (New Haven: Yale Univ. Press, 1953); R.L. Duffus and L. Emmett Holt, Jr., *L. Emmett Holt: Pioneer of a Children's Century* (New York: D. Appleton and Co., 1940); G. F. McCleary, *The Early History of the Infant Welfare Movement* (London: H.K. Lewis and Co., Ltd., 1933); Henri Siebert, "The Progress of Ideas Regarding the Causation and Control of Infant Mortality," *Bulletin of the History of Medicine* 8 (April 1940): 546-98; and Manfred J. Waserman, "Henry L. Coit and the Certified Milk Movement in the Development of Modern Pediatrics," *Bulletin of the History of Medicine* 46 (July-August 1972): 359-90.

The health center provided early twentieth century Americans with a strategy for combating the problems of poor health. Although not much has been written on the rise of the urban health center or on its relationship to child health, the following sources, Robert C. Bishop, "Health Center in a Large City," *American Journal of Nursing* 17 (August 1917): 1054-60; Michael M. Davis, *Clinics, Hospitals and Health Centers* (New York: Harper and Bros., 1927); Michael M. Davis, "The Health Center Idea: A New Development in Public Health Work," *Public Health Nurse Quarterly* 8 (January 1916): 22-39; Michael M. Davis, "Social Planning and the Medical Sciences," *Publication of the American Sociological Society* 29 (August 1935): 70-80; Michael M. Davis and Andrew R. Warner, *Dispensaries: Their Management and Development* (New York: Macmillan Co., 1918); Ralph E. Pumphrey, "Michael M. Davis and the Development of the Health Care Movement 1900-1928," *Societies* 2 (Winter 1972): 27-41; C.-E. A. Winslow, *The Evolution and Significance of the Modern Public Health Campaign* (New Haven: Yale Univ. Press, 1923); and C.-E. A. Winslow, "The Health Center Movement," *Modern Medicine* 1 (August 1919): 327-28, offer an introduction to the subject.

The social unit organization and its Cincinnati experiment stimulated a significant amount of contemporary literature. Studies that provide descriptions of the development of the social unit organization and its subsequent activities include Warwick Black, "The Social Unit Ended in Cincinnati," *National Municipal Review,* January, 1921, 72-73; Robert A. Chaddock, "Municipal Statistics and the Social Unit Organization," *Quarterly Publication of the American Statistical Association* 16 (December 1919): 549-50; Edward T. Devine, "The Social Unit as a Means of Democratizing Social Work," *Journal of Delinquency* 5 (January 1920): 9-14; Courtenay Dinwiddie, *Community Responsibility: A Review of the Social Unit Experiment* (New York: New York School of Social Work, 1921); Phyllis Duganne, "Country Neighborliness in City Blocks," *World Outlook,* July, 1919, 12-13; Seba Eldridge, "Community Organization and Citizenship," *Social Forces* 7 (September 1928): 132-40; S. Gale Lowrie, "Social Unit: An Experiment in Politics," *National Municipal Review,* September, 1920, 553-66; "Mr. and Mrs. Wilbur C. Phillips' Big Idea," *Everybody's Magazine,* June 1916, 784-85; "Mrs. Tiffany on the 'Social Unit,' " *The Review,* January 1920, 7; National Social Unit Organization, *Beginning of Work in the Social Unit,* Bulletin 5 (Cincinnati: National Social Unit Organization, 1918); National Social Unit Organization, *Creation and Purpose of the Cincinnati Social Unit Organization,* Bulletin 3 (Cincinnati: National Social Unit Organization, 1918); National Social Unit Organization, *Description of the Social Unit Plan,* Bulletin 4 (Cincinnati: National Social Unit Organization, 1917); National Social Unit Organization, *History of the Unit Plan,* Bulletin 1 (Cincinnati: National Social Unit Organization, 1917); National Social Unit Organization, *Outline of the Unit Plan,* Bulletin 2 (Cincinnati: National Social Unit Organization, 1917); National Social Unit Organization, *A Statement of the Practical Experience on Which the Unit Plan Is Based,* Bulletin 2-A (Cincinnati: National Social Unit Organization, 1918); National Social Unit Organization, *The Unit Experiment from the Standpoint of Popular Control, Theoretical Soundness, Practical Efficiency, Educational Value and Cost,* Bulletin 6 (Cincinnati: National Social Unit Organization, 1919); N.A. Nelson, "Neighborhood Organization vs. Tuberculosis," *Modern Medicine* 1 (October 1919): 515-21; Elsie Phillips, "Cincinnati's 'Social Unit,' " *Vassar Quarterly* (1919): 271-76; Elsie Phillips, "A Plan for Community Organization," *Vassar Quarterly* 2 (February 1917): 75-81; Elsie Phillips, "The Social Unit," *School and Community,* January 1, 1920, 6, 13; Elsie Phillips, "The Social Unit Plan for Cincinnati," *Woman's City Club Bulletin,* December 1916, 7-11; Charles A. Reed, "The 'Social Unit' in Cincinnati," *American Review of Reviews,* May, 1919, 523-24; Gertrude Mathews Shelby, "Extending Democracy, What the Cincinnati Social Unit Has Accomplished," *Harpers Maga-*

zine, April 1920, 688-95; "Social Work by Blocks," *Literary Digest*, December 6, 1919, 34-35, 90, 92; Dorothy Thompson, "The Social Unit: A Social Organization That Should Appeal to Labor," *Shipbuilders News and Navy Yard Employee*, November 1919, 3-4; Dorothy Thompson, "Social Unit Organization, Cincinnati, Ohio, *Social Service Review* 8 (September 1918): 12-13; Dorothy Thompson, "The Unit Plan of Health Administration," *National Municipal Review*, November 1918, 596-99; and Katrina Ely Tiffany, "The Social Unit at Cincinnati—Is It a Soviet?" *The Review*, January 3, 1920, 11-12.

Despite a high level of contemporary interest, relatively little information about the social unit organization can be found in the secondary literature. Of the studies that do discuss the social unit, Michael J. Austin and Neil Betten, "The Unwanted Helping Hand," *Environment* 19 (January/February 1977): 13-20; Robert Fisher, *Let the People Decide: Neighborhood Organizing in America* (Boston: Twayne, 1984); and Anatole Shaffer, "The Cincinnati Social Unit Experiment, 1917-1919," *Social Service Review* 45 (June 1971): 159-72, rank among the best.

Index

Academy of Medicine, 81-82, 91-92,
131, 143, 191 n. 4, 200 n. 22
Addams, Jane, 20
Adler, Felix, 67
Agin, C.C., 91-92
Alinsky, Saul D., 159, 172
Allen, Arthur M., 70
American Red Cross, 113
Anti-Tuberculosis League, 74, 77, 79,
92, 110-11, 139, 148, 190-91 n. 70,
191 n. 4
Associated Charities, 92, 118-19, 139,
148, 191 n. 4

Babies Milk Fund Association, 152,
203 n. 71
Bading, Gerald, 53-55
Baker, S. Josephine, 31, 44
Baltimore, Maryland, 25, 66, 73
Battle, George Gordon, 161-62,
205 n. 15
Beffel, John, 46-47, 70, 73, 189 n. 47
Bend, Beatrice, 67
Better Housing League, 116-18, 148
Bigelow, Herbert S., 131
Bodman, C.M., 74, 139
Bogen, Jessie, 80, 87, 90, 95
Brand, John, 136
Brichard, A.D., 150
Brinkerd, Robert S., 69
Bruère, Henry, 70
Bruère, Robert, 5, 35
Bull, Mrs. Henry Adsit, 70

Burgess, Ernest W., 1-2, 159
Buss, Eugene, 140

Cabot, Richard C., 64-66, 72, 189 n. 31
Carothers, Robert C., 131
Carsten, C.C., 70, 72
Chaddock, Robert E., 115, 147
Chapin, Charles V., 115, 184 n. 25
Chicago, Illinois, 171-72
Chicago sociologists, 1, 159
child health, 27-56, 68, 97, 156-58
Child Welfare Commission (CWC), 6,
56-57, 64, 70, 133; demise of, 53-55;
establishment of, 45-47; organization
of the station, 49-53; selection of
experimental district, 47-49
Children's Year. See Mohawk-Brighton
Social Unit Organization
Cincinnati, Ohio, 6-8, 24-26, 73-159,
163, 165, 169
Cincinnati Americanization Bureau, 116
Cincinnati Social Unit Organization
(CSUO), 6-7, 26, 87, 96; attacks on,
127-29, 134-58; disbanding of, 151;
establishment of, 77-81, 127, 191-92
n. 4; and MBSUO, 101; and NSUO
Conference, 144-50, 160; Physicians'
Council of, 81-82, 131-32; and selec-
tion of Mohawk-Brighton, 82-84, 193
n. 25; Statisticians' Council of, 82,
114-16
Cincinnati War Chest, 138-40
Clark, Mrs. Mowbray, 69, 189 n. 47

Clark, Ralph, 138-40
Cochran, William F., 66, 70, 189 n. 47
Coit, Henry L., 30, 182 n. 11,
    184 n. 25
Coit, Stanton, 21-22
Cole, Mrs. Frank, 136
Coleman, George W., 69, 130
Collier, John C., 145, 149, 189 n. 47
community centers, 3, 23-24
Community Councils of National Defense (CCND), 160, 171
Community Councils of New York, 161, 205 n. 14
community organization, 2-3, 6, 149, 160, 162, 164; definition of, 174 n. 4; and health organization, 28; history of, 8-9; in organic city, 19-26, 166-67, 169; in pluralistic metropolis, 160, 169-72; strategies of, 3-4
Community Service, Inc., 205 n. 14
Condon, Randall, 79-80, 82, 107, 136, 145
Converse, Mary, 70
cooperative society. See organic theory of society
Council of National Defense, 81, 131-32, 160
Council of Social Agencies (CSA), 128, 138-45, 150, 191 n. 4, 201 n. 39, 203-04 n. 85
Court of Domestic Relations, 92, 119
Crandall, Ella Phillips, 70, 109
Croly, Herbert, 59, 67, 70, 72
Cross, Mrs. Whitman, 70
Crum, Frederick S., 115
Culkins, W.C., 79

Davis, Michael M., 73, 190 n. 47
Department of Health (Cincinnati), 76, 92, 109, 112-13, 132, 143, 155
descriptions of reality, 1-2, 175 n. 14, 175-76 n. 9
Destler, Louis, 151
Detroit Community Fund, 128, 199 n. 12
Devine, Edward, 14, 147-49, 153
Dinwiddie, Courtenay, 62, 74, 87, 110, 121-22, 128, 132, 139, 141, 143-44, 152
Dublin, Louis I., 115

Duncan, J.C., 80

Eastman, Roe, 80
Edison, Charles, 70
Edson, John Joy, 66, 69, 73, 189 n. 47
Elliot, John L., 21-22, 67, 69, 145
Emerson, Haven, 122, 146
environment, 27
Evans, E. Walter, 82, 115
Evans, William A., 87-88, 96, 120, 195 n. 75
Ewing, William C., 165

Feiker, Frederick M., 165
financial federations, 155, 203-04 n. 85
Fisher, Irving, 115
Flinchbaugh, F.L., 135, 138
Follett, Mary P., 12, 58, 153-54
Frankfurter, Felix, 70, 72
Freiberg, Maurice, 140
Friedlander, Walter, 138

Galbraith, F.W., 80
Galvin, John, 9, 107, 124, 130-35, 142, 148, 151, 154
Gaston, R. E., 99
Gaveling, G.H., 87
Geier, Fred A., 140
Goldwater, S.S., 70, 73, 189 n. 47
Goler, George, 30, 182 nn. 12, 25
Gottlieb, Ruth, 83, 87, 195 n. 75
Greenbaum, J. Victor, 131
Grothaus, John, 91-92, 101, 195 n. 75
Guggenheim, Daniel, 67, 134
Guggenheim, Mrs. Daniel, 67, 70, 134, 205 n. 15
Gwynn, Mary, 70

Haines, W.B., 131
Hardcastle, E.E., 82, 115
Harding, Mrs. Charles, 136
Harriman, Mrs. J. Borden, 66-69, 72
Hart, Thomas, 138, 146
Hartley, Robert M., 28-30
Haynes, Rowland G., 70
health organization, 6, 27-28, 45, 56, 156-57
Hebble, C.R., 127
Helen S. Trounstine Foundation, 128-29, 141, 155

Hicks, Mary, 83, 90, 95, 106, 120
Hills, Joseph A., 115
Howe, Frederic, 12, 15
Hudson Guild, 21-22, 145
Humane Society, 119
Huyck, Edmund, 70
Hymans, Isabel, 70

ideas, relationship to action, 10-11
Ihlder, John, 70
infant mortality, 28-31, 37, 46, 49,
  52-53, 65-66; statistics, 31-33, 40-41,
  183 n. 17
interdependence, 2, 11-13, 37
Jack, William T., 93, 195 n. 75
Jenkins, Helen Hartley, 67, 70,
  205 n. 15
Jones, Mark, 149
Julian, W.A., 144-45
Juvenile Protection Agency, 119

Kellogg, Paul U., 67
Kennedy, Albert J., 84
Kober, George M., 70
Kohut, Mrs. Alexander, 67, 70
Koplik, Henry, 31, 182 n. 14
Kotler, Milton, 2, 9
Kreidler, A.G., 101, 105-06, 121-22,
  133

LaForge, Zoe, 146
Lamont, Mrs. Thomas, 67
Landesco, Alexander, 94, 195 n. 75
Landis, John, 74, 78, 81, 110, 127-28,
  130-31, 137, 139, 141
Lane, Franklin P., 129-30, 164
Lathrop, Julia, 65, 104-06, 189 n. 47
Lee, Alice, 70
Lee, Porter R., 70
Lent, Mary, 109
Lewisohn, Adolph, 67, 70
Loeb, William Jr., 69-70, 189 n. 47
Loughman, Anna, 117
Lower North Community Council
  (LNCC), 171-72

McKenzie, Roderick D., 170, 172
Magee, James, 82, 115
Marquette, Bleeker, 117
Martin, Franklin, 81, 131-32

Mason-Knox, James, 72, 189 n. 47,
  200 n. 22
Melish, Howard J., 70, 79
Meyers, Curtis, 82, 115
milk: efforts to improve quality of,
  28-31, 33-45, 182-83 nn. 11-15; and
  infant mortality, 31-33
Miller, John D., 131
Milwaukee, Wisconsin, 6, 45-55, 57, 60,
  62, 75, 101
Mitchell, E.W., 129, 131, 138
Mitchell, Wesley C., 115, 166
Mithoeffer, William, 131
modern city, 2, 15-16
Mohawk-Brighton, Cincinnati, 7, 82-97,
  193 n. 36
Mohawk-Brighton Social Unit Organization (MBSUO), 77, 165; adult
  examinations by, 98, 113; attacks on,
  127-29, 134-58; and Better Housing
  League, 116-18; block elections in,
  125-127, budget (1918), 96,
  195 n. 78; budget (1919), 125-26,
  199 n. 3; Businessmen's Council, 93,
  118-19; and Children's Year, 98, 103-
  08, 197 n. 29; Clergymen's Council
  of, 93, 118-19; cooperation with other
  organizations, 116-18; and Council of
  Social Agencies, 138-44, 150; critique
  of, 168-69; defense of, 134-38; demise
  of, 151-52; establishment of, 87-97,
  195 nn 74-76; fund-raising by, 150-51;
  generalized nursing service of, 108-
  09, 146; and influenza epidemic,
  111-13, 122, 125, 142; Labor Council
  of, 93-94, 118-19; neighborhood census by, 113-16; Nurses' Council of,
  92, 99-103, 107-13; opening of baby
  station by, 98-101, 196 n. 9; Physicians' Council of, 91-92; 98-103, 105-
  07, 113, 121-22; postnatal program of,
  98-102; postpartum program of, 98,
  103; prenatal program of, 98, 102-03;
  Recreational Council of, 119-21; and
  Red Cross, 113; selection of child
  health program, 97-101; Social Workers' Council of, 92-93, 118-19;
  Teachers' Council of, 93
Monasmith, Harry B., 69, 189 n. 47
Mullen, Michael, 127

Municipal Tuberculosis Committee, 74, 78, 110, 191 n. 71

nation, definition of, 12
National Community Center Association, 23, 145
National Social Unit Organization (NSUO), 57, 77, 78-79, 96-97, 130, 159; establishment of, 68-71, 189-90 n. 47; and MBSUO, 98, 123, 125, 140-52; National Advisory Council of, 131-32; NSUO Conference, 144-50, 160; and NYCC, 160, 162-65, 167, 205 nn. 14-15; selection of host city by, 71-76; Statistical Council of, 70, 115
neighborhood: and the social unit theory, 60-64; definition of, 3, 17-18
Neighborhood Guild, 21-22, 179 n. 51
neighborhood health, 55-56, 64-66, 146, 158
neighborhood improvement associations, 3, 24-25
neighborhood organization. See community organization
Neighbors' Day, 164
Nelson, N.A., 111
Newman, Oliver P., 66, 69, 73-74, 189 n. 47
New York Association for Improving the Condition of the Poor (AICP), 5, 28, 33-35, 37, 42-43; clean milk crusade of, 28-30; and "Clean Milk for New York City," 33-35, 184-85 n. 25
New York City, 5-6, 20-22, 28-45, 55-56, 66-76, 104, 132, 145-46, 149, 159-65
New York Citywide Tenants' Council, 172
New York Community Councils (NYCC), 159-65, 205 nn. 14-15
New York Department of Health Bureau of Child Hygiene, 31, 44
New York Milk Committee (NYMC), 6, 55-57, 64, 66, 133, 158; campaign to save depots, 43-44; dairy environment programs, 44; examination of milk depot work, 35-37; experimental milk stations, 37-43, 45
Nordman, Kathryn, 94, 195 n. 75

North, Charles E., 72, 189 n. 47
Norton, William, J., 74, 128-29

Ogburn, William F., 115
Ohio Health and Old Age Insurance Commission, 116
Ollesheimer, Mrs. Henry, 68, 70, 205 n. 15
Oppenheimer, Benton S., 74, 79
organic theory: of society, 11, 13-14, 58-59; of urban organization, 1-2, 4, 8, 15, 17, 24-26, 56-57, 178 n. 30

Pandorf, S.W., 94
Park, Robert, 158
Perkins, Mrs. Henry C., 70, 189 n. 47
Peters, William, 131-33
Phillips, Elsie, 64, 69, 76-77, 80, 94, 140-41
Phillips, Wilbur C., 9, 26, 57, 158, 166; Adventuring for Democracy, 165; background, 4-5; and Child Welfare Commission, 6, 45-56; and Consumers' and Producers' Association, 165-66; and CSA investigation, 138-44; defends MBSUO, 135-38; and establishment of CSUO, 77-82; and establishment of NSUO, 64-73; Galvin's attack on, 130-33; and MBSUO, 99-101, 103-05, 108, 114, 116, 123, 128, 159-61, 205 n. 15; and New York Milk Committee, 5-6, 35-45; resigns from MBSUO, 149-50, 160; and Social Science Research Council, 166; and selection of Cincinnati, 73-76; and Social Unit Institute, 166-67; and social unit theory of organization, 7-8, 57-64
Pinchot, Gifford, 67, 69, 73, 129-30
Pinchot, Mrs. Gifford, 67, 69
Porter, W.D., 131
Potter, Virginia, 68-70, 205 n. 15
preschool examinations. See Children's Year
Progressive Era historiography, 8-9
Puchta, George, 79, 80
Putnam, Mrs. William Lowell, 70, 72, 190 n. 47

Rainey, Mrs. George, 70

Rauh, Sidney
Reinhardt, Mrs. Charles, 150-51
Richard, Alice E., 118-19
Roberts, Abbie, 99, 102, 109
Rochester, New York, 23
Rubinow, I.M., 115

St. Cyril's Parish, Milwaukee, 6, 49-53, 62, 73, 75, 101
Schilling, H.E., 99
school centers. *See* community centers
Schneider, Gustave C., 135
Seidel, Emil, 45, 53
Seligman, E.R.A., 70
settlements, social, 3, 19-23
Severett, Caroline, 151
Shiels, Albert, 161-62, 205 n. 15
Shinkle, A. Clifford, 140
Siddons, Frederick L., 66, 189 n. 47
Simkhovitch, Mary, 20
Smith, E.O., 131
Smith, Luke W., 129
Socialism, 9, 130-31, 133, 155
social unit theory of organization, 4, 7-10, 25-26, 57, 75, 160; description of, 60-64; development of, 59-60; implications for social work, 155-56; political implications of, 152-55; search for supporters, 64-68
Spargo, John, 70, 72
Spencer, Herbert, 13-14
Stammel, C.A., 99
Steighthoff, Frank, 115
Steiner, Jesse, 22
Stelzle, Charles, 68-70
Stokes, Helen Philips, 70
Storrow, Mrs. James, 70
Straight, Mrs. Dorothy Whitney, 67-70, 72, 205 n. 15
Straus, Nathan, 31, 182-83 n. 15, 184 n. 25
Strong, Josiah, 14

Tawney, Guy A., 129, 138
Taylor, Graham, 20
Thompson, Dorothy, 134, 205 n. 15
Tiffany, Mrs. Charles, 69, 130, 134, 162, 189 n. 47, 205 n. 15
Twitchell, G.B., 99

United States Children's Bureau, 65-66, 103-06
urban definition, 1-2, 11, 27

Valentine, R.G., 70, 73
Vaughan, John, 68
Visiting Nurse Association, 92, 109, 138-39, 142, 152, 155, 191 n 4
Vocational Bureau of the Board of Education, 116

Waldman, Morris, 68-69
Walker, John, 149
Wall, Joseph P., 66
Ward, Edward, 23
Washington, D.C., 65-66, 68, 70, 73-75, 132, 164
Westcott, Edith, 66
Wherry, William B., 138
Whitaker, Mrs. A.L., 136-38
White, James O., 79, 127, 131
White, Mrs. James O., 80
Wilbur, Cressey, 70
Wiley, Harvey W., 165
Williams, E.W., 70
Wilson, Margaret, 66
Wittpenn, Mrs. H., 70, 190 n. 47
Wofstein, D.I., 131
Woodbury, Mrs. Robert M., 115
Woods, Robert A., 12, 14-15, 17-18, 20, 56, 58, 84
Wooley, Helen T., 116
Wooley, Mrs. Paul, 138

Zone of Emergence, 84, 86
Zorbaugh, Harvey W., 159, 170-72